D1306153

Progress Tests for the Developmentally Disabled

Progress Tests for the Developmentally Disabled:
An Evaluation

John Doucette
Ruth Freedman

Distributed Exclusively
In The U.S. By:
BROOKLINE BOOKS
P.O. Box 1046
CAMBRIDGE, MASSACHUSETTS 02238-1046

The research reported herein was performed pursuant to Contract No. HEW-105-77-5005 with the U.S. Developmental Disabilities Office. Contractors undertaking such government-sponsored projects are encouraged to express freely their professional judgement in the conduct of the project. Points of view and opinions stated do not, therefore, necessarily represent the official position or policy of the U.S. Developmental Disabilities Office.

Library of Congress Catalog Card Number 79-55773

Printed in the United States of America.

ISBN: 0-89011-539-7

Contents

Contents

Acknowledgments

This book, based on a study conducted by Abt Associates Inc. for the United States Developmental Disabilities Office, involved the dedication and contribution of a large number of individuals. First, we wish to thank the Abt Associates staff who have worked hard throughout the course of this project. Special thanks go to Karen Keefe who served as administrative and research assistant. Among her many tasks, she was responsible for coordinating, abstracting, and editing the reviews of individual instruments contained in this book. Credit also goes to Suzanne Simenson, who was involved in the abstracting and editing of reviews; Judy Agard, who assisted in the reviews of instruments and contributed to the development of the guidelines for users; and Elinor Gollay, who served as senior consultant to the project. We would also like to extend special thanks to Karen Tropeano who served as project secretary during the initial stage of the study and Carole Chu who served in this capacity during the middle and final phases.

We received invaluable assistance from our national review panel members who not only gave generously of their time during the three panel meetings, but also in reviewing and evaluating the primary instruments contained in this book. The panel members were Tony Arangio, Graduate School of Social Work, University of Texas; Gerry Bensberg, Texas Research and Training Center; Frances Berko, Suffolk County Department of Developmental Services; Robert Bruininks, University of Minnesota Develop-

Acknowledgments

mental Disabilities Project on Residential Services and Community Adjustment; James Budde, Kansas Center for Mental Retardation and Human Development; Carolyn Cherington, Social Planning Services Inc. of Watertown, Massachusetts; Maurice Dayan, Pinecrest State School, Louisiana; Robert Gettings, National Association of State Mental Retardation Program Directors, Arlington, Virginia; Andy Halpern, Oregon Research and Training Center; Lynda Kahn, Columbus State University Deinstitutionalization Project; Ron Wiegerink, University of North Carolina Developmental Disabilities Technical Assistance Project; and Angela Yaron, Colorado Department of Institutions, Division for Developmental Disabilities.

Our project officer, Kristen Rogge, deserves personal thanks for her continued support throughout the conduct of the study. And finally, we wish to thank all of the authors and publishers of instruments who took the time to send us materials and to review our descriptions of their assessment tools. We hope that the contributions of all these individuals to the development of this book will result in increased and more knowledgeable utilization of existing assessment instruments and new directions for research and development of instruments appropriate for developmentally disabled persons.

John Doucette
Ruth Freedman

Chapter 1

Introduction

This book summarizes the major findings of a review and evaluation of instrumentation utilized by programs for the developmentally disabled. Conducted by Abt Associates Inc. for the United States Developmental Disabilities Office (now part of the Rehabilitation Services Administration) under contract HEW-105-77-5005, the study had as its purpose to provide the background information necessary for service providers and planners to make informed decisions concerning the use of developmental assessment tools.

The information presented in this book is intended for use by a variety of persons and programs involved with developmentally disabled persons. It should prove to be extremely useful to planners designing services, service providers planning and serving clients, administrators evaluating the outcomes of services, and advocates determining whether clients' interests are being addressed.

The major focus of this book is on assessment instruments which measure the developmental progress of developmentally disabled persons. Two major kinds of assessment instruments are reviewed: (1) client assessment instruments which measure various aspects of an individual's adaptive functioning (e.g., self-care, communication, socialization) and (2) environmental assessment instruments which assess the characteristics of the individual's environment(s) (e.g., school, home, or work settings) which may affect personal growth and development. These instrument evaluations are presented in order to introduce users to varying perspectives and approaches to measuring the developmental progress of developmentally disabled persons.

CONTEXT

Before presenting the instrument reviews, it is important to examine why such progress is being measured. Until recently, assessment instruments have been used primarily to assess periodically the developmental status and progress of individual clients. These periodic review data have traditionally been used for such clinical purposes as screening, determining eligibility, predicting or measuring progress in an individual's treatment program, and making placement decisions. However, recent trends in the human services and developmental disabilities fields have led to the use of assessment instruments for other purposes as well, such as the development of individual service plans and overall program evaluation. The following are some of the trends which have contributed to the importance of assessments:

In recent years greater emphasis has been placed on individualized programming and the development of treatment, service, education, and rehabilitation plans.

Disabled persons are demanding their own rights and organizing into a potent political force.

There is now more emphasis placed on adaptive behavior in training programs.

Increased concern with the effectiveness and outcomes of services for disabled persons is developing.

Accountability at all levels of programs is being stressed more.

Perhaps the greatest impetus for the development of assessment instruments has been the various legislative actions mandating assessments of developmentally disabled persons. Some of the major pieces of federal legislation which have provisions for client assessments or evaluations include the following:

Developmentally Disabled Assistance and Bill of Rights Act of 1975 (PL 94-103)

Concerned with the protection and advocacy of individual rights of the developmentally disabled, this act contains various provisions relating to assessments of developmental progress. Specifically, the act requires that an evaluation system be developed which "shall provide objective measures of the developmental progress of persons with developmental disabilities using data obtained from individualized habilitation plans."

The Education of All Handicapped Children Act of 1975 (PL 94-142)

This law assures that a free, appropriate public education will be available for all handicapped children. An analysis and evaluation of the effectiveness of procedures is required in order "to assure that all handicapped children receive special education and related services." The evaluation must include information relating to educational achievement.

Medicaid Title XIX, 1977 Standards for Intermediate Care Facilities for the Mentally Retarded (PL 92-223)

There are several aspects of these standards which relate to client assessments. First, facilities "shall admit only residents who have had a comprehensive evaluation covering physical, emotional, social, and cognitive factors." Secondly, the law requires that there shall be "a regular, at least annual, joint review of the status of each resident by all relevant personnel." And finally, specific evaluation and program plans are mandated for each resident.

Rehabilitation Act of 1973 (PL 93-112)

This 1973 act requires both HEW and state vocational rehabilitation agencies to provide services on a priority basis to "those with the most severe handicaps so that they may prepare for and engage in gainful employment." This is to be accomplished through individualized written rehabilitation programs which set forth long-range goals and intermediate objectives as well as objective criteria, procedures, and schedules for review and evaluation of progress toward objectives and goals.

3

Large numbers of instruments currently exist which are intended to meet a variety of assessment needs. In this study several hundred instruments were initially identified as being used to measure individual adaptive functioning or environmental characteristics in programs serving developmentally disabled persons. Other research projects have also identified numerous instruments, many of which are published, well-researched, and widely-distributed tests. Others are unpublished "homegrown" tools developed or adapted for use in a specific local program.

STUDY PROCEDURES

Review Panel

Throughout the course of the study a national review panel consisting of 12 experts in the fields of developmental disabilities and instrumentation assisted project staff. Serving as a resource pool from which project staff drew, the panel participated in three formal panel meetings and reviewed instruments and materials sent to them. These experts, separately and collectively, are the authors of the instrument reviews which appear in Chapters 3 and 4.

The next phase of the process involved sending copies of the draft abstracts and reviews to the instruments' authors for their review and comments. With the exception of five cases, responses were received by at least one of the instruments' authors for each of the primary review instruments. In general, authors were quite satisfied with the abstracts and reviews, although many offered some factual corrections and editorial suggestions. These corrections were incorporated, where deemed appropriate by project staff. In some cases, authors responded by sending additional materials and research findings which were not available at the time the reviews were conducted. In a small number of cases, these additional materials had a major effect on the accuracy of the review; the instrument and new materials were therefore reviewed again by project staff and the review was revised accordingly. In other cases, additional materials were informative but not essential to the review and reference was made to these materials but the instruments were not reviewed again.

Instrument Selection

The first step in the review process was the identification of appropriate instruments for study. Certain inclusion and exclusion guidelines were established to help determine which types of instruments should and should not be considered. Inclusion criteria were fairly simple: an instrument was included in the study if it measured an aspect of development relevant to the delivery of services to developmentally disabled persons. Figure 1.1 presents a list of domains considered relevant measures of developmental progress for the purposes of this study.

Figure 1.1
Assessment Domains

A. COMMUNICATION

Includes verbal and nonverbal, receptive and expressive communication skills.

Examples: Language, receptive language, expressive language, listening, understanding, auditory comprehension, verbal, speech, speaking, voice, sign language, lip reading, conversation

B. SELF-CARE SKILLS

Skills that enable an individual to meet his/her own basic self-care needs.

Examples: drinking, eating, toileting, dressing, hygiene, appearance, cleanliness, washing, showering, bathing, grooming, toothbrushing, meal behaviors, manners, personal and bedtime routines

C. INDEPENDENT LIVING SKILLS

Skills that enable an individual to function independently in the home and the community.

Examples: care of clothing, clothes selection, laundry, cooking, domestic activities, housecleaning, health care, safety, transportation, travel, postal, telephone, shopping, money management, time management

D. LEARNING AND PROBLEM SOLVING ABILITIES

Includes general cognitive competence and academic and preacademic skills.

Examples: reading, writing, quantitative skills, recognition, perception, reasoning, memory, knowledge, cognition.

Figure 1.1 (continued)

E.   MALADAPTIVE BEHAVIORS

Extreme behavior problems which involve antisocial or deviant behaviors, or danger to self or to others.

Examples: aggression, hyperactivity, violence, extreme acting out of temper tantrums, withdrawal, delinquency, suicidal tendencies, self-injurious behavior.

F.   PHYSICAL DEVELOPMENT

Includes both motor development (those behaviors that primarily involve muscular, neuromuscular, or physical skills and that involve varying degrees of physical dexterity) and sensory development (development of perceptual skills).

Examples: gross motor, basic motor, body-motor, fine motor, visual-motor, perceptual-motor, hand-motor, manual dexterity, coordination, perception, sensory-motor, balance, posture, sitting, ambulation, locomotion, crawling, walking, climbing.

G.   EMOTIONAL DEVELOPMENT

Behaviors that affect an individual's relationship with other people and the individual's interests, attitudes, values, or emotional expressions.

Examples: emotion, initiative, self-management, self-direction, self-esteem, self-concept, self-confidence, social maturity, social awareness, cooperation, emotional stability.

H.   SOCIALIZATION

Refers to an individual's social relationships and interactions in social activities.

Examples: peer relationships, family relationships, friendships, interpersonal or social interactions, involvement in social and leisure time activities.

I.   WORK HABITS AND WORK ADJUSTMENT

Ability to perform assigned job tasks independently, to maintain proper work habits, and to work well with fellow employees and employers.

Examples: job finding skills, job learning skills, work habits, work performance, adjustment to work or work training.

Figure 1.1 (continued)

J. ENVIRONMENTAL CHARACTERISTICS

> Characteristics of the individual's environment, such as normalization aspects of the individual's residential and work situation, community attitudes, barriers, and aspects of the service delivery process.

Because of their increasing importance in planning and monitoring programs, formal measures of environmental conditions in programs serving developmentally disabled persons were also included in the review. While they are not, strictly speaking, measures of developmental progress, they nevertheless assess aspects of the process of service delivery which are important to evaluating both programs and individual clients.

Excluded from the review process were measures of domains that have already been studied extensively and reported in the literature, for example, intelligence and personality tests. While intelligence and personality testing are important in evaluating developmentally disabled clients, numerous reviews of such instruments already exist; there was no need to duplicate work that has already been done.

Based on these guidelines, potentially appropriate instruments were identified through a literature review and contacts with national review panel members, governmental and program staff, and other relevant research projects. These instruments were then screened by project staff to determine which met most closely the following selection criteria:

> appropriateness for assessing the developmental progress of developmentally disabled persons or of assessing the environments in which developmentally disabled persons function;

> widespread usage as indicated by references in the literature, by program staff and consumers, and by national review panel members;

> noteworthy, promising, or unique in its approach to the assessment of developmentally disabled persons and/or the environments in which they function;

> sufficient information available on test purposes, administration procedures, test development, and research and validation efforts to warrant in-depth reviews by national review panel members and project staff.

7

Based on this screening process, 47 primary instruments were selected to be reviewed in-depth by staff and panel members.

Instrument Review

The instrument review process involved a series of steps. First, Abt Associates project staff collected descriptive information and prepared a brief abstract of each instrument based on authors' statements regarding test purpose, administration procedures, test content, and research efforts. This information was obtained from test manuals, articles, and supporting materials available for each instrument.

Second, each primary instrument was reviewed and evaluated by one or, in some cases, two national review panel members. An instrument review recording form, organized according to the seven dimensions of content, administration, interpretation, utility, test development, reliability, and validity, was developed for use in the review. The form included rating scales and some close-ended questions for overall analysis purposes as well as open-ended questions to assist panel members in conducting their individual reviews.

The third step of the review process involved the preparation of a narrative review of each instrument. Based on the panel members' comments provided in the instrument review recording form, the narrative review summarized the strengths and weaknesses of each instrument in terms of the seven major dimensions stated above.

After an instrument's abstract (based on descriptive information) and the narrative review were completed they were reviewed by a second panel member (where possible, someone already familiar with the particular instrument) and a project staff person for substantive and editorial comments. And the final step, in cases where the opinions of the initial panel reviewer and the second reader were discrepant, was further review of the instrument. Conducted by project staff this review was aimed at resolving or at least reporting different viewpoints.

Chapter 2

Guidelines for the Selection and Use of Assessment Instruments

This chapter is designed to guide readers through the process of selecting and using instruments which measure developmental progress, and is a nontechnical discussion of issues which are important yet often overlooked in test selection.

The guidelines presented in this chapter identify certain crucial characteristics of assessment instruments which you should consider when selecting a test. The instrument descriptions and reviews which follow in Chapters 3 and 4 are keyed to these characteristics and were designed to facilitate the screening of instruments for selection. The reviews are not intended to be a substitute for following the procedures described in this chapter. Rather, they are the raw data that the user must have to make informed decisions about assessment instruments.

OVERVIEW OF THE PROCESS

When choosing and implementing an assessment strategy, you should always keep in mind that your objective is to obtain information about a program or its clients, and not simply to "pick a test." The process of instrument selection requires a clear understanding of the *purpose* of the assessment and of the *context* in which it will be used since there can be no rational basis for selecting an assessment procedure without knowledge of the reasons for and the context of the planned data collection effort.

There are five basic steps in the selection of an instrument and the collection of assessment data. Each of the following steps will be discussed further in the following sections of this chapter:

specification of the characteristics of your situation;

examination of the dimensions or characteristics of an instrument which are relevant to the situation;

review of the available tests in terms of the dimensions;

selection of an assessment approach based on the dimensions; and

collection of data according to standardized administration procedures.

According to this approach the "quality" of an instrument is, in large part, situational and depends on how well an instrument meets the demands of the intended application and context. What may be a perfectly acceptable approach in one setting may be completely inappropriate in another because of characteristics of the situation, not because of anything inherent to the instrument itself. For this very important reason, we will not recommend specific instruments for use by programs. It is up to you, the user, to determine which of a number of potentially useful scales is most appropriate for your purposes and situation. However, we have evaluated a number of instruments in terms of their appropriateness for a variety of typical applications and setting (e.g., program evaluation or Individual Habilitation Plan (IHP) development). This information is intended to assist you in forming a judgement, not to replace the judgement of a program and its staff in the instrument selection process.

CHARACTERISTICS OF THE SITUATION

This section offers guidelines for the first step in the instrument selection process—specifying the characteristics of a particular situation in which the data collection will take place. Instrument selection cannot take place in a vacuum; the particular aspects of each individual situation greatly affect the kind of instrument that should be chosen. There are a series of questions to ask when considering the characteristics of a situation. In general, they all deal with specification of the *purpose* of the data collection and the *population* from which data will be collected. Table 2.1 summarizes these considerations.

Table 2.1
Characteristics of the Situation: Data Collection

I. Purpose of Data Collection

    A. Application: What decisions or actions will be performed on the basis of the data to be collected?

        Initial IHP development
        Progress measurement
        Screening or eligiblity determination
        Program planning
        Program evaluation

    B. Level: At what level should the data be aggregated — individual client level or group/program level?

    C. Content areas: What is the substance or content of the information which needs to be collected?

        Communication
        Self-care
        Independent living
        Learning and problem solving
        Maladaptive behavior
        Physical development
        Emotional development
        Socialization
        Work habits and adjustment
        Environmental characteristics

    D. Ultimate user(s) of data: Who will use the data collected with the instrument?

        Service delivery staff (teachers, etc.)
        Provider administrators or planners
        Administrators outside of the provider (e.g., system-level staff)

    E. Data collection requirements: Is the data collection activity required?

        If so, does the mandate prescribe procedures and characteristics for the data collection, such as the name or content of the instrument, the frequency of data collection, etc.?

11

Table 2.1 (continued)

II. Population Characteristics

    A. Population: What are the basic characteristics of the population of clients to be assessed?

        Disability type and severity
        Age (calendar)
        Sex
        Ethnicity/SES

    B. Setting: In what general settings or environments does the data need to be collected?

        Residential institution
        School
        Work
        Community residence
        Home

Purpose

The first issue, the purpose of the data collection, relates to the *application* of the data: What decisions or actions will be performed on the basis of the data to be collected? We have identified the following five general types of applications for use in assessing the instruments reviewed in this book:

1. screening or eligibility determination of prospective clients;
2. development of an individualized plan for a client;
3. measurement of the progress of a client or group of clients over time;
4. collection of program data to determine and plan for general service needs; and
5. collection of program data for evaluation.

Despite apparent economies, it is very unlikely that the same instrument will be equally useful for all of these purposes. As will be discussed in a later section of this chapter, the characteristics required of an instrument for effective use for each of these purposes are sometimes in conflict. A more fruitful strategy to follow, for example, if you have the need for both individualized plan development and evaluation data would be to select different instruments for each purpose.

12

For the purposes of this discussion, it is possible to combine the data collection applications into three basic types of decisions, at both the client and program administration levels, which reflect the major stages in the delivery process:

planning decisions, required to determine eligibility and need and to make placement and programming recommendations;

monitoring decisions, required to determine whether services are being delivered in accordance with some predetermined plan or standard and whether changes or modifications are needed in the existing intervention or allocation of services; and

evaluation decisions, required to determine the effectiveness of a treatment or program.

The next question is what the level of aggregation (individual or group) will be for the data collected. This distinction will have major implications for instrument selection. Again, data which are useful at the individual client level may not be practical for use when aggregated. Likewise, data collected with an instrument designed for group data collection (as in a program evaluation) may not be useful for making inferences about individual clients.

The two levels of aggregation when crossed with the three types of decisions yield six possible purposes for an assessment. Examples of these purposes are displayed in Table 2.2. In each box of the table are listed the possible types of decisions to be made which have direct implications for the selection of an assessment instrument.

Planning decisions at the individual (client) level are concerned with initial screening decisions such as preliminary detection, eligibility determination, and disability classification, as well as intensive diagnostic decisions related to IHP planning, such as determining behavior strengths and weaknesses, generating behavioral objectives, specifying treatment strategies, and interventions. Planning decisions at the group or program level involve describing the characteristics of a population to determine the need for services and to assist in specific program planning and resource allocation.

Individual client monitoring decisions involve tracing the progress of a client over time to determine if behavioral objectives are being achieved, whether intervention or treatment is appropriate, and if IHP modifications are necessary. Monitoring at the group or program level is concerned with determining monitoring compliance with established standards and assessing the need for changes in program resource allocation.

Table 2.2
Decision and Assessment Purpose Chart

| | DECISION TYPE | | |
Aggregation	Planning Decisions	Monitoring Decisions	Evaluation Decisions
Individual Client Level	Provide for early detection of disability Screen clients for eligiblity Classify clients in disability or treatment category Provide diagnosis of strengths and weaknesses Determine strategies, interventions, treatments to be used Predict success of intervention Provide profile or total picture of client Provide information about needs, treatment to parents, service providers, client Develop IHP's specifying interventions to be used Generate behavioral objectives and long term goals Determine starting point for intervention Anticipate performance deficits in new behavior areas	Track progress over time Determine if IHP followed Determine if IHP should be modified Assess need for changes in intervention strategies Aid in counseling client Monitor client treatment Assess behavioral changes in small units Determine impact of environmental manipulation Assess whether behavioral objectives being met	Determine success or failure of treatment or intervention Reassess client strengths, weaknesses Assess client change, growth development Determine continued eligibility Determine whether client may be discharged Determine if goals were attained Reclassify place in different program
Group or Program Level	Provide descriptive information on client population Determine need for program Determine specific program needs Establish program priorities Develop program plan, operational guidelines Predict potential value of program	Determine needed program changes Assess allocation of services, resources Assess compliance with standards Assess specific program aspects that are effective Determine specific program weaknesses, problems	Study trends in program impact Assess change in groups of clients (whole programs or administrative units) Evaluate programs Determine impact of program on client Study trends in program impact Assess effectiveness of service Determine benefits of program Ascertain barriers to program success Compare effectiveness of alternative programs or interventions

Evaluation decisions at the client level are related to reassessment of growth and progress and continued eligibility. Client evaluation decisions also involve determining the success or failure of a particular intervention. And at the group or program level, evaluation decisions involve comparative evaluations of program impact and benefits, assessment of changes in program effectiveness over time, and the discovery of barriers to program success.

These six assessment purposes should help guide those selecting an instrument since the level and type of decision will help determine the qualities important in the selection of an appropriate assessment instrument.

Another important decision is the specification of the content area or areas about which data are to be collected. This requires some understanding of the wide range of content areas that exist so that, when reviewing tests, you will be able to determine if a particular instrument that claims to assess a particular content area does so in a manner that is consistent with your own evaluation of its appropriateness. Since many important constructs are ambiguously defined, it will be necessary to examine the author's claims about content by review of individual items and supporting test materials, such as the manual.

We have utilized nine content areas for use in subsequent reviews. Of course, your concept of these constructs may vary somewhat, so it is essential that you are sure of what it is you wish to measure so that you can determine if the content of a particular instrument is consistent with your conceptualization.

For example, what an author calls a test of "independent living" may measure skills quite different from those that you think should be measured. If an instrument was developed for a moderately retarded population living in a community residence, some of the content of the independent living scale could refer to the ability to go to a store or participate in some other community activity. However, if the clients you wish to assess are physically handicapped, the items in the scale requiring mobility may be inappropriate. Likewise, if your population is severely retarded and is located in a residential institution, there may be no practical opportunities to "go to the store," regardless of a client's level of functioning.

To determine the congruence between your concept of the trait to be measured and the author's operationalization of it in the scale, it is necessary to examine both the supporting materials for the instrument (the manual, etc.) as well as specific items in the scale. Often, the items will be the most illuminating and their interpretation requires no technical expertise. You should ask one simple question of each item: "Is this behavior being measured as part of the concept as I want it measured for my client population and setting?"

The next consideration is who will use the data collected with the instrument. This question has a number of implications for the selection process. If the data are to be used by individual service delivery staff (teachers, etc.) to assist them in working with individual clients, the data must be readily available and interpretable for an individual client. If, however, the data are to be used by the administration or planning staff of the provider institution to make general decisions about services, or if they are to be reported to some outside agency for the purposes of evaluation, then the data must be readily aggregated and should be highly quantitative.

In addition to the issue of the level of aggregation necessary introduced by the nature of the data user, the additional concern of interpretability emerges. Information of a highly detailed, clinical nature that describes a client's behaviors in great detail may be exactly what a teacher needs to plan an individualized program for the client. However, planners and evaluators will be quickly overwhelmed by such detailed data. These individuals need instruments which yield a small number of scale scores rather than detailed item-level information. On the other hand, service delivery staff and the planners/administrators of a single provider institution need some kind of performance standard for the instrument so that they can judge whether a particular client (or group) is performing as well as possible for his or her age and disability. A standard for client performance which can be easily interpreted and applied by the user is required. This is not always necessary for interprogram comparisons of the sort that are often made in statewide program evaluations. In such cases, variation among clients (or providers) serves to set relative expectations.

A final consideration for data collection is whether the activity is required. Do state or federal laws or program requirements mandate the collection of data from these clients? If so, one must consider the specific requirements of the mandate when selecting a test. The regulations surrounding such a requirement could specify the content to be assessed, the frequency of assessment, the population that should be assessed, the administration procedures to be followed, the agency to which data are reported or, in some cases, the specific instruments that should be used. It is therefore necessary to become familiar with the requirements of a mandated testing program so that you can be assured that your data collection is in compliance.

Population Characteristics

The second major set of variables relevant to instrument selection are *population characteristics*. Most instruments are designed for a particular reference population, whether that group is explicitly defined or only hinted at by the authors. The likely performance characteristics of a population suggest types of skills or behaviors that should be measured and those that should not. The reference population therefore sets certain expectations for the functioning of the clients to be assessed. It is important that these expectations be appropriate for your population and understood by you.

In comparing your population with the reference population of an instrument you should consider both client characteristics and setting. Client characteristics simply describe the population of clients to be assessed in terms of such variables as disability type and severity, calendar age, sex, ethnicity, and socioeconomic status. When considering an instrument, you should determine if it has been developed for or used in a population similar to your own. Very often an instrument will claim to be appropriate for "all types and levels of disability." While this may be true to some extent, you should still examine the instrument's supporting materials and item content to be sure it is appropriate for your clients. The question of setting raises many of the same issues stated above. Certain settings have particular expectations for the behavior of clients and what is appropriate in one setting may not be appropriate in another.

EXAMINING TEST DIMENSIONS

The second task in the selection of an instrument is to understand the dimensions that characterize different instruments. The dimensions used in this guide and in the accompanying reviews were selected to be comprehensive—they include major criteria considered important in theory and practice by both researcher and instrument users. The seven basic dimensions described below are derived from many sources, including agency standards, research guidelines, legislation, and administrative regulations

Content—Specification of the behavior domains to be measured, the depth and breadth with which those domains are measured, the appropriateness of the content for specific populations, and the sensitivity of the instrument to change

Administration—The procedures and personnel involved in completing the instrument and guaranteeing client rights

Interpretation—The existence and utility of different methods of assigning meaning to instrument scores for specific populations

Utility—The applicability and acceptability of the instrument to particular populations, settings, and decision purposes, and the degrees to which instrument manipulatability and cost affect its utility

Development—The methods used to construct and field test the instrument

Reliability—The internal consistency and stability of the instrument scores

Validity—The ability of the instrument to measure what it purports to measure, and the legitimate inferences that can be drawn from the instrument

We have chosen not to develop specific criteria or cutoff points for each of these dimensions. The particular criteria which you apply will depend on the specific purposes and needs of your program. The following sections describe the various elements to consider within each of these dimensions, and information about the individual instruments, as well as ratings, are provided on these dimensions in the instrument reviews found in Chapters 3 and 4.

Content

The content dimension involves determining the nature of the behavior domains included in the instrument, the appropriateness of the instrument for particular populations, and the sensitivity of the content to change. The content dimension provides information about the following questions:

What are the behavioral domains included in the instrument?

What range of skill does the instrument cover?

Are the items stated clearly and objectively?

Are the items developmentally sequenced?

For what types of clients is the instrument appropriate?

How sensitive is the instrument to client change?

In order to select an instrument for any purpose, it is obvious that one must ascertain its substantive content, particularly the number and type of behavior domains covered by the instrument. Some instruments will assess multiple domains but not in depth; others will concentrate on only a few domains but assess those few more extensively.

Instruments that cover more than one domain should offer evidence that the domains are independent either conceptually or analytically. For instance, an instrument may be reported to measure two domains—speech and language, but if the items on the two scales seem similar and the scales are highly correlated, they might better be considered as representing only one domain.

Beyond determining which domains are included in the instrument, it is important to determine whether the content and format of the items are appropriate for assessing the domain, as well as whether the instrument items are expressed clearly and objectively. It is also essential to consider whether the instrument requires that the client actually perform a particular behavior or that an informant report that the client can or has performed the behavior. Consideration should also be given to whether the items are unambiguous and objective. Whenever possible, instrument items should have clear behavioral referents.

Another concern when considering content is the range covered by the instrument items. Some instruments cover a wide range of behavior from no skill to complete mastery, while others target on a more limited range. The performance range of the items should be consistent with that expected in your client population. Items on some instruments are developmentally sequenced, suggesting that if a client can perform one item in the sequence, he or she should be able to perform all those preceding it. However, the validity of such sequences should be proven.

Having determined the behavior domains included in the instrument and the comprehensiveness and preciseness of the instrument in measuring those domains, we must now determine the population for whom the instrument is appropriate. Some instruments are designed for certain specific age/disability/severity levels; others are more widely applicable. But whatever the level, all instruments should be culture-free and minimize burdens imposed by language (except, of course, when assessing language). They should also be contemporary in idioms and in content. Tests developed long ago may contain items that are outdated, irrelevant, or inappropriate to current standards.

Of special concern should be any requirement of the assessment that presents a bias against some of your clients. For example, if you have a number of hearing-impaired clients and the instruments require a response to some verbal stimulus, obviously, there is a bias. In such a case, you might be able to overcome the bias by providing instructions in writing or sign.

Many instruments include content or behavior expectations that are inappropriate for clients with mobility impairments. Others, especially certain types of cognitive tests and emotional development measures, have been considered by some to have ethnic or cultural biases because of their response expectations. If this is of concern to you, be sure to examine the content of the instrument to assure that there are no inappropriate or sensitive items or, if such items do exist, that you can make allowances for them. Look specifically for scoring instructions detailing what should be done if a client does not have the opportunity to perform a particular behavior; is it assumed that the client is able to perform, unable, or is the item simply ignored? If it is ignored, how does that affect the scoring and interpretation of the instrument?

The appropriateness of the instrument for the setting must also be judged when reviewing instruments for developmentally disabled individuals. Many instruments were initially developed for institutional use and may not be applicable to clients in natural, foster, or group homes, or in independent or sheltered work environments. Related to the appropriateness of the instrument for different settings is the extent to which clients to be tested have had prior opportunities to learn, practice, or perform a skill. Many instruments do not take into account that some clients may not perform a particular skill because there is no opportunity for them to do so in their setting. Therefore, since the setting determines the types of opportunities available, instruments for which prior experience is important may not be easily transferable from one setting to another.

Administration

The administration dimension provides information related to the procedures and personnel involved in administering the instrument and insuring that client rights are respected. The following questions about this dimension must be answered:

What is the design and format of the instrument?

Is there a comprehensive instructional manual accompanying the instrument?

Are the instrument administration procedures clearly defined?

How long does it take to administer the instrument?

What type of person is required to administer the test?

What procedures exist to protect client rights?

In selecting an instrument you must consider the mechanics of information gathering and recording: Who provides the information (client, parent, service provider, psychologist, clinician), how it is obtained (observation, interview, written response) and, how it is recorded (narrative description, open-ended comments, rating scales, check lists). These mechanics are directly related to the accuracy and expense of the test, as well as the time involved.

Instruments vary in the degree to which their administrative procedures are standardized, that is, clearly defined, detailed, and explicit. Some instruments will be accompanied by a comprehensive manual or set of administrative procedures. Such manuals state the purpose and suggested use of the instrument, how and why the instrument was developed, as well as outline administrative procedures and scoring, including interpretation. Other manuals will provide only general guidelines under the assumption that the instrument administrator will have had the necessary training or experience to administer the instrument. Instructions also vary in the discretion they permit administrators to develop rapport and encourage attention, motivation, and task persistence. The degree to which the examiner is free to manipulate these attitudinal factors has important implications for the behavior demonstrated and the scores obtained on the instrument. Other factors such as time required for instrument administration and the size of the group involved substantially affect the cost of administering the instrument and thus are important practical factors in its selection.

The second element in the administration dimension involves the number and expertise of the personnel involved in administration. The use of multiple observers or informants (including the client's family or guardians) may increase the accuracy of the assessment but adds to the time and cost involved. Instruments vary in the extent to which training, experience, or professional certification is required for instrument administration.

This aspect also has implications for the cost of an instrument as well as the confidence one might place in the information it provides.

Client rights, the third element, are the result of recent government and agency directives at the federal, state, and local levels. Such directives call for certain rights for clients, particularly informed consent prior to testing, assurance of confidentiality, and freedom of access to all information. The instrument administration and subsequent data storage and release procedures must be in accordance with these directives.

Interpretation

The interpretation of instrument findings is the third dimension to be considered in selecting an instrument. This dimension provides information related to the following questions:

What types of raw and standardized scores are provided by the instrument?

Are confidence intervals provided for the scores?

What was the reference population from which the standardized scores were derived?

How difficult is it to communicate instrument findings to lay personnel and personnel from various professional disciplines?

An important consideration in interpretation is the type of score yielded by an instrument. Is only a raw score (number of items passed, frequency of occurrences of certain behaviors) used, or must the raw score be converted to some kind of standard score? If standard scores are used, it is important to be sure that the population on which the standardization was performed is similar to your client population.

Confidence intervals (probabilistic statements indicating the degree of confidence that the true score of the client is within a certain range) are helpful when discussing the accuracy of the score with others. Graphic presentations of scores and confidence intervals, including those provided in computerized reports, are helpful in communicating results to the client, parents, and other nonprofessional personnel.

In order to understand the applicability of the normative data to the intended population, the clients used in the normative sample must be described in terms of the characteristics that might be related to their performance, namely, age, socioeconomic status, disability type and severity, and setting. It is especially useful if normative data is available for certain subpopulations such as specific disabilities, ages, and settings.

The availability of normative data from a relevant population, confidence intervals, and graphic displays all contribute to the interpretability of instrument results. In addition, one needs to consider the need for training and/or clinical expertise to score and/or interpret the findings to nonprofessional personnel. The terminology involved in interpreting the results should be understood by nonprofessional individuals and professional personnel from other disciplines or service areas.

Utility

The utility dimension characterizes instruments in terms of their application for certain populations, settings, and purposes and considers their acceptance, manipulability, and cost. This dimension provides information on the following questions:

How appropriate is this instrument for the particular client population, setting, and decision needs?

How acceptable is this instrument to state and local administrators, parents, advocacy groups, legislators, and service providers?

Are the findings from this instrument quantifiable and aggregatable?

Is this instrument adaptable for computer scoring and analysis?

What are the direct and indirect costs involved in using the instrument?

In order to select an assessment instrument, it is important to know the population, setting, and purpose for which the instrument was originally designed and is recommended. Although many instruments are developed for specific populations, settings, and purposes, often an instrument developed for a particular application can be extended to other applications without serious loss of reliability or validity. Sometimes, however, an instrument can be revised to meet a program's specific requirements.

The acceptance of the instrument by other users, particularly those in similar situations and with similar decision needs, is an important indication of an instrument's utility. One of the best indications of acceptability is the extent of current use. However, often well known instruments that are widely used may not be completely satisfactory, and others might be used more widely if they were better known. Instrument acceptance by other users is important, but acceptance by client families, consumer advocacy groups, researchers and state and local administrators should also be considered. The extent to which an instrument meets legally mandated assessment requirements is another significant aspect of acceptance.

Manipulatability, particularly the extent to which an instrument yields scores that can be quantified and aggregated, and the ease with which scores can be calculated and standardized is the third aspect of instrument utility. Also included in the characteristics of manipulatability are the availability of computerized scoring services and/or the adaptability of the instrument for in-house computer manipulation.

The manipulatability of an instrument is enhanced when the instrument contains relatively independent modular scales or subscores that can be added, subtracted, or modified depending on the instrument's intended use. In addition, instruments are more adaptable if analytic procedures (i.e., formulas for profile construction) are available which suggest how the instrument scores may be used for particular purposes.

Another consideration of instrument utility is cost: both the direct cost of obtaining instrument materials and the indirect cost of personnel time. In estimating personnel time, you must include time involved in training or preparing to use the instrument, administering and scoring the test, and interpreting its results. It is useful if costs are expressed on a per pupil, per administration basis. Of course, this accounting will generally show that group-administered instruments are cheaper on a per client basis.

Development

The fifth dimension, the development process, takes place during instrument construction and field testing. This dimension provides information regarding the following questions:

What was the original purpose for the construction of the instrument?

What method was used to select and sequence the items?

What was the population used in the field test of the instrument?

It is important to understand the purpose for which the instrument was originally developed since many of them are originally created for a specific research purpose or to meet a specific program need such as screening, diagnosis, or program evaluation. Related to the question of original purpose is that of the theoretical framework (e.g., Piaget) upon which the instrument was based and which guided the selection and sequence of the items. The final aspect of the instrument construction involves the extent to which pilot testing and subsequent modification (addition, removal, rewording, rearrangement) took place prior to actual field testing.

The field test is the first major administration of the instrument from which are derived the psychometric properties of the instrument, particularly item analysis, reliability, and validity. The field test population should be described in terms of age (developmental level), ethnic group, socioeconomic status, and disability/severity, and the results of all psychometric analyses discussed. Item analysis of the field test must also be conducted to determine item difficulty, sequence verification, internal consistency, and the independence of scales and subscales.

Reliability

The last two dimensions of an instrument that may be considered as selection criteria are psychometric properties of reliability and validity. Reliability refers to the consistency and stability of an assessment instrument. This dimension provides information regarding the following questions:

What type of reliability evidence is provided for the instrument?

What are the characteristics of the population from whom the reliability evidence was obtained?

In reviewing reported reliability data, it is important to be precise about the nature of the reliability of the coefficient being reported. Is the report related to an internal consistency measure of reliability, to a test-retest assessment, or to interrater agreement? What are the conditions under which the reliability data were collected? For example, an interrater study which had different raters assess the behavior of the same client (observed simultaneously or from videotape) may show a higher interrate correlation than a study that has the same raters assess the behavior of clients at different times. Another common approach is to have day and evening staff rate the behavior of institutionalized clients and to correlate their ratings. However, it is possible that the client's behavior was actually different at these times and that inconsistent observations are not indicators of unreliability of the procedure.

The concept of stability must be introduced here. When comparing scores of the same individual at different times, is it reasonable to assume that the client's "true score" on the instrument is likely to be unchanged? When measuring development over long periods, one hopes for some growth. However, there is often short-term change in behavior. For example, measures of the incidence of maladaptive behavior are prone to instability and are related to the setting of the observation. So, in assessing the reliability expected of a test, some consideration must be given to the expected stability of the test score given the conditions under which data were obtained.

The reliability coefficient for a specific test will fall between 0 and 1, regardless of whether interval consistency, test-retest, or interrater reliability is being measured. What level of reliability is acceptable in an instrument? Psychometricians disagree, but none advocate a single criterion which ignores the use to which the test will be put. In particular, it is recognized that the measurement of individual performance requires substantially higher reliability than the measurement of group performance, and that for both individual and group measurement, internal consistency reliability must be higher if the objective is to measure change in performance over time than if the objective is to measure performance at a given point.* From a practical or programmatic standpoint reliability is important because it determines the extent to which scores obtained from different groups, by different testers (or raters), or for the same group at different points in time can be compared.

---

*Short-term test-retest reliability which is not affected by the instability of test scores must also be higher if change over time is to be assessed. The measurement of change, however, is psychometrically complex. Paradoxically, for example, the test-retest correlation over the span of time in question, which does not include instability, must not too closely approximate the test's internal consistency at the individual time points, or even the most sophisticatedly computed change scores will have very poor reliability (Bache 1979, Stanley 1971).

Validity

The validity dimension indicates the degree to which the assessment instrument is capable of achieving certain aims. The validity dimension provides answers to the following questions:

What type of validity evidence is provided for the instrument?

Are separate validity estimates provided for each scale?

What are the characteristics of the population (including environmental setting and geographic area) from which the validity evidence was obtained?

Three particular aspects of validity—content, criterion, and construct—are typically considered in this test dimension. Content validity is the extent to which the instrument items are representative of the behavior or domain about which conclusions are to be drawn; criterion validity is the extent to which the instrument scores are related to the probable performance of the subject on another instrument or different situation; and construct validity is the extent to which the instrument scores are reflective of the psychological qualities or developmental stages they are intended to reflect.

The documentation for an instrument should discuss the types of validity appropriate for the instrument and its potential use, and should describe the validation studies that have been conducted using the instrument. Whenever possible, validity investigations conducted by persons other than the instrument developers should be examined.

SELECTING AN ASSESSMENT INSTRUMENT

After clarifying the context of the assessment that is contemplated and gaining some understanding of the characteristics that describe instruments, it is possible to begin the search for an instrument that is best suited for your needs.

This instrument selection process (described in Figure 2.1) begins with identification of potential instruments. Detailed reviews of measures of various aspects of developmental progress which are suited for use with developmentally disabled clients in a variety of settings are contained in this book. These may serve as a starting point. Using the summary tables on subsequent pages, you may first identify those instruments that assess the content area(s) in which you are interested. This can be determined from

Figure 2.1
Steps in Selecting an Instrument

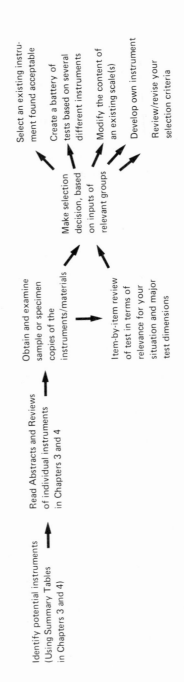

the content columns of the table or by inspection of the titles of instruments although these are sometimes nonspecific or misleading. Those instruments which, based on other information contained in the table, appear definitely to be unsuitable for your purpose or population can be screened out. At this stage of the process you should be generous in your assessments; continue to examine as many instruments as possible and keep a list of the names of instruments that seem to have potential.

Next, read the reviews of these instruments; they will provide more detail on instrument content (administration time, costs, etc.) and give some subjective assessment of the general suitability of the instrument for the developmentally disabled population. The reviews represent the collective opinions of a number of experts in measurement and service delivery but should *not* be taken as the last words on an instrument. However, they will point out some of the strengths and weaknesses of each instrument and should highlight issues for you to be aware of as you continue the selection process.

The next and most important stage of the process is to obtain and examine sample or specimen copies of the instruments, and to supplement that with materials such as the manual and other available technical reports. However, only through detailed study of the instrument itself can a final judgement of appropriateness be made. It is important to realize, though, that there may be some instruments in addition to those reviewed in this volume that may be appropriate. You may come across reference to these in journal articles, other instrument reviews, publishers' catalogs, and so forth. Use whatever descriptive information is available to perform the initial screening of these scales and then subject them to the same examination as the instruments reviewed in this volume.

Any instrument examination should begin with an explicit restatement of the developmental or educational goals of your program. This strategy applies equally to the use of tests for individual client planning and for large-scale, statewide program evaluations. Then, study each item in the scale to see if its content is relevant to these objectives. For each item, record which objective(s) are assessed. This will be useful information for diagnostic purposes should you eventually use the scale. After going through this exercise, you should note whether all important aspects of your objectives are adequately covered by the content of the instrument and observe the proportion of "irrelevant" items. If you have multiple objectives that can be prioritized, see if the relative coverage of objectives is in proportion to their priority.

Don't expect to find an existing scale that is perfectly congruent with your objectives or curriculum goals. Most scales were designed to measure fairly general traits (e.g., adaptive behavior) and are therefore attempts at incorporating a wide range of behaviors. Other scales have been designed with specific reference to a particular set of objectives or an educational program in use somewhere. While these instruments may be a perfect fit for this other program, what is important is how it fits yours.

The items provide information in addition to their substantive content and you must judge it, too. Are terms vaguely defined? Is there some implicit bias in the setting? Do items (and their response categories) contain ethnic or sex role stereotypes? You will have to judge the appropriateness of items for your population and setting from their content and language.

Going beyond the items, it is necessary to examine closely other attributes of the instrument (such as those outlined previously). To conduct this type of examination, you will need, at minimum, access to the test manual. The manual should contain background information on the rationale for and development of the instrument, detailed instructions for administration and scoring, and guidance for score interpretation, as well as information on the psychometric properties of the instrument (reliability and validity). The manual may be supplemented by other information sources such as journal articles to provide more detail, clarification of certain points, or additional empirical evidence of the properties of the scale.

Armed with this knowledge about all candidate instruments, you will have to make a selection. The selection process will generally be a difficult one because a number of potential instruments, each having unique strengths and weaknesses, may be found, and it will be necessary to balance their various attributes to make the most appropriate selection. Content considerations must be weighed with practical constraints such as the time and effort needed to administer a scale, and psychometric quality. For example, in general, longer scales (i.e., those with more items) are more reliable than shorter ones. You may have to decide if for your intended purpose the additional cost of using a longer and more reliable scale is offset by additional confidence in the accuracy of its scores.

The final selection process should include inputs from a variety of relevant groups. The most essential group consists of those who will ultimately use the data the scale provides. Their decision must be the result of examining sufficient data about the instrument selected. Service delivery staff should also be consulted about the appropriateness of the instrument's content and level of difficulty for the intended client population. Given informed consent and open disclosure of records requirements, it is advisable that clients be represented in the decision process personally or by advocates to be sure that the content is not considered offensive or inappropriate. Finally, measurement or research methodologists can provide useful observations to guide the selection process by interpreting the technical information obtained about potential instruments.

The above process should lead to a conclusion, at which time a single, optimal, if not perfect, instrument is selected for use. However, it is possible that no existing instrument is acceptable for a particular application. What alternatives are then available? If the problem is simply one of coverage of domains, it is possible to use several instruments in conjunction. Many comprehensive scales consist of such combinations, but you may wish to chose your own scales from several sources to combine. The drawback here is that a total score cannot be interpreted and that the various norming populations for the separate instruments (if they exist) will probably not be directly comparable. However, for applications requiring a profile of data on clients, but not a total score, use of multiple measurements may be advisable.

Also, it may often seem appropriate to modify the content of a particular scale to make it more appropriate for your population or setting. For example, you may wish to rephrase items which seem institutionally oriented for use in a population of community residents. Or you may want to drop some items entirely, perhaps substituting some of your own. If modification does take place, you have essentially created a new instrument and existing data about the original version no longer applies. Scoring procedures may be invalidated and all reference norms must be considered inapplicable. Although it is entirely possible that the revised scale may be more appropriate for your population, you cannot assume very much about its psychometric characteristics. If you intend to publish your results or compare scores obtained with the revised version of the score with those based on the original, then this course of action is not recommended. But, if the instrument is to be used locally for diagnostic purposes and scores are not to be compared to existing norms, such revisions may be feasible. However, if the content is changed drastically or the length of the scale is reduced, the risk is one of reduced reliability and validity. Still, the changes may enhance the content validity with respect to your program and, on balance, be justified.

An even further departure would be the development of an original instrument. This is an expensive and time-consuming process and should not be undertaken without a clear understanding of what is required to produce an instrument of high quality.

After reviewing the available instruments, you may find that no alternative seems attractive. It may then be necessary to review your criteria and constraints; it is possible that the demands you have set for an instrument are simply not feasible. Your willingness to settle for less (e.g., an instrument that does not include assessment of a particular content area), however, may immediately suggest an appropriate scale. The decision to change your criteria can actually come at any point in the selection and review process when it becomes apparent that the demands are too stringent.

In summary, the selection process is one of compromise. It will be necessary to trade off considerations of content against practicality, practicality against psychometric quality, and quality against content. If all possible options are explored fully and objectively and you have taken the time to examine several possible instruments and allow people with divergent perspectives on assessment to present their opinions you will ultimately make the best decision. This is especially true if you intend a wide range of staff members to participate in the assessment process of supplying, using, or interpreting data.

ADMINISTRATION OF INSTRUMENTS

Having selected an assessment instrument, you are now almost ready to begin collecting data. First, you should obtain sufficient copies of the assessment materials for your purpose. Then, review once again, in detail, the administration procedures for the instrument; be sure you have available the right number and type of staff to collect data. And, if training sessions are required, plan to have them before the data collection effort begins. Then, with materials in hand and with trained staff ready, you can start data collection.

In this section we will present some of the various considerations related to the administration and use of tests. Many of the points made here can be found in standard textbooks on psychological assessment and are also an integral part of the American Psychological Association's *Standards for Educational and Psychological Tests* (1974). We urge readers who are responsible for an assessment program but are not familiar with the standards or have not had some formal training in psychological assessment to read and become familiar with these materials. Ultimately, the quality and usefulness of data are determined by the procedures followed in obtaining it.

A basic principle in assessment is the concept of *standardization*. Because it is important to reduce the probability of bias in scores due to variation in procedures the procedures for quantifying behavior (e.g., testing environment, instructions to the examinee or rater) must be kept consistent (standardized) across all administrations of the test. Standardization of procedures is particularly important when decisions such as program placement or IHP development are to be made on the basis of scores or when data from several different locations, as in a statewide evaluation, are to be compared or combined. Unless administration procedures are followed exactly, you cannot assume that published performance standards (norms, etc.) can be used validly.

Standardization is especially important for rating scales. Precise, objective definitions of criterion behaviors are necessary to assure that data obtained from different raters are comparable—that two raters who view the same behavior will be able to provide the same rating. Many manuals provide data on interrater reliability (correlations or percent agreement) but this should be interpreted as the *maximum* likely agreement because most studies of reliability of this sort are conducted under the direction of the instrument's developer and generally include extensive training and close supervision of raters.

When giving instructions to instrument administrators, be sure to stress the need for consistency of procedures over time and across settings. If the instrument is to be used repeatedly (such as for regular periodic progress monitoring or as an intake screening device) it is possible that even the best training and instructions will be less effective over time; people forget and there will inevitably be staff turnover. In this case, it may be advisable to prepare your own procedures manual which includes not only the instructions provided by the scale's author but also any local elaboration and specification of the procedures that have been established.

Most instruments specify to some extent the qualifications required of the staff members who will administer the instrument. While many authors state that "no special training or qualifications" are required, this can be misleading. Although it may not be necessary for staff members to participate in an extensive, formal training program to learn how to administer an instrument, it is essential that they have some practice with the form and procedures before entering the field to collect data. Otherwise, aspects of the procedures could become confusing in a data collection situation and cause a problem which may unfairly bias the score obtained by the client being assessed. Likewise, while graduate training or degrees in psychology may not be necessary for a user, he or she must fully understand the administration procedures and their rationale and should have some basic grasp of the issues in data collection discussed in this section (especially the need for standardization of procedures).

Most assessment situations have a *social context* and the interaction between the tester and the client can have major effects on the performance observed and, therefore, on the validity of the data. This is especially true in a situation in which the person conducting the assessment requires the client to respond explicitly to some stimulus. The client's attitudes are not directly involved in an assessment in which there is unobtrusive observation or in which the data are provided by a rater in retrospect (i.e., without direct observation but based on familiarity with the client). In these cases, however, the biases of the rater can affect the scores.

The primary determinant of the social context of the assessment is the person who conducts the assessment (the rater, observer, etc.) and his or her perception of the assessment situation itself. Does he or she resent having to provide the data considering it a useless imposition? If so, the procedures may be treated cursorily and any number of errors can creep in. Does the assessor have objections to the overall assessment process (especially likely in an evaluative context)? If so, there is the danger that ratings will be enhanced. The rater may, consciously or not, give better ratings to clients than they truly deserve in an effort to make their (and, perhaps, the rater's) performance appear better. Does the rater have a bias against some irrelevant characteristics of the client (e.g., race or physical handicap)? If so, these biases can affect the validity of ratings. A very common problem observed in the assessment of disabled clients is that the staff members conducting the assessments are service delivery staff and care a great deal about the clients and their welfare. For this reason, they are often lenient in assessments, giving higher scores than an objective observer would, often because they "know" that the client can perform a particular behavior even though he or she does not perform in the formal assessment situation. These biases are natural and common in all forms of psychological assessment. Sensitization of data collection staff to their existence and to the dangers associated with them should be an integral part of the training process.

When the client has to provide a response in direct reaction to a stimulus, the rater must provide some support and instruction. Clients may be unmotivated or hostile and the rater must get them to perform as well as possible. The rater should develop rapport with the client and be sure that all instructions are clearly understood without coaching a particular response. There is a fine line between motivating and helping a client. The rater must be sure that the input provided to the client being assessed in no way gives that particular client any advantage over other clients with whom the current client's scores will in some way be compared. This is especially a problem with clients having some sort of communications impairment and requires very sensitive tailoring of instructions to the specific needs and abilities of the client. If your population has a significant proportion of such clients, it is important to select an assessment procedure which depends as little as possible on direct communication with clients or which is designed to allow a range of communication methods.

Likewise, instruments which require physical mobility or coordination but which are not direct measures of these skills (e.g., a measure of cognitive skills that requires the client to identify and move blocks) must be used with caution in the case of a disabled population. You should select an instrument which minimizes the problem and not leave it to the discretion of a rater to modify an item to respond to the limitations of a client. If items are to be modified, the procedures to be followed should be specified explicitly in advance and made part of the training process for raters at your facility.

Scoring and Interpretation

Once data are collected, it is generally necessary to score the instrument. This process can be very simple (count the number of behaviors checked) or can require complex statistical manipulation of a number of variables. The individual raters are responsible for the clerical accuracy and legibility of their report forms, just as the person(s) scoring the test are responsible for the quantitative accuracy of the scoring. Be sure that the scoring procedures and formulas are clear in advance, and that someone is designated to implement them. If the task is large or complex, you should investigate computerized scoring or processing of results. Some instruments offer this as an optional service from their distributors.

Interpretation of scores is a clinical and subjective process. Most instruments in use provide some basis for interpreting scores such as norms or criterion behaviors. The interpretation procedures should be described in some detail in the manual. Some knowledge of statistics may be helpful in interpretation, especially if group data are being used. We assume that there will be a qualified research methodologist involved in the project as a staff member or consultant.

Client Rights

Throughout the assessment process, from test selection to the storage of results, the rights of clients must be understood and respected. A number of recent federal and state laws grant the following rights to all clients being assessed:

Informed consent. The client, or someone acting in his or her behalf, such as a parent or guardian, has the right to know why data are being collected and can refuse to participate. Participation in most educational programs constitutes implicit consent for data collected as a routine part of the instructional process (e.g., periodic evaluations of progress).

Privacy. Client records, including scores and interpretations of them, must be protected from unauthorized release. Professional staff may have access to the data but other agencies (potential employers, for example) cannot be given the data without the explicit permission of the client. The privacy provisions also apply to computerized data. If data are stored in computerized form the data files must be constructed to keep the identity of individual clients obscured to all except authorized parties.

Freedom of information. The client, or the client's parent or guardian, has the right to see information maintained in the client's files, including scores and their interpretations. For this reason, care must be taken to assure that data are accurate and that interpretations are clear to a lay person and logically follow from the data.

SUMMARY

In general, the selection of an instrument to assess the developmental progress of a developmentally disabled client is a process of identifying available measures and selecting the one (or set) best suited for your own purposes and situation. This requires initially a clear and explicit understanding of the reasons for which you want to collect data, the domains (content areas) about which you want data, and the population from which the data will be collected. Use this information to screen available instruments to locate a small number for extensive review. The instrument reviews in this volume are one source of tests, although there are others.

When you have identified some candidate instruments, obtain specimen copies of the forms, manuals, and other available supporting materials. Examine them closely to be sure that the content of the instrument is consistent with your needs; different authors may operationalize the same construct in quite different ways. Find the instrument with the best match of features for your setting; do not expect to find a perfect fit. Making the final selection will therefore be a compromise, so all interested parties should be involved in the decision, including both programmatic staff (e.g., teachers) and measurement specialists.

When the instrument is used in your facility, be sure all administration instructions are followed exactly and consistently, otherwise that data may be invalidated and comparisons with other settings (including norms) may be inappropriate. The staff who collect data should receive some (even if brief) explicit training and practice with the instrument under the supervision of a senior professional before they collect data from clients. Throughout the process the rights of clients must be protected and compliance with appropriate federal and state regulations must be assured.

References

American Psychological Association, Inc. *Standards for Educational and Psychological Tests*. Washington, D.C., 1974.

Bache, W.L. "The Reliability of Three Measures of Change." Unpublished manuscript. Cambridge, Mass.: Abt Associates, Inc. 1979.

Cronbach, L.J. & Furby, L. "How We Should Measure Change — or Should We?" *Psychological Bulletin*, 1971, *74*, 68-80.

Stanley, J. "Reliability." In R.L. Thorndike (ed.), *Educational Measurement*, Washington, D.C.: American Council on Education, 1971 (2nd ed.).

Chapter 3

Primary Client Assessment Instruments

In this chapter, the reviews of 47 client assessment instruments selected for primary review are presented. The following information is presented for each instrument:

Summary tables. Major instrument characteristics are presented as a screening device for readers in helping them identify instruments of particular interest for which they should pursue further review information. (Tables 3.1 and 3.2)

Abstract. A brief description of each instrument as reported by author(s) in test manual and other supporting materials is presented. The abstracts include information on intended purposes, domains, procedures, and costs of instruments.

Review. The narrative review of each instrument is based on the reviewer's evaluation of the instrument in terms of seven major dimensions—content, administration, interpretation, utility, test development, reliability, and validity.

These three sets of information are intended to be used as a unit. The reader should first refer to the summary tables to determine which instruments are of particular interest for his or her purposes or needs. After identifying these instruments, both the abstracts and reviews of those tests should be read. The summary tables should not be used separately from the other sources of information because the data in the tables are too cursory to be useful for other than screening purposes. The abstracts and reviews present the detailed factual and assessment data and serve as the basis for the summary table.

Readers should not select particular instruments for use in their programs based solely on the abstracts and reviews presented in this report since they are intended to serve as the foundation for further investigation. The reference and citations listed at the end of each review, where available, can assist readers in identifying additional sources of information about specific instruments.

SUMMARY TABLES

Two summary tables (3.1 and 3.2) are presented to assist readers in screening client assessment instruments of particular interest to them. Table 3.1 summarizes the major characteristics of primary client assessment instruments based on authors' statements (obtained from test manuals and supporting materials). Table 3.2 presents a summary assessment of these instruments based on the reviewers' evaluations.

Both tables are presented because they provide somewhat different perspectives of the instruments. The information in the reviewers' table is more selective in many cases than that reported in the authors' table. For example, an author might claim that his/her test measures communication, independent living, and emotional development, so three checks would appear under the "domains" column. However, the reviewer may judge that only the communication domain was measured adequately by the test, so only one check mark would appear in the reviewers' table.

Description of Terms

Descriptions of the terms used in Tables 3.1 and 3.2 are presented below.

Purposes

In Table 3.1, the authors' intended purposes of the instrument are listed. In Table 3.2, the reviewers' recommended purposes are listed. The specific purposes included are:

Individual plan development. Plans of intervention and action for individual clients such as the federally mandated Individual Habilitation Plans (Developmentally Disabled Assistance and Bill of Rights Act of 1975, P.L. 94-103) and the Individual Education Plan (Education of All Handicapped Children Act of 1975, P.L. 94-142) are developed. These and other related plans focus on client abilities and needs, specified goals and objectives for client progress, procedures for implementation and review of the plan, and client progress.

Monitoring client progress. Progress made by the individual over time is measured, implying the existence of baseline data and follow-up assessment.

Screening/needs assessment. Individual clients or groups of clients are screened to determine the nature and extent of their disabilities and needs.

Overall program planning. Based on information about groups of clients, plans and decisions regarding what services are needed and should be provided, and who should provide these services are made.

Overall program evaluation. Assessment of program process and impacts at the individual service provider level or at broader levels of program (e.g., local or state-wide evaluation of service systems) are made.

Population

Disability Type (Severity). In Table 3.1 the descriptions of type and severity of disability are based on the authors' statements. In Table 3.2, the descriptions of these terms are based on either the authors' statements—in those cases where the reviewer was in agreement with the authors' or the reviewers' judgement—in those cases where the reviewer disagreed with the authors' statements.

Age. In Table 3.1, the age ranges presented are based on the authors' statements. Again, in Table 3.2, the age range is based on either the authors' statements when the reviewer and the author(s) are in agreement, or the reviewer's judgement if there is disagreement.

Setting Characteristics (Table 3.2 Only)

Setting characteristics are the general settings for which an instrument is appropriate, based on the reviewer's opinion. The specific settings include institutions, community programs, schools, and workshops.

Domains

Domains refer to the aspects of development which the instrument is intended to measure (Table 3.1) or is judged by the reviewer to measure adequately or better (Table 3.2), and consist of the following:

Communication. Includes verbal and nonverbal, receptive and expressive communication skills.
> *Examples:* Language, receptive language, expressive language, listening, understanding, auditory comprehension, verbal, speech, speaking, voice, sign language, lip reading, and conversation.

Self-care skills. Skills that enable an individual to meet his or her own basic self-care needs.
> *Examples:* Drinking, eating, toileting, dressing, hygiene, appearance, cleanliness, washing, showering, bathing, grooming, toothbrushing, meal behaviors, manners, and personal and bedtime routines.

Independent living skills. Skills that enable an individual to function independently in the home and the community.
> *Examples:* Care of clothing, clothes selection, laundry, cooking, domestic activities, housecleaning, health care, safety, transportation, travel, postal, telephone, shopping, money management, and time management.

Learning and problem-solving abilities. Includes general cognitive, competence, and academic and preacademic skills.
> *Examples:* Reading, writing, quantitative skills, recognition, perception, reasoning, memory, knowledge, and cognition.

Maladaptive behaviors. Extreme behavior problems that involve antisocial or deviant behaviors, or danger to self or to others.

Examples: Aggresion, hyperactivity, violence, extreme acting out or temper tantrums, withdrawal, delinquency, suicidal tendencies, and self-injurious behavior.

Physical development. Includes both motor and sensory development.

Examples: Gross motor, basic motor, body-motor, fine motor, visual-motor, perceptual-motor, hand-motor, manual dexterity, coordination, perception, sensory-motor, balance, posture, sitting, ambulation, locomotion, crawling, walking, and climbing.

Emotional development. Behaviors that affect an individual's relationships with other people and the individual's interests, attitudes, values, or emotional expressions.

Examples: Emotion, initiative, self-management, self-direction, self-esteem, self-concept, self-confidence, social maturity, social awareness, cooperation, and emotional stability.

Socialization. Refers to an individual's social relationships and interactions in social activities.

Examples: Peer relationships, family relationships, friendships, interpersonal or social interactions, involvement in clubs and organizations, and involvement in social and leisure time activities.

Work habits and work adjustment. Ability to perform assigned job tasks independently, to maintain proper work habits, and to work well with fellow employees and employers.

Examples: Job-finding skills, job-learning skills, work habits, work performance, and adjustment to work or work training.

Environmental characteristics. Characteristics of the individual's environment, such as normalization aspects of the individual's residential and work situation, community attitudes, barriers, and aspects of the service delivery process.

Summary Ratings (Table 3.2 Only)

The summary ratings are organized according to the seven major dimensions on which instruments were evaluated by reviewers—content, administration, interpretation, utility, test development, reliability, and validity.

Table 3.1
Characteristics of Primary Client Assessment Instruments
(Based on Authors' Statements)

CLIENT ASSESSMENT INSTRUMENTS	Individual Plan Development	Client Progress Measurement	Screening/Eligibility Determination	Program Planning/Evaluation	DISABILITY TYPE (SEVERITY)	AGE	Communication	Self-care Skills	Independent Living Skills	Learning and Problem-solving Abilities	Maladaptive Behavior	Physical Development	Emotional Development	Socialization	Work Habits and Work Adjustment	Environmental Characteristics
AAMD-Becker Reading-Free Vocational Interest Inventory	X		X		Retardation (Mild)	14-25+									X	
AAMD Adaptive Behavior Scale	X		X	X	Retardation, Emotional Disturbances	6-69	X	X	X	X	X	X	X	X		
AAMD ABS Public School Version	X		X	X	Retardation (Trainable and Educable), Educational Handicaps, Normal Intelligence	7-13	X	X	X	X	X	X	X	X		
Adaptive Functioning Index	X	X	X		Developmental Disabilities	14+	X	X	X	X				X	X	
Balthazar Scales I. Functional Independence	X	X		X	Retardation (Severe and Profound)	5-57		X	X							
Balthazar Scales II. Social Adaptation	X	X		X	Retardation (Severe and Profound)	All	X	X			X		X	X		
Behavior Development Survey	X	X	X	X	Developmental Disabilities	All	X	X	X			X	X	X		
Bristol Social Adjustment Guides	X	X	X		Emotional Disturbances, Social Immaturity, Neurological Impairments	5-14					X		X	X	X	
Bruininks-Oseretsky Test of Motor Proficiency	X	X	X	X	From Retardation (Severe) to Normal Intelligence	4½-14½						X				
Cain-Levine Social Competency Scale	X	X	X	X	Retardation (Trainable)	5-12	X	X	X					X		
California Preschool Social Competency Scale	X	X	X	X	Normal Intelligence	2½-5½	X	X	X					X		
Callier-Azusa Scale	X	X	X	X	Deaf-blind and Other multiple Handicaps)Severe and Profound)	All	X		X	X		X	X	X		
Camelot Behavioral Checklist	X	X	X		Retardation (All Levels)*	2-Adult*	X	X	X	X		X		X	X	
Child Behavior Rating Scale		X	X		Normal Intelligence, Emotional Handicaps	5-9					X		X	X		
Client-Centered Evaluation Model	X	X	X	X	All Disabilities	1-Adult	X		X	X			X	X	X	X
Community Adjustment Scale		X	X		Retardation	Adults	X	X	X	X	X	X	X	X	X	X
Denver Developmental Screening Test		X	X		Developmental Impairments	0-6	X	X		X			X	X		
Fairview Scales Self-Help	X	X	X		Retardation (Severe and Profound)	2-9	X	X	X	X			X	X		
Fairview Scales Language Evaluation	X	X	X		All Disabilities	0-6	X									
Fairview Scales Problem Behavior Record	X	X	X		Retardation	All					X		X			
Fairview Scales Development	X	X	X		Retardation (Severe and Profound)	0-2	X	X						X	X	
Fairview Scales Social Skills	X	X	X		Retardation (Severe and Profound)	2-9	X	X	X	X			X	X		
Learning Accomplishment Profile	X	X	X		Developmental Delays	Children	X	X		X			X	X		
Lexington Developmental Scales	X	X	X		Learning Handicaps	0-6	X	X	X			X		X		

*Not specified by the author; this is the reviewer's assessment.

Table 3.1 (continued)

CLIENT ASSESSMENT INSTRUMENTS	Individual Plan Development	Client Progress Measurement	Screening/Eligibility Determination	Program Planning/Evaluation	DISABILITY TYPE (SEVERITY)	AGE	Communication	Self-care Skills	Independent Living Skills	Learning and Problem-solving Abilities	Maladaptive Behavior	Physical Development	Emotional Development	Socialization	Work Habits and Work Adjustment	Environmental Characteristics
MDC Behavior Identification Form	X	X	X	X	Retardation, Developmental Disabilities	Adolescents - Adults									X	
Mid-Nebraska Basic Skills Screening Test	X	X	X	X	Retardation (Borderline, Mild, Moderate, Severe)	NS**										
Mid-Nebraska Independent Living Screening Test	X	X	X	X	Retardation (Borderline, Mild, Moderate)	NS**	X		X			X	X	X	X	
Mid-Nebraska Competitive Employment Screening Test	X	X	X	X	Retardation (Borderline, Mild)	NS**										
Minnesota Developmental Programming System Behavioral Scales	X	X	X		Mental Retardation and Developmental Disabilities (All Levels, except Total Dependence)	All but very young and very old	X	X	X	X		X		X	X	
O'Berry Developmental Tests— Behavior Maturity Checklist			X		Retardation (Severe and Profound primarily, but also younger, trainable and educable)	0-16		X								
Ohio Performance Scale	X	X	X		Retardation (All Levels)	NS**	X	X	X	X	X	X	X	X	X	
Pinecrest Behavior Meters of Primary Functioning	X	X	X	X	Retardation	All	X	X				X				
Preschool Attainment Record	X	X	X		All Developmental Disabilities	0-7	X			X		X		X		
Progress Assessment Chart of Social and Personal Development	X	X	X		Retardation (All Levels)	0-Adult	X	X	X			X			X	X	X
San Francisco Vocational Competency Scale	X	X	X		Retardation (Mild to Severe)	18+									X	
Santa Cruz Behavioral Characteristics Progression	X	X	X		All Disabilities	3-18	X	X	X	X	X	X	X	X	X	
School Behavior Profile		X	X		Physical, Intellectual and Emotional Handicaps (Mild to Moderate)	5-9	X				X		X	X	X	
Social and Prevocational Information Battery	X	X	X	X	Retardation (Educable)	15-65	X	X	X				X		X	
Social and Prevocational Information Battery — Form T	X	X	X	X	Retardation (Trainable)	15-65	X	X	X				X		X	
TARC Assessment System	X	X	X	X	Retardation (Severe and Profound), Autism, Cerebral Palsy	3-16	X	X	X			X	X			
Test of Social Inference			X		Retardation (Mild)	7½+							X			
TMR School Competency Scales	X	X		X	Retardation (Trainable)	5-17+	X	X		X		X	X	X		
Uniform Performance Assessment System	X	X	X	X	All Disabilities	0-6						X		X		
Vineland Social Maturity Scale	X	X	X		All Developmental Disabilities	0-Adult	X	X	X					X	X	
Vocational Behavior Scale (Experimental)	X	X	X		Special Needs	NS**									X	
Vulpé Assessment Battery	X	X	X	X	All Developmental Disabilities	0-6	X	X	X	X	X	X	X	X		X
Work Adjustment Rating Form	X	X	X	X	Retardation	NS**									X	

**Not specified.

Table 3.2
Summary Assessments of Primary Client Assessment Instruments
(Based on Reviewers' Statements)

Client Assessment Instruments	Recommended Purposes: Individual Plan Development	Client Progress Measurement	Screening/Eligibility Determination	Program Planning	Program Evaluation	Applications: Disability type (Severity)	Age	Setting Characteristics	Domains: Communication	Self-care Skills	Independent Living Skills	Learning and Problem-solving Abilities	Maladaptive Behavior	Physical Development	Emotional Development	Socialization	Work Habits and Work Adjustment	Environmental Characteristics	Summary Ratings: Content	Administration	Interpretability	Utility	Test Development	Reliability	Validity
AAMD-Becker Reading-Free Vocational Interest Inventory	X		X			Retardation (Educable)	14-25	Educational Programs in the Community or in Institutions									*		X	X	X		X	X	X
AAMD Adaptive Behavior Scale	X	X	X	X	X	Retardation (All Levels) and Emotional Disturbances	6-69	Institutions	X	X	X		X	X	X	X									
AAMD ABS Public School Version	X	X	X	X	X	Retardation (All Levels) and Emotional Disturbances	7-13	Schools	X	X	X		X	X	X	X			X	X	X	X	X	X	
Adaptive Functioning Index	X	X	X	X		Retardation (Mild and Moderate)	14+	Institutions and Community Training Programs		X	X				X	X	X		X	X	X	X			
Balthazar Scales I. Functional Independence	X		X			Retardation (Severe and Profound)	All	Institutions and Community Training Programs		X									X	X	X	X		X	

Table 3.2 (continued)

CLIENT ASSESSMENT INSTRUMENTS	Recommended Purposes: Individual Plan Development	Client Progress Measurement	Screening/Eligibility Determination	Program Planning	Program Evaluation	Applications: Disability type (Severity)	Age	Setting Characteristics	Domains: Communication	Self-care Skills	Independent Living Skills	Learning and Problem-solving Abilities	Maladaptive Behavior	Physical Development	Emotional Development	Socialization	Work Habits and Work Adjustment	Environmental Characteristics	Summary Ratings: Content	Administration	Interpretability	Utility	Test Development	Reliability	Validity
Balthazar Scales II. Social Adaptation	X	X				Retardation (Severe and Profound)	All	Institutions and Community Training Programs	X	X		X			X				X			X			
Behavior Development Survey					X	Retardation (All Levels)	3+	All, primarily Institutions	X	X	X		X			X	X		X	X	X			X	
Bristol Social Adjustment Guides			X	X		All Disabilities	5-16	Schools		X	X		X		X	X			X	X	X				
Bruininks-Oseretsky Test of Motor Proficiency	X	X	X	X		All Disabilities except Non-Ambulatory Individuals (All Levels)	4½-14½	Research, Clinical and Educational Programs						X					X	X	X	X	X	X	X
Cain-Levine Social Competency Scale			X			Retardation (Trainable)	5-12	Institutions and Public School Special Education Classes	X	X	X					X			X	X	X	X	X	X	
California Preschool Social Competency Scale	X		X		X	Normal Intelligence	2½-5½	Preschools	X	X	X					X			X	X	X	X	X	X	X

Recommended Purposes (judged acceptable or better for the following purposes)

Applications — Population Characteristics; Setting Characteristics

Domains (judged acceptable or better for measuring the following domains)

Summary Ratings (given the potential applications, rated acceptable or better on the following dimensions)

Table 3.2 (continued)

CLIENT ASSESSMENT INSTRUMENTS	Recommended Purposes (judged acceptable or better for the following purposes)					APPLICATIONS			DOMAINS (judged acceptable or better for measuring the following domains)										SUMMARY RATINGS (given the potential applications, rated acceptable or better on the following dimensions)						
	Individual Plan Development	Client Progress Measurement	Screening/Eligibility Determination	Program Planning	Program Evaluation	Disability type (Severity)	Age	Setting Characteristics	Communication	Self-care Skills	Independent Living Skills	Learning and Problem-solving Abilities	Maladaptive Behavior	Physical Development	Emotional Development	Socialization	Work Habits and Work Adjustment	Environmental Characteristics	Content	Administration	Interpretability	Utility	Test Development	Reliability	Validity
Callier-Azusa Scale	X	X				Retardation (Severe), Deaf-Blind and Other Multiple Handicaps	All	Schools or Training Situations	X		X	X		X	X	X			X	X	X	X	X	X	
Camelot Behavioral Checklist	X	X		X		Retardation (All Levels)	2-adult	Institutions or Community Programs	X	X	X			X		X			X	X	X	X	X		
Child Behavior Rating Scale						Emotional Handicaps	5-9	School primarily, also the Home												X					
Client-Centered Evaluation Model	X		X			Developmental and Other Disabilities	1-adult	Residences or Day Care Programs	X	X	X			X	X	X	X		X	X	X	X			
Community Adjustment Scale	X	X	X	X		Retardation (Mild)	Adults	Community Programs	X	X	X					X	X		X	X	X	X	X		
Denver Developmental Screening Test			X	X		This instrument is a screening tool for detection of developmental impairments.	0-6	Early Childhood Programs	X	X	X			X				X	X	X	X	X	X	X	X

Table 3.2 (continued)

CLIENT ASSESSMENT INSTRUMENTS	Recommended Purposes (judged acceptable or better for the following purposes)					Applications — Population Characteristics			Domains (judged acceptable or better for measuring the following domains)										Summary Ratings (given the potential applications, rated acceptable or better on the following dimensions)						
	Individual Plan Development	Client Progress Measurement	Screening/Eligibility Determination	Program Planning	Program Evaluation	Disability type (Severity)	Age	Setting Characteristics	Communication	Self-care Skills	Independent Living Skills	Learning and Problem-solving Abilities	Maladaptive Behavior	Physical Development	Emotional Development	Socialization	Work Habits and Work Adjustment	Environmental Characteristics	Content	Administration	Interpretability	Utility	Test Development	Reliability	Validity
Fairview Scales Self-Help	X	X	X			Retardation (Severe and Profound)	2-9	Institutions		X	X			X		X									
Fairview Scales Language Evaluation	X	X	X			All Disabilities	0-6	Institutions	X																
Fairview Scales Problem Behavior Record	X	X	X			Retardation	All	Institutions					X		X										
Fairview Scales Development	X	X	X			Retardation (Severe and Profound)	0-2	Institutions	X	X	X			X	X										
Fairview Scales Social Skills	X	X	X			Retardation (Mild and Moderate)	10+	Institutions	X	X	X					X	X	}	X	X	X	X	X	X	X
Learning Accomplishment Profile	X	X	X			Developmental Disabilities (All Levels)	0-6	Preschools, Developmental Day Care Centers	X	X	X	X		X		X	X		X	X	X	X	X	X	X

Table 3.2 (continued)

CLIENT ASSESSMENT INSTRUMENTS	Individual Plan Development	Client Progress Measurement	Screening/Eligibility Determination	Program Planning	Program Evaluation	Disability type (Severity)	Age	Setting Characteristics	Communication	Self-care Skills	Independent Living Skills	Learning and Problem-solving Abilities	Maladaptive Behavior	Physical Development	Emotional Development	Socialization	Work Habits and Work Adjustment	Environmental Characteristics	Content	Administration	Interpretability	Utility	Test Development	Reliability	Validity
	Recommended Purposes (judged acceptable or better for the following purposes)					**APPLICATIONS** — Population Characteristics		Setting Characteristics	**DOMAINS** (judged acceptable or better for measuring the following domains)										**SUMMARY RATINGS** (given the potential applications, rated acceptable or better on the following dimensions)						
Lexington Developmental Scales	X	X				Cerebral Palsy, Retardation and Multiple Handicaps	0-6	Early Childhood Programs	X					X					X	X	X	X	X		
MDC Behavior Identification Form	X	X		X		Retardation (Moderate to Mild)	Adolescent-Adult	Workplace (Regular or Sheltered)									X			X	X	X			
Mid-Nebraska Basic Skills Screening Test	X	X	X			Retardation (All Levels)	18+	Institutions, Community Programs or Job Training Programs	X	X	X	X		X	X	X		}	X	X	X	X		X	
Mid-Nebraska Independent Living Screening Test	X	X	X			Retardation (Moderate and above)	18+	Institutions, Community Programs or Job Training Programs		X	X	X				X		}							
Mid-Nebraska Competitive Employment Screening Test	X	X	X			Retardation (Mild and above)	18+										X	}							
Minnesota Developmental Programming System Behavioral Scales	X	X	X			Retardation (excludes the Near Normal and the Totally Dependent)	Children and Young Adults	All service settings within the mental retardation system		X										X		X	X	X	

Table 3.2 (continued)

CLIENT ASSESSMENT INSTRUMENTS	Recommended Purposes (judged acceptable or better for the following purposes)					APPLICATIONS			DOMAINS (judged acceptable or better for measuring the following domains)										SUMMARY RATINGS (given the potential applications, rated acceptable or better on the following dimensions)						
	Individual Plan Development	Client Progress Measurement	Screening/Eligibility Determination	Program Planning	Program Evaluation	Disability type (Severity)	Age	Setting Characteristics	Communication	Self-care Skills	Independent Living Skills	Learning and Problem-solving Abilities	Maladaptive Behavior	Physical Development	Emotional Development	Socialization	Work Habits and Work Adjustment	Environmental Characteristics	Content	Administration	Interpretability	Utility	Test Development	Reliability	Validity
O'Berry Developmental Tests—Behavior Maturity Checklist	X	X	X			Retardation (Severe and Profound)	Children	Institutions		X										X		X		X	
Ohio Performance Scale	X	X		X		Retardation (All Levels)	All	Institutions	X	X	X	X	X		X	X			X	X	X	X			
Pinecrest Behavior Meters of Primary Functioning	X					Retardation (Severe and Profound)	All	Institutions	X	X										X		X			
Preschool Attainment Record	X	X		X		All Disabilities (All Levels)	0-7	Preschools	X	X		X		X		X	X		X	X	X	X			
Progress Assessment Chart of Social and Personal Development	X	X	X	X		Retardation (All Levels)	0-adult	Institutions or Community Programs	X	X	X	X	X			X			X	X	X	X			
San Francisco Vocational Competency Scale		X	X			Retardation (Mild to Severe)	18+	Workshops								X	X		X	X			X	X	
Santa Cruz Behavioral Characteristics Progression	X	X	X			All Disabilities, particularly Retardation (All Levels, particularly Severe)	3-18	Schools or Homes	X		X	X	X	X	X	X			X	X	X	X			
School Behavior Profile		X				Physical, Intellectual or Emotional Impairments	5-9	Schools			X	X	X	X	X	X			X	X			X	X	X

Table 3.2 (continued)

CLIENT ASSESSMENT INSTRUMENTS	Recommended Purposes (judged acceptable or better for the following purposes)					APPLICATIONS — Population Characteristics		APPLICATIONS — Setting Characteristics	DOMAINS (judged acceptable or better for measuring the following domains)										SUMMARY RATINGS (given the potential applications, rated acceptable or better on the following dimensions)						
	Individual Plan Development	Client Progress Measurement	Screening/Eligibility Determination	Program Planning	Program Evaluation	Disability type (Severity)	Age	Setting Characteristics	Communication	Self-care Skills	Independent Living Skills	Learning and Problem-solving Abilities	Maladaptive Behavior	Physical Development	Emotional Development	Socialization	Work Habits and Work Adjustment	Environmental Characteristics	Content	Administration	Interpretability	Utility	Test Development	Reliability	Validity
Social and Prevocational Information Battery	X	X		X		Retardation (Educable)	14-20	Community Residences, Schools, Training Programs	X	X	X			X			X		X	X		X	X	X	X
Social and Prevocational Information Battery – Form T	X	X		X		Retardation (Trainable and Low Educable)	15-62	Community Residences, Schools, Training Programs	X	X	X			X			X		X	X		X	X	X	
TARC Assessment System	X	X				Retardation (Severe and Profound)	3-16	Institutions or Community Programs	X	X	X			X						X				X	
Test of Social Inference					X	Retardation (Mild)	7½+	Research Settings	X	X	X														
TMR School Competency Scales	X	X	X			Retardation (Trainable)	5-17+	Schools	X	X	X	X				X			X	X		X	X	X	X
Uniform Performance Assessment System	X	X	X	X		All Disabilities (All Levels)	0-6	Educational Programs	X	X	X	X				X			X	X		X	X	X	X
Vineland Social Maturity Scale	X	X	X	X		All Disabilities (All Levels)	1-adult	Institutions or Community Programs	X	X	X	X				X	X		X	X		X			
Vocational Behaviors Scale	X	X				Retardation (Mild and Moderate), and other Developmental Disabilities	Adolescents and adults	Vocational, Prevocational Settings			X	X					X		X	X		X			
Vulpe Assessment Battery	X	X			X	Developmental Handicaps	0-6	Institutions, Schools or Homes	X	X	X	X	X	X	X	X						X			
Work Adjustment Rating Form	X	X			X	Retardation	16-21	Workshops	X	X	X	X					X		X	X			X	X	

American Association on Mental Deficiency (AAMD)—
Becker Reading-Free Vocational Interest Inventory

Author Ralph L. Becker	**Distributor** American Association on Mental Deficiency 5101 Wisconsin Ave., N.W. Washington, D.C. 20016
Alternative Version None	**Date** 1975
Revisions in Progress None	**Test Manual** AAMD-Becker Reading-Free Vocational Interest Inventory Manual, Ralph L Becker, 1975

INTENDED PURPOSES

The American Association on Mental Deficiency (AAMD)—Becker Reading-Free Vocational Interest Inventory (RFVII) is a nonreading vocational preference test intended for use with mentally retarded persons, particularly educable mentally retarded students at the high school level. The Inventory was devised to provide systematic information on the interest patterns of mentally retarded males and females engaged in occupations at the unskilled and semiskilled levels. Thus, according to the author, the instrument helps to identify areas in which individuals have vocational interests. Identifying areas and patterns of interest is intended to aid counselors in the vocational planning, training, or job placement of individuals.

There are two forms of the AAMD-Becker Inventory—one for males and one for females. Each is designed to test mildly retarded individuals ranging in chronological age from 14 to 25 years. Testing can be carried out at community-based schools and within institutions.

DOMAINS

The Inventory measures a client's attitudes along one domain—vocational interest. The male version of the instrument contains 11 interest areas or subdomains and 55 items, while the female version consists of 8 interest areas and 40 items.

PROCEDURES

This self-administered instrument can be used with individuals or groups. It consists of a series of pictures which illustrate activities related to different vocations. The pictures are presented in groups of three and the individual is asked to circle the one describing the job he or she likes best. According to the author, the test can be administered and scored by a trained clerical assistant, but must be interpreted by someone familiar with the principles of psychological measurement and with guidance practices. The manual states that administration can be completed within 45 minutes, including distribution of test materials, reading of test instructions, selections by examinees, and collection of test materials. It is estimated by the author that the average examinee will complete the Inventory in 20 minutes or less.

A score is reported for each interest area. With the aid of conversion tables, these scores are converted into T scores and then into percentile ranks. The percentiles are then presented graphically as a profile of the individual's vocational interests.

COSTS

Test (inventory booklet—male)	$ 1.00
Test (inventory booklet—male), 10-99	.80
Test (inventory booklet—male), 100 or more	.50
Test (inventory booklet—female)	1.00
Test (inventory booklet—female), 10-99	.80
Test (inventory booklet—female), 100 or more	.50
Specimen set	11.00
Manual	6.00
Manual, 10 or more	5.00

REVIEW

CONTENT

Although most of the interest items which appear on the Inventory are good choices, the content is not representative of all the job options available to mildly retarded people. The two forms of the scale—male and female—also make certain options available only to males or only to females, which is certainly an outmoded concept.

ADMINISTRATION

Instructions are clear, and the tasks are relatively easy for the examinee to perform.

INTERPRETABILITY

The test should be interpreted only by a person who is knowledgeable in the field of psychological measurement. Given this restriction, the scores are presented in a reasonable way, and raw scores can be converted to standard scores and percentiles. Percentile norms are presented for several norm groups that constituted a well-designed national sample. These norms, in their extremes, present a good way of identifying *apparently* very strong or very weak vocational interests. Interpreting middle-range scores is more risky.

TEST DEVELOPMENT

The initial stages of test development appear to follow standard procedures, but they are not thoroughly reported in the manual and cannot, therefore, be evaluated accurately. The final steps of development, however, are excellent, including the utilization of a representative national sample for statistical verification of the instrument's psychometric properties.

RELIABILITY

Test-retest reliabilities were mostly in the .70s and .80s, with a two-week interval between testings. Internal consistency reliabilities ranged from .67 to .96, with a median value around .81. Except for an occasional small sample (N = 50), the reliability studies were good ones and outcomes were also good.

VALIDITY

The content validity procedures appear to be fairly standard and adequate, involving the logical clustering of items that are subsequently confirmed by item-test discrimination indices. The front end procedures for logical clustering were only partially described.

Concurrent validity was investigated by correlating scores on the RFVII with scores on two similar instruments, the Geist Picture Interest Inventory and the Picture Inventory Test. Correlations were low to moderate (most below .50).

A type of criterion validity labeled "occupational validity" was investigated by examining the RFVII profiles of people employed in each instrument category, and comparing these profiles with those of people who were employed in other instrument categories. People scored higher on their own scale than on scales outside their work area.

SUMMARY OF UTILITY

On the surface, the Becker Reading-Free Vocational Interest Inventory appears to have some utility in helping mildly mentally retarded people, aged 14-25 years, make wise vocational choices as part of the Individual Habilitation Plan process. However, because of the limited and sex-biased vocational options presented in the instrument, it should be supplemented by other material including job sampling opportunities. There is a real danger that exclusive use of the instrument will narrow the thinking of the retarded person and his or her counselor. This, however, is a problem with any vocational interest inventory.

There is a problem which resides in the general utility of *any* vocational interest inventory that is used with mentally retarded people. The development of vocational interests is known to be affected by the quantity and quality of vocational experiences that are part of an individual's background. Mentally retarded people, almost by definition, are limited in vocational experience, especially during adolescence. It is important, therefore, to question the long-range stability of measured interests if vocational training decisions are going to be made with a long-range impact. The stability coefficients presented for this instrument involved only two-week intervals, appropriate for one aspect of reliability, but not appropriate for the purpose indicated here. The instrument is not intended to measure client progress.

American Association on Mental Deficiency
Adaptive Behavior Scale*

Authors Kazuo Nihira, Ray Foster, Max Shellhaas, and Henry Leland	**Distributor** American Association on Mental Deficiency 5101 Wisconsin Ave., N.W. Washington, D.C. 20016
Alternative Version Public School Version	**Dates** 1969, 1975
Revisions in Progress Children's Adaptive Be- havior Scale (BEH grant); scheduled for publication in 1980	**Test Manual** AAMD Adaptive Behavior Manual, Arnold Madow, Henry Leland, Bruce Libby, Kazuo Nihira, and Charles Fogelman (editor), 1975

INTENDED PURPOSES

The American Association on Mental Deficiency (AAMD) Adaptive Behavior Scale (ABS) was designed to provide an objective description and evaluation of an individual's effectiveness in coping with the natural and social demands of his or her environment. It is intended to provide a description of the way an individual maintains his or her personal independence in daily living and how that person meets the social expectations of his or her environment. It can be used to help determine an individual's adaptive behavior level in conjunction with other assessment devices and techniques.

The ABS is intended for mentally retarded (as defined in the current AAMD Manual on Terminology and Classification in Mental Retardation), emotionally maladjusted, and developmentally disabled individuals, but can be used with other handicapped individuals. It can serve a population with a chronological age range of 6 to 69 plus years.

The ABS has many uses according to its authors. The instrument can identify areas of deficiency, provide an objective basis for comparison of ratings over a period of time, and compare ratings under different situations. This can be used to facilitate the

---

*This scale and the one following it, the American Association on Mental Deficiency (AAMD) Adaptive Behavior Scale Public School Version, are reviewed together.

assignment, comparison, and development of curriculum, training programs, and Individual Habilitation Plans. The authors point out in the manual that the ABS should be used in conjunction with other assessment techniques to determine an individual's level of adaptive behavior.

DOMAINS

The ABS has 24 domains, 21 subdomains, and a total of 110 items.

Part I is organized along developmental lines, evaluating an individual's skills and habits in the ten behavior domains of independent functioning, physical development, economic activity, language development, numbers and time, domestic activity, vocational activity, self-direction, responsibility, and socialization.

Part II provides measures of maladaptive behavior related to personality and behavior disorders in the 14 domains of violent and destructive behavior, antisocial behavior, rebellious behavior, untrustworthy behavior, withdrawal, stereotyped behavior and odd mannerisms, inappropriate interpersonal manners, unacceptable vocal habits, unacceptable or eccentric habits, self-abusive behavior, hyperactive tendencies, sexually aberrant behavior, psychological disturbances, and uses of medications.

PROCEDURES

Data are collected about an individual client by obtaining information from a person knowledgeable about the client or his or her program. Three types of administrative procedures may be used: observation of the client, completion by a knowledgeable person, and interview of a knowledgeable person. The instrument utilizes rating scales and checklists which measure the presence or absence of specific behaviors, the frequency of specified behaviors, or the highest level of performance of given behaviors.

A score is reported for each domain and each subdomain. Norms are provided for a comparison with an institutional population.

COSTS

Test (scale booklet)	$1.00
Test (scale booklet), 100-499	.50
Test (scale booklet), 500 or more	.40
Specimen set	6.00
Manual	5.00
Manual, 10 or more	4.00

American Association of Mental Deficiency (AAMD) Adaptive Behavior Scale Public School Version

Authors
Kazuo Nihira, Ray Foster, Max Shellhaas, and Henry Leland. Revised and standardized by Nadine Lambert, Myra Windmiller, and Linda Cole

Alternative Version
AAMD Adaptive Behavior

Revisions in Progress
Scheduled for publication in 1978, the revision will provide norms on regular and special education pupils from age 3 to 16 and will be based on stratified samples of school subjects in California and Florida. In addition, the revised version will describe procedures and provide norms for five factor scores derived from scale items and domains.

Distributor
American Association on Mental Deficiency
5101 Wisconsin Ave., N.W.
Washington, D.C. 20016

Dates
1972, 1974

Test Manual
AAMD Adaptive Behavior Scale Public School Version
Nadine Lambert, Myra Windmiller, and Linda Cole, 1974

INTENDED PURPOSES

The American Association of Mental Deficiency (AAMD) Adaptive Behavior Scale (ABS) Public School Version is primarily intended to aid school personnel in obtaining a measure of a child's adaptive behavior and, secondarily, to suggest those areas of functioning where special recommendations for remediation may be applied. The objective of this method of assessment is to provide educationally relevant information about the status of children and the ways in which they respond to their environments.

The instrument is intended for a population of children with a chronological age range of 7 to 13. It is used with individuals in the public school setting who are mentally retarded, educationally handicapped, and normal.

DOMAINS

The ABS Public School Version is a two-part instrument with a total of 21 domains, 18 subdomains, and 95 items. Each item contains from three to nine behavioral descriptions associated with the adaptive behavior attribute being assessed in the item.

Part I is organized along developmental lines. It is designed to evaluate an individual's skills and habits in nine areas considered important to the development of personal independence in daily living: independent functioning, physical development, economic activity, language development, numbers and time, vocational activity, self-direction, responsibility, and socialization.

Part II is designed to provide measures of maladaptive behavior related to personality and behavior disorders in the 12 areas of violent and destructive behavior, antisocial behavior, rebellious behavior, untrustworthy behavior, withdrawal, stereotyped behavior and odd mannerisms, inappropriate interpersonal manners, unacceptable vocal habits, unacceptable or eccentric habits, hyperactivity tendencies, psychological disturbances, and use of medications.

PROCEDURES

The ABS Public School Version is designed to get information from teachers, parents, school psychologists, speech therapists, social workers, and other school personnel who have an opportunity to observe the behavior of the child closely. Data are collected about an individual client by three types of administrative procedures: observation of client, completion by teacher or parent, and the interview of a person knowledgeable about the client. The instrument utilizes rating scales and checklists to assess adaptive behaviors of children.

The scale is designed to permit administration by people without a great deal of special training. The authors recommend that administration be under the supervision of a school psychologist or special educator. The amount of time required to complete the scale for an individual client is 15 to 20 minutes.

Scores are reported for each domain and each subdomain. Scoring programs are available from the AAMD.

COSTS

Test	$ 1.00
Test, 100-499	.50
Test, 500 or more	.40
Specimen set	10.00
Manual	7.00
Manual, 10 or more	6.00

REVIEW

CONTENT

For the purposes intended, the ABS domains represent a good gross measure of competency in the areas covered. Bhattacharya (1973) points out that, particularly for the Public School Version, the inclusion of other areas such as self-concept, self-confidence, and environmental awareness in the instrument would be useful. The scale is comprehensive with respect to coverage of domains of functioning. However, it was developed in an institutional setting and is most comprehensive for a retarded person living in a sheltered environment, although it is useful and valid for other populations. In the Public School Version certain sensitive items such as "wipes self at the toilet" have been eliminated. These items were not replaced, however.

Items within domains in Part I are sequenced in a developmental order. Although the items in Part I specify desired behaviors clearly and objectively, the items in Part II are much less definitive. Part II is written from a negative orientation, emphasizing maladaptive behaviors. This is of particular concern in the Public School Version since these items are seldom observed in children in school ("kicks others, bites others, spits on others, throws self on floor, kicking and screaming") and they might cause raters, particularly teachers, to expect or even search for deviant behavior. The problem is with both the relative infrequency with which these behaviors occur and the potential for bias in the recall of a rater or teacher. Is such a highly detailed and quantitative procedure really necessary to tabulate occurrences of severe maladaptive behavior? One can envision situations in which a classroom teacher "recalls" more instances of maladaptive behavior—severe and otherwise—than actually occur for a child who is a chronic classroom discipline problem. The result is an overstatement of the child's problem and the potential for misclassification. Given the highly skewed distribution of scores in Part II, the measurement error potential is great—one or two instances of overreporting of the frequency of maladaptive behavior for an individual client could have a major effect on his or her percentile ranking.

ADMINISTRATION

As compared with some assessment instruments, both versions of the ABS are relatively easy to become familiar with and to administer. However, training or experience in a service delivery field would be helpful, particularly for interpretation. The number of items are manageable and a person who is acquainted with the child or client can complete administration in about 20 minutes or less. Data storage and retrieval should not be difficult and could be easily programmed for a computer.

The comprehensiveness and clarity of the manual and supporting materials are considered very good when compared with other such scales. More work has gone into all elements of the scale than is the case with any other instrument. It does not share the content problems some other scales have because it behaviorally defines criteria for scoring and reference norms for comparison.

INTERPRETABILITY

The Public School Version includes more information regarding test results than did the 1974 revision of the ABS. Both versions, however, rely upon face validity in reaching conclusions about the characteristics of a client and his or her training needs. There has been a number of studies which have utilized the ABS to develop individualized client plans with some success. McDevitt et al. (1977) indicate that one should be particularly careful in interpreting Part II of the scale because it is markedly skewed, with some 40 to 50 percent of the standardization sample displaying no inappropriate behavior on the Public School Version. Nevertheless, these individuals received ratings that significantly elevated their profile scores, giving the impression of a moderate number of instances of inappropriate behavior. For example, on three of the scales for some age levels, an individual with no rated behavior received a score as high as the eighth decile. There is also the problem that an individual who scores positive for many "mildly inappropriate" behaviors will have a higher scale score than one who is rated on one of more kinds of severe antisocial behavior. It would seem that importance rather than frequency would be a better scoring guide. Other investigators (Arnold 1974, Fitzpatrick and Rogers 1977) suggest that the interpreter should look at individual items and compare them with norms of the institution or community before making decisions or value judgements.

TEST DEVELOPMENT

The investigators certainly followed appropriate steps in developing the ABS and its revisions. The fact that the test does present some problems reflects the difficult nature of developing a test which measures adaptive behavior. It was difficult (and remains difficult) to obtain concensus among all users on what adaptive behavior is (despite the existence of a standard definition—with which the ABS is consistent) and to obtain normative groups on which to base individual test scores.

The test development has a solid history. In the original version items were selected from other instruments, crisis behaviors in institutional settings, as well as from the normal growth and development literature. The items were field tested on a large sample of institutionalized persons aged 3 to 69 years. Items with high interrater reliability, ability to discriminate different degrees of retardation and adaptive behavior were retained. The items have been sequenced on the basis of percent of passes for each subdomain. This does not apply to most items in Part II. In the original version of the scale there were separate forms for children and adults. These have been combined in the 1974 version. Although all items were retained, the revised version contains several wording changes.

Items were rejected in the Public School Version if they could not be scored by teachers or did not fit a school setting. Items which did not discriminate among different class (grade) levels were also eliminated. Because of the amount of attention given the earlier versions of the scale, the Public School Version appears well organized, with items properly sequenced and internally consistent. The Public School Version was standardized on groups of California public school children ages 7 to 13 who were normal, trainable mentally retarded, educable mentally retarded, and educationally handicapped.

RELIABILITY

Reliability of the 1974 version of ABS was assessed by comparing the ratings given institutional residents by two independent ward personnel from the same shift. Interrater reliabilities for Part I ranged from .71 (self-direction) to .93 (physical development), with a mean reliability of .86. Reliabilities for Part II were low; only one scale (use of medication) had a reliability above .70; the others ranged from .37 (unacceptable vocal habits) to .68 (antisocial behavior). The mean reliability for Part II domains is .57. Obviously, the Part II reliabilities present problems in making individual predictions in such matters as future growth, class or program placements, and individualized rehabilitation planning. This problem is related to deficiencies in norms noted above. Part II domains have too few items to be very useful.

No reliability studies on the Public School Version were conducted by the test developers. They argue, probably correctly, that the reliabilities would be the same as the 1974 revision. Internal consistency reliability studies of the domains are not reported. It is expected that Part II domains would have lower reliabilities.

VALIDITY

A number of concurrent validity studies (Arnold 1974, Christian and Malone 1973, Edmonsen and Wish 1975, Malone and Christian 1974) have been conducted using the 1974 version of the ABS. These studies find that the domains of the test correlate with other tests in the same domain. In general, Part I domains have been found to correlate significantly with IQ. Lower and insignificant correlations were found with achievement tests. Part II domains are independent of both IQ and achievement measures.

In general, factor analytic studies have been in agreement in finding three factors related to adaptive behavior: personal self-sufficiency, community self-sufficiency, and personal social responsibility. (Cunningham and Presnall 1978, Guarnaccia 1976, Lambert and Nicoll 1976, Nihira 1976, Nihira et al. 1974).

Most studies which have used the ABS 1974 version to assess program needs and to place clients in programs have found it helpful. It has also been found useful in selecting and screening participants for educational programs and for measuring client progress following special programming.

Studies of the validity of the Public School Version reported by the developers, as well as those of several other investigators, have found the instrument to separate children of different placements (regular or special education) or levels (EMR, TMR, educationally handicapped, normal).

Although the ABS separates students with different levels of impairment, there is considerable overlap between the scores of the different levels, particularly at the upper ages; this makes it less useful for assigning individual classifications. As the authors point out, many of the maladaptive behaviors in Part II would preclude school attendance. Hence, public school students receive low scores on this part. The instrument has little bias related to sex, race, or socioeconomic status.

The fact that the ABS was based directly on the *AAMD Manual on Terminology and Classification in Mental Retardation* is strong evidence for the content validity of the instrument.

SUMMARY OF UTILITY

The 1974 version is a good instrument to give a gross measure of adaptive behavior in the major domains for moderate to profoundly retarded adults and all levels of children in institutional settings. It could be used for noninstitutionalized adults as long as the user recognized that the normative data would no longer be applicable and that reliability and validity evidence is not available to support the application of the instrument to this population.

The instrument has been used for IHP development, program planning, program placement, program evaluation, evaluation of treatment progress, and to differentiate between levels of handicap and type of emotional disorder. Most investigators feel that Part I has greater utility for these purposes than Part II (Aanes and Moen

1976, Bogen and Aanes 1975, Cohen et al. 1977, Congdon 1973, Cunningham and Presnall 1978, Lambert and Nicoll 1976, and Malone and Christian 1974). Christian and Malone (1973) state that the ABS can measure change as a result of programming and can serve as a test of program effectiveness. Attempts to use the scale to measure more subtle behavior changes have generally been found to be ineffective. For example, Coburn et al. (1973) used the ABS as one of the measures in a test of variant diets with children with phenylketonuria, and although some differences were found on scores in Part II, they were not definitive.

Part I of the instrument, because of its sequential nature, can be used to indicate an overall need for service, the specific domain(s) that need attention, and the level within the domain that could serve as a starting point for intervention. Because the subdomains and individual items lack reliability and validity, the use of the instrument for the formation of a detailed IHP must proceed cautiously. Since there are many more items at the lower developmental levels of the scales, it may be more appropriate for use in developing IHPs for more severely retarded clients. The instrument could be used to monitor client progress.

The Public School Version may serve as a supplement to other instruments in determining individual need for service and the domains needing attention. Because of the relatively large overlaps in scores of different severity levels, it should be used cautiously for making classification or placement decisions. Engleman (1974) found the Public School Version to be helpful for client assessment in grades 2 through 6, but observed that normal subjects began hitting a ceiling by age 12. Standard deviations on the scale scores are large, suggesting that the diagnostic value of the instrument is limited.

Part II of both versions had lower reliability, a negative value-biased tone, item content that includes infrequently occurring behaviors, and skewed distributions. For these reasons, its usefulness, particularly in public school settings, is questionable.

Overall, the ABS is a very widely used instrument appropriate for use at the state and local level for needs assessment, program evaluation, and monitoring of client progress. Its use for diagnosis, classification, and placement is more limited. Part I appears more appropriate than Part II, especially in the public school setting, and the instrument is most useful at the client planning level for lower functioning clients.

Adaptive Functioning Index
Social Education Test, Vocational Check List,
Residential Check List

Author Nancy J. Marlett	**Distributor** The Vocational Rehabilitation Research Institute 3304 - 33 Street N.W. Calgary, Alberta T2L 2A6
Alternative Versions Adaptive Functioning for Dependent Handicapped (for young children, chronological age up to 14 months, and profoundly handicapped persons), 1975. Work is underway in the development of a French version, a supplement for the blind, one for those with perceptual-motor impairments, and British, New Zealand, and Australian cultural adaptations of the form.	**Dates** 1971, 1973
Revisions in Progress None	**Test Manual** Adaptive Functioning Index-Administration Manual, Nancy J. Marlett, 1973, 1976

INTENDED PURPOSES

The Adaptive Functioning Index is a training and assessment tool to be used by those working with developmentally handicapped adolescents and adults (above fourteen years of age). According to the author, it is designed for use with clients who are generally characterized by a lack of social independence caused by inadequate intellectual functioning, a history of institutionalization, or social disadvantage.

The AFI consists of three separate but compatible program units: social education, vocational, and residential. It is designed primarily for centers whose training aim is relative independence for their trainees. According to the author, it will, therefore, be of most use to community facilities and institutions which try to assimilate community standards.

DOMAINS

The total Index consists of 15 domains, 68 subdomains, and 274 items. The Social Education Test contains 39 items within 9 domains: reading, writing, communication, concept attainment, number concepts, time, money handling, community awareness, and motor movements. The Vocational Check List contains 85 items within 3 domains: basic work habits, work skills, and acceptance skills. The Residential Check List contains 150 items within 3 domains: personal routines, community awareness, and social maturity.

PROCEDURES

All three AFI indices have been designed for administration and use by direct service personnel (teachers, supervisors, nurses, houseparents, workshop staff) as well as by the individual's parents or employer. The administration manual recommends that professional backup be available for consultation and monitoring, but states that the indices can be used by any staff who follow the manual directions carefully. The manual further states that some guidance is available through the publisher.

The Social Education Test is an objective one with criteria for marking correct and incorrect responses; the vocational and residential units are behavior check lists that use a three-point rating for each behavior. None of the AFI materials estimate the actual time involved in the administration and use of the instrument.

COSTS*

Complete AFI	$40.40
Administration manual	3.95
Standardization manual	3.95
Social education test booklet	10 for $3.75, 50 for $17.00

*The price list is in Canadian funds and there is a 20 percent discount available when ordering 50 or more of the training package and a 30 percent discount on orders of 25 or more.

Vocational check list booklet	10 for $2.45, 50 for $10.00
Residential check list booklet	10 for $2.45, 50 for $10.00
AFI wheels	50 for $5.85
Research package	12.00

(includes one each administration manual, standardization manual, #1, #2, and #3 booklets, target and
program workbooks)

Rehabilitation programs manual	11.50

(includes target workbook and program workbook)

Target workbook	10 for $3.75, 50 for $17.00
Program workbook	10 for $3.75, 50 for $17.00

REVIEW

CONTENT

The Adaptive Functioning Index is a measurement tool intended to assess most of the behaviors and skills relevant to the independent functioning or community integration of an adolescent or adult. In assessing "some of the basic skills relevant to community living," the AFI touches several domains: self-care, independent living, and communication skills; learning and problem-solving abilities; emotional development; socialization; and work habits and work adjustment (predominantly in the residential AFI). The perspective of the AFI is that all of these skills are necessary for community integration and are measures of independent living ability and readiness. The AFI is most comprehensive in measuring self-care and independent living skills when all three indices (Social Education Test, Vocational Check List, and Residential Check List) are used as a package, instead of independently.

These three indices overlap in some of the behaviors measured. For example, appearance is assessed in both the Residential and Vocational check lists, although from slightly different perspectives. There is also some overlap of domains within the Social Education Test and the two check lists. In recognition of this overlap, the AFI Wheel is used as a pictorial display which shows the juxtaposition of domains and their relationship to other program areas.

Only a few of the items in the two check lists have criteria included in the descriptions which make them more easily and clearly observable—such as "60-80% industrial standard—almost as fast as supervisor" (an item under "Speed—Working Fast" in the Vocational Check List). Although some of the items include

69

italicized examples in order to make more clear the behavior's observable qualities, the check lists, for the most part, are subject to rater interpretation or subjectivity.

Many of the item descriptions encompass too broad a range of behaviors (e.g., in the appearance category on the Residential Check List, the item examples under "dresses himself neatly" include "shirt tucked in," "buttons, zippers fastened"). The check list does not take into account that a client may be able to perform some but not all of these skills; many of the items deserve to be broken down into more discrete categories.

In scoring the Vocational and Residential check lists, no credit is given "if the trainee does not show or has not had the chance to show the behavior." This scoring procedure is inadequate in the case of individuals who are nonambulatory or have other physical disabilities. For example, in the Residential Check List subdomain of transportation, none of the items recognize that different kinds of skills, opportunities, or equipment may be necessary in the area of transportation mobility for individuals who are not ambulatory or have other physical disabilities. This kind of bias is also found in the Social Education Test under motor movements. In the items which deal with posture and gait, there is space to note the presence of a physical disability, but no alternative, appropriate set of items is included for individuals with such disabilities.

ADMINISTRATION

The Adaptive Functioning Index has a very good administration manual and supporting materials which help facilitate the use and application of the instrument. The administration manual gives a brief historical background of the AFI and describes each of the indices, giving specific instructions for administration. Also described are various uses and applications of the AFI Wheel, a pictogram displaying assessment results of an individual client on all three program units.

Other supporting materials include a training manual which covers in greater depth the applicability, uses, and interpretation of the AFI, as well as training exercises to prepare staff to maximize the utility of the AFI and to apply rehabilitative techniques. The manual is written for field use—for staff already working in rehabilitative programs such as community workshops, group homes, and activity centers. It is recommended that a resource person with an education or psychology background and experience with the handicapped be available for the training sessions described in the manual. The training manual is a very strong and valuable supporting piece in the utility of the AFI in that it helps bridge the gap that too often exists between assessment results and a staff's ability to apply those results to individualized program planning and training.

Also available is a target workbook which outlines a step-by-step process, from assessment to training. The process described is expanded upon in Chapter 3 of the AFI Training Manual. Lastly, the author of the AFI has devised and compiled a Social History Information Booklet for agencies and institutions which deal with handicapped individuals. It summarizes social history information in a way intended to allow transferability between agencies and ease of computer storage and retrieval.

Based on a review of the AFI and supporting materials, the author's recommendations for administration seem very sound. (See procedures section.) Relative to administration of the Social Education Test, the author suggests that anyone who has familiarity with and some training in objective measurement should be able to administer the test. Each item has specific standardized instructions to the test giver which describe what is to be said or done in the administration of that item. The correct answer is given, as are scoring criteria and instructions for marking responses to each item. A test kit containing all the equipment needed to administer the Social Education Test is also available from the publisher. On this test there is a great degree of interaction between the test administrator and the individual being assessed.

In considering the Vocational and Residential check lists, ease of administration would seem to be affected by the opportunity of the rater or test administrator to observe the client, relative to the behaviors found in the check lists. Familiarity with the individual's behavior and skills would reduce test administration time. Although the Vocational Check List has fewer items than the Residential (82 and 150, respectively), the former may be slightly more time-consuming to complete due to the inclusion of a Task Analysis Sheet which requires the rater to record regular tasks done by the individual being rated relative to skill level and competence.

INTERPRETABILITY

Interpretation procedures of the AFI are unique in that they go beyond the traditional assignment of scores and development of profiles. The interpretation procedures, as outlined in the administration and training manuals, include these additional steps:

1. Identification of training needs of the individual. The AFI approach suggests the trainee should be integrally involved in choosing the skill area to be worked on for the next two to six months. A developmental priorities list, found in the AFI Training Manual, can be used to facilitate identification of need.

2. Specification of target behavioral objectives and training approach to be used in addressing training needs. The AFI Target Workbook provides technical assistance in objective writing.

3. Calculation of incentive rates based on the trainee's functioning level. These calculations are to be used in negotiating with the trainee and in setting goal(s) and implementing training to accomplish goal(s) or target objective. The AFI Training Manual expands upon utility of incentive options.

This approach to administration, scoring, and interpretation aims at bridging the gap between assessment and application and is, without question, significant strength in the utility and methodology of the AFI.

After the assessment results of the trainee's functioning are recorded and a training need is subsequently identified, interpretation occurs. To facilitate the determination of training needs, the AFI Training Manual includes an appendix that lists developmental priorities. This information can be used by the test administrator/trainer and the trainee to choose the skill that the trainee would like to work toward for the next two to six months. At this point, the AFI Training Manual and Training Workbook become extremely helpful in providing a step-by-step approach to the development of behavioral objectives. These materials were designed for use with the AFI or other related training/assessment techniques.

Finally, the AFI Wheel can be useful in pictorially describing a trainee's level of functioning in the training areas found within any or all of the AFI indices. Elaboration on the wheel's utility is provided in the administration manual which discusses its use for single-client assessments, multiple assessments of the same client over time, and as a reporting system between agencies.

Scoring and interpretation limitations may exist in some areas of the test where ambulation is a necessary requirement for performance of the behavioral goal statements included in a training area. As discussed in the content section, there are no appropriate behavioral goal statements or training sequences provided in the indices for individuals with a physical disability.

TEST DEVELOPMENT

The initial generation and selection of items is slightly unclear in the standardization manual. The Progress Assessment Chart* is cited as a widely used assessment tool which "presents many adaptive behaviors in a precise, easily understood format." Although the manual states "some of the same concepts are present in the AFI, " it is not explicit as to whether any of the items found in the PAC served as a basis for the AFI.

Concretization of items or training goals and refinements of the AFI are discussed in the manual. However, studies or instruments from which the items or goals were initially selected are not specifically mentioned. The training goals were "grouped statistically into uniform training hierarchies and tested for effectiveness." Reported results of such studies of effectiveness, the mention of specific populations used, and any subsequent item analysis were not included in the data tables of the standardization manual. These training hierarchies in the AFI are intended to provide the standard against which the trainee's functioning is assessed.

The manual does describe a thorough item refinement process in terms of scope of effort. What is not stated explicitly is the nature of the population used in the studies contributing to the refinement process: "The AFI forms (1973) have been refined as a result of numerous standardization projects across Canada, extensive research at the VRRI (Vocational and Rehabilitation Institute in Calgary, Alberta), and a series of training courses in major Canadian centers funded by Federal Manpower, the Ontario ARC, and the National Institute on Mental Retardation. The Check Lists have been reworded to make them more relevant to trainees, and the range of skills was broadened to include more prevocational and preresidential skills."

AFI Profiles for five representative populations are presented in the manual for general information only. These include a large

---

*The Progress Assessment Chart is also reviewed in this book.

heterogeneous mental health population in a rural institution (n=48); a community-based institutional training program for the mentally retarded (n=65); a community-based training program for developmentally handicapped (n=121); graduates from a community-based training program (n=34); and institutionalized retarded (n=256). The manual states that national norms are not a relevant part of the AFI because it is "a training system for individuals and small groups, not a classification system." There is, however, a more detailed section of the manual which presents a description of various facilities and group scores for each training sequence of the AFI. The stated purpose here is simply for the user's information, so that a comparable facility and group scores can be located and reviewed for comparison purposes only—not as a group norm or standard.

RELIABILITY

The design of the reliability studies conducted for the AFI was very good, given the intended purposes of the instrument. Interrater reliabilities and test-retest reliabilities for all three indices were calculated, and the data are included in the standardization manual. The tests were conducted at a variety of facilities whose demographic characteristics are provided in the comparative data tables of the manual.

All items in the AFI check lists met an interrater reliability significant beyond the .05 level. This is a very high rating and tends to indicate that, given the same trainee, AFI assessments yield highly similar test results.

As would be expected, the AFI Social Education Test interrater reliabilities have a much higher reliability than the check lists because of the concreteness of the items and the standardized format for administration and scoring. The social maturity training sequences of the Residential Check List have the lowest interrater reliabilities of the AFI. This is probably due to the potential for rater bias, introduced by the use of vague terms such as "proper" and "appropriate" in these items.

In one data table in which unfamiliar, untrained raters were used for the Vocational Check List, the overall reliability coefficient was .81 for the raters, as compared with three studies using trained observers with overall coefficients of .96, .97 and .99.

Although the use of trained observers yields higher reliabilities, the reasonably high coefficients (range of .54 to .83) obtained by using untrained observers indicates that the extensive training of observers may not be absolutely necessary.

The above findings suggest that some ongoing training or periodic discussions among staff may serve as a means of maintaining interrater reliability and providing an informal check of interrater reliability. A marked decrease in interrater reliabilities was found for the two check lists when they were used extensively over a long period of time without communication among staff, or when there was confusion in the program. In one case, a short, intensive training session on marking the Vocational Check List was the only intervening difference after two years without an interrater check. The training session yielded differences in the mean reliability coefficients from .51 before training to .89 after intervention. In the area of self-expression, the jump in interrater reliability was from .04 to .90.

Test-retest reliabilities were also very high for each form of the AFI. A two-week interval was used in all test-retest studies. For the Social Education Test reliabilities reported were .97 in one study and .99 in another. For the Vocational Check List, the test-retest reliability was .97, and for the Residential Check List a coefficient of .96 was achieved for the test-retest reliability. High reliabilities are indicative of the ability of the AFI to yield consistent assessment results for that which it intends to measure.

VALIDITY

The AFI Standardization Manual contains no validation studies or data, per se. There is a table which suggests that the training hierarchies have been appropriately grouped in the three test forms, but there is no specific data which document that the items fit the content or training categories within each AFI index. Nor are there data which provide an analysis of the AFI items, and an assessment of the items' ability to measure that which they are intended to measure. There are also no studies of validity included in the manual which document the developmental nature and sequencing of the items or behavioral goals within each training sequence.

Despite the fact that the validation studies and results were not included expressly in the manual, it would appear from both the procedures described in the standardization manual and the comparison data which are included that the AFI does in fact have some content and construct validity. Profiles of various populations assessed with the AFI emerge as one would predict, given the nature of the populations—an institutionalized mental health population in a community-based institution and in a rural area.

SUMMARY OF UTILITY

One of the most exciting and innovative features of the AFI is its deliberate attempt to link assessment with training. The approach of the AFI is to provide a positively stated, goal-directed assessment instrument that involves the client and the trainer in determining training needs, goals, and expectations.

Due to its training approach, the AFI could be used as a basis for: (a) needs assessment at the client and program level; (b) program planning information at the group level; (c) individualized program planning or habilitation planning information; (d) program implementation and monitoring information; (e) client progress information; and (f) some client screening and eligibility information. Of the applications described above, the potential use of the AFI in the area of Individual Program Plan (IPP) or Individual Habilitation Plan (IHP) development is one of the strongest and best supported by the approach and supplemental materials.

The AFI Training Manual provides a strong basis for training staff in rehabilitation and training techniques appropriate to the needs of trainees. In addition, the AFI Training Workbook provides a cookbook approach to developing training objectives and the equivalent of an IPP or IHP for a client based on the results of the AFI. Also very useful in the program planning process are the developmental priorities of the AFI found in the appendix of the training manual.

One of the other features of the AFI that allows it to be useful in IPP and IHP development is its provision for incentive options. Many training programs use token economies or incentive pay schedules to provide a reward and incentive to the trainee for accomplishing a goal or maintaining a behavior or skill. The AFI provides guidelines for the use of incentive options, and has found utilization of incentives effective in negotiating training objectives with trainees and in determining training approaches to be used.

The Adaptive Functioning Index was designed for use by facilities whose training aim is the relative independence of its trainees. Thus, community facilities and institutions that try to assimilate community standards should find it most helpful, as differentiated from institutions with a traditional ward type program that is not oriented toward community integration of the individuals within the program.

Although the author does not specify the mental age range of the intended population, this reviewer thinks the AFI would apply to individuals who are functioning at mild, moderate, or severe levels of mental retardation. In fact, the AFI has been used with these populations in the community and in rural institutions, yielding profiles presented in the AFI Standardization Manual.

The AFI training sequences do, however, include goal statements and developmental type steps that seem *most* appropriate for individuals functioning at the moderate and mild levels of mental retardation. The refinements at the lower end of the developmental sequences do not seem fine enough for much use with profoundly retarded individuals, and their use with the severely retarded seems marginal. In addition, some verbal and communication skills are certainly required for the Social Education Test, and in order to really apply and find appropriate training sequences as stated in the Vocational and Residential check lists, these same skills seem requisite. Auditory and visual skills are also necessary for appropriate administration of the AFI. The authors are currently developing a supplement for the blind, and one for those with perceptual-motor impairments.

As mentioned earlier in this review, there is some scoring discrimination against individuals who are nonambulatory or who have other physical disabilities. It would seem this can be compensated for through some modification of the training sequences affected. Goal statements which are appropriate for this population could be included in the AFI, without sacrificing its orientation toward community integration and independent living.

Balthazar Scales of Adaptive Behavior
For the Profoundly and Severely Mentally Retarded
Scales of Functional Independence (BSAB-I)*

Author Earl E. Balthazar	**Distributor** Consulting Psychologists Press, Inc. 577 College Avenue Palo Alto, California 94306
Alternative Version None	**Dates** 1971, 1976
Revisions in Progress Presently in press	**Test Manual** Balthazar Scales of Adaptive Behavior—Part I: Handbook for the Professional Supervisor, Part II: Handbook for the Rater Technician, Earl E. Balthazar, 1971, 1976; Part IV: Workshop and Training Manual, Earl E. Balthazar, 1971

INTENDED PURPOSES

The Balthazar Scales of Adaptive Behavior—Scales of Functional Independence (BSAB-I) were developed to document and measure changes in the self-care experiences of the client without evaluating on the basis of external norms. The scales are intended for use with severely and profoundly mentally retarded and younger less retarded individuals in the identification of specific target behaviors in ongoing treatment programs. Changes in individual behavior form the basis of program development and evaluation. The scales are intended to be applied to males and females in institutional, day care, and other clinical community centers.

---

*This instrument and the following one, Scales of Social Adaptation, are reviewed together.

In addition to the Scales of Functional Independence, there is a second set of Balthazar scales, the Scales of Social Adaptation. These two scales may be administered jointly or independently; together, they can evaluate improvements in self-care skills and the effects of such improvements on social behaviors.

DOMAINS

The BSAB-I contains 132 items and 22 subdomains across the four self-help domains of eating, dressing, toileting, and supplementary eating.

PROCEDURES

Some scale items, based on an interview with a person familiar with the client, are rated from 0 (indicating that a behavior does not occur) to 6 or 10 (indicating that the behavior occurs all the time). A system of item indentation is indicative of the order of complexity of various skills. Additional items involve rating of performance of a behavior upon command, and require direct observation of the client. Specialized professional training is not required, but the test administrator must complete a five-day training workshop. Observational and assessment skills and an understanding of testing methodology are required. When nonprofessional raters are used, a training manual is provided which may be used to set up a training program. The scales are completed over a period of several days. The author makes no statement regarding the specific amount of time required to administer the scales.

A score is obtained for each domain and subdomain.

COSTS

Supervisor's handbook	$ 4.00
Rater's handbook	4.00
Training manual (optional)	1.75
Scoring forms, package of 25	8.00
package of 100	27.50
Specimen set	10.00
(includes all handbooks plus sample forms)	

Balthazar Scales of Adaptive Behavior
Scales of Social Adaptation (BSAB-II)

Author Earl E. Balthazar	**Distributor** Consulting Psychologists Press, Inc. 577 College Avenue Palo Alto, California 94306
Alternative Version None	**Date** 1973
Revisions in Progress Yes	**Test Manual** Balthazar Scales of Adaptive Behavior II, Scales of Social Adaptation. Part I: For the Professional Supervisor: Purposes and Development of BSAB-II. Part II: For the Rater Technician: Purposes and Use of BSAB-II. Earl E. Balthazar, 1973

INTENDED PURPOSES

The Balthazar Scales of Adaptive Behavior — Scales of Social Adaptation (BSAB-II) are a system devised to develop normative studies of the emotionally disturbed and severely and profoundly mentally retarded individual at any age. As a baseline assessment instrument, it is designed to provide precise objectives for program planning. It may also be used to evaluate programs on the basis of retest. According to the author, the scales are especially useful for correlational studies examining the relationships among behavior diagnosis and prognosis along cross-disciplinary lines. Testing is best done in a clinical or institutional setting.

DOMAINS

The BSAB-II contains 84 items in 20 subdomains to form the basis for measurement along 8 domains: unadaptive self-directed behaviors, unadaptive interpersonal behaviors, adaptive self-directed behaviors, adaptive interpersonal behavior, verbal communication, play activities, response to instructions, and a personal care and other behaviors checklist.

PROCEDURES

The checklist format items are tallied following direct observation of subjects in their own environment while engaged in typical activities. The observation takes place on several days and at different times. To be effective, the rater must have knowledge of the content area of the scales, of research methodology, and awareness of rater error in testing of this type. According to the author, training of inexperienced raters with some college background typically takes about ten days to two weeks. With adequate pretesting and rater training the scales can be completed in six blocks of ten minutes over a three-day period or longer.

A score is obtained for each subdomain, each of which is a separate scale. Scores are recorded on the BSAB-II Tally Sheet and Scoring Summary Sheet. In addition, the optional Prebaseline Information Sheet (based on subject history), the Ward Supervisor and Staff Information Sheet, and the Program Information Sheet are used to tabulate supplementary information for programming purposes.

COSTS

Specimen set	$ 5.00
Additional manuals	4.75
Complete kit	16.00
(manual and material for 20 subjects)	
Tally sheets, pad with 50 sheets	3.50
5 pads	16.00
Scoring summary sheets, package of 25	2.00
package of 100	7.50
Information/program sheet, package of 25	2.00
package of 100	7.50

REVIEW

CONTENT

Together the BSAB-I and BSAB-II scales are very comprehensive and make allowances for special problems and environments. The developmental sequencing of items is excellent. Items are behaviorally expressed and the author gives an excellent detailed description of what the items mean. Their internal consistency is good.

ADMINISTRATION

While the author claims that no special credentials are required to administer the BSAB-I, review of this instrument indicates that some professional training is useful. While special training in a specific degree program may not be necessary, good observation, assessment, and interpretation skills are necessary, as are the need for consistency of observations, control of bias, and an understanding of the "why" of all of it for successful administration. However, these needs can be met if raters without a professional background are supervised by an experienced professional.

To the author's credit, his instructions on administration and training are rigorous, and point out the penalty for not administering the test correctly. This attention to detail and scientific rigor in pretesting and training before actual administration, and then administration over days or weeks to make accurate observations costs a great deal in time and effort of the rater-technician. This investment in training, together with subsequent experience, will reduce the burden of administration if the scales are used for a large number of clients.

Except for cases of research interest and use, the BSAB-I appears too costly for general use. Excessive costs are due to the need for well-trained and experienced observers and the need to time sample a variety of behavioral activities across time and settings. The rater really must have knowledge of the content area, research methodology, and awareness of types of rater error to be very effective. It is not a parsimonious instrument.

INTERPRETABILITY

The BSAB-I is easy to interpret if the data collected are representative and accurate. The author provides very detailed instructions for the rater-technician regarding the aggregation of data, the setting of standards for each institution using the instrument, the setting of norms, etc. He also states very clearly the limitations of the scales and suggests ways to minimize these. The author cautions the user against spurious interpretation.

The results of the BSAB-II require little interpretation. Data are recorded in frequencies of occurrence. Because norms are not presented, the results might not be readily meaningful. The author includes interpretation statements for the rater-technician and team. He also very carefully describes the limitations of the instrument and extraneous variables not controlled for which may alter or change interpretations. The author recommends that users not rely on norms, correlations, and reliability figures given, but stresses the aggregation of data by users.

The interpretation section of the BSAB-II manual is extremely weak. Although group data are presented, they are not intended to be norms. It is advised that each setting develop its own norms and interpretations. This would make cross-setting comparisons most difficult.

TEST DEVELOPMENT

Not enough information is presented to determine the quality of the development for either scale. No procedures are given for the selection and refinement of individual items other than to state that they were developed from "direct observation" of the behavior of target clients. However, the techniques used to translate these observations into quantifiable form and to structure the infinity of behaviors were not specified. While the instrument has been used for numerous studies at its development site, very little data and information are presented regarding its development process. No item analyses are presented.

Examination of secondary sources cited in the Scale's manual indicates that observational studies for the BSAB-I began in 1964 and continued through 1968. Over 450 ambulant residents in one institution and "several" in three others were observed. The data gathered were used to develop an item pool. Items were selected and transformed into subscales which were used for profile study purposes. One hundred twenty-two subjects with IQs of less than 20 to 35 and Level IV and V AAMD ratings (i.e., severely and profoundly retarded), were used with this scale. The author did not include the above data in the manual. Secondary sources and journal articles confirm the adequate testing of items but not all procedures. The author, who was so rigorous in other areas, did not include these data in the manual.

RELIABILITY

Reliability figures presented are high for both interrater and test-retest, but only after extensive supervision and training in the cases mentioned. Therefore, except under controlled research circumstances, data produced would not be highly reliable. The author presents no evidence for the instrument's reliability in general use in the manual. A study reported informally by the author does show potential for high reliability in more general use.

VALIDITY

No data concerning the instrument's validity is presented by the author, but it appears acceptable based on its face value alone. The items tap important aspects of social adaptation and are similar to those in other instruments examining the same modalities.

The author notes that behavioral observations designated in the subscale items constitute the criterion measure itself and therefore it is considered not relevant to inquire if the observer judgements are valid. What must be assessed is whether the observer has had sufficient training and experience to rate the behaviors of a subgroup of retarded people. What apparently cannot be questioned is the validity of the behavioral criterion.

SUMMARY OF UTILITY

The BSAB-I has been constructed to make fine discriminations in the behavior of the person who is severely or profoundly retarded in the areas of eating, toileting, and dressing. The author emphasizes that these fine discriminations or "micro-behaviors" should be accomplished in order to continue to observe progress or institute specific individual training for persons who might get lost or isolated, especially in an institutional setting. The author points out very sensitively that such improvements, albeit in small increments, not only benefit the institutions, but also enhance the dignity of each of the individuals.

The author's attention to detail and rigor in the design turns out to be a major drawback to the use of the instrument. It is easily administered after the rater has undergone a great deal of training.

While the BSAB-II has some potential for valuable use, it would not be appropriate in a client progress evaluation program. It is of particular usefulness in the area of individual program planning. As a broader instrument it would be too unreliable, costly, and unmanageable—the latter because the data presented are not readily reducible, comparable, and interpretable for purposes of evaluating and monitoring the progress of a large number of clients.

BSAB-I and BSAB-II are unique in their emphasis on measurement of the adaptive behavior of severely and profoundly retarded individuals, based on immediate observational methods. Both scales have usefulness for the purposes of needs assessment, individual program planning, program evaluation, and research. Data would be useful primarily at the client service level.

Behavior Development Survey

Author Not Specified	**Distributor** Neuropsychiatric Institute, UCLA Research Group at Pacific State Hospital P.O. Box 100-R Pomona, California 91766
Alternative Version None	**Date** 1977
Revisions in Progress None	**Test Manual** Interpretation of Behavior Development Survey Client Profile, Sharon Borthwick, 1977

INTENDED PURPOSES

The Behavior Development Survey (BDS) is designed to assist in the evaluation of the adaptive behavior of developmentally disabled individuals. It can be administered to clients of all chronological and all mental ages. No special setting is recommended.

The BDS was developed in order to provide a shortened version of the AAMD Adaptive Behavior Scale (ABS), a well-standardized behavior rating instrument. According to the authors, whenever possible, the more comprehensive ABS is the preferred instrument over the BDS, as it allows for greater stability and reliability of the data, and the interpretation is more meaningful to the user. The BDS, however, is intended to prove valuable in evaluation by giving an overview of client progress and development.

BDS information, according to the authors, can be used for two major purposes: (1) individual client planning and evaluation, and (2) group/administrative planning and evaluation.

At this time, the BDS is considered to be an experimental form, intended for use in research and demonstration settings.

DOMAINS

BDS domains are grouped as either adaptive or maladaptive behaviors. Adaptive behaviors include personal self-sufficiency, community self-sufficiency, and personal-social responsibility. The maladaptive behavior domains are social adaptation and personal adaptation. The BDS contains a total of 66 items, compared to 110 items in the ABS.

PROCEDURES

The BDS collects data about the client by obtaining information from a person knowledgeable about the individual's behavior. Procedures are identical to those used in the ABS. The instrument contains both checklist and rating items. The rating scale describes either the level of performance of adaptive behaviors or the frequency of occurrence of maladaptive behaviors. The test administrator needs experience in counseling or a related field because some of the questions about maladaptive behaviors could be threatening to, or difficult for, a parent or other informant with close ties to the client. Therefore, interviewing skills are important. The authors expect that ten to fifteen minutes are required for administering the survey.

A score is recorded for each domain. Domain scores are then either plotted directly onto a profile histogram, or they are converted to percentages and/or percentiles and then plotted to form a profile histogram.

COSTS

Not available.

REVIEW

CONTENT

The value of the content of the BDS is that it allows for a summary representation of the client. However, because there is no direct observation of the client, the representation could be distorted due to biases in the perception of the rater of the client's behavior. This problem is a characteristic common to all scales which do not use direct observation for data collection.

Although domain conceptualization is logical, the instrument would probably be more useful for application to individual clients if domains were grouped according to finer areas of developmental skills and behaviors, rather than composite abilities required for personal self-sufficiency, community self-sufficiency, and personal-social responsibility. Item examples of abilities that could better be included in separate domains are personal self-sufficiency domain—body balance and toilet training; community self-sufficiency domain—eating in public and time; personal-social responsibility domain—care of clothing and initiative. However, the intent of the BDS was to obtain gross descriptive data. Its authors would refer a user to the complete ABS if more detailed data were needed.

In a test claiming to be comprehensive (as does this test), items measuring cognitive, emotional, and vocational development should be included. The BDS only has several cognitive and vocational items and no emotional development items, except for the maladjustment scale. However, emotional development and maladjustment are not synonymous.

ADMINISTRATION

Administration is simple, but the interviewer must be sensitive to emotional and threatening material in the questions. Instructions for administration are not included in the BDS materials; users are referred to the ABS manual. Instructions for interpreting are clear. Training requirements are not mentioned by the authors, but a rater should have some counseling experience because of the content of many of the questions.

The test was designed to shorten the ABS, yet virtually the same costs are present in the BDS. Both tests obtain information about the client from a person other than the client, both require a person with some counseling experience as the interviewer, and both tests are computerized (obviously, a benefit). While the BDS is much shorter, it still takes a long time to administer (about one hour per client, according to this review). The BDS materials, which exclude much important information except by reference to the ABS manual (i.e., administration, development, reliability, and validity procedures), even note that "Whenever possible, the more comprehensive ABS is the preferred instrument over the BDS, as it allows for greater stability and reliability of the data, and the interpretation is more meaningful to the user." Consequently, it is not clear that the loss of data is balanced by the reduction in administration time for individual client applications or even small-scale research studies.

INTERPRETABILITY

The histograms are very good. They simplify interpretation of client strengths and weaknesses at one point in time, and also enable clients' progressions and regressions over time to be identified. One histogram presents actual domain scores, the second presents the percentage of possible points for each domain, and the third is a normative ranking histogram comparing individual clients with all individuals in a selected group of test scores. However, as noted elsewhere in this review, use of BDS scores for individual client assessment is problematic.

The authors point out that scores obtained with the BDS should be considered to be estimates of what would have been obtained with the full ABS. However, statistical data on the accuracy of the estimate (i.e., the standard error of measurement) are not provided.

TEST DEVELOPMENT

Development procedures are not discussed. The reviewer understands that a factor analysis of ABS items was performed to select items for the BDS. The procedures are not described except to state that items were selected to correlate $\geq .80$ with the ABS. The ABS manual describes the development of the initial pool of BDS items.

RELIABILITY

Reliability data are not presented, and this review questions the test's reliability, because of the authors' statement that the ABS is preferable because of its higher reliability (of domain scores), and because the reliability of tests is generally a function of length. Interrater reliability should be comparable to that of the ABS, given that individual items and administration procedures are the same.

VALIDITY

Although validity studies are not reported in the manual, the test may be weak in this area because the authors imply the superior validity of the ABS, and there is no direct observation of the client. An extensive national norming sample (14,675 retarded persons in residential settings) could have been used explicitly for validation. For example, performance generally improves with age, except in the maladaptive behavior domains where all client groups aged 10 and above have similar norms.

SUMMARY OF UTILITY

The value of the test is that it gives *summary* information for client, as well as program, planning and evaluation. However, even this summary information is questionable because of the lack of client observation and sound psychometric evidence. The relationship between the interviewee and the client is critical to the appropriate use and validity of this instrument. The interviewee must be very familiar with the client in order to answer all the questions accurately.

The scale's most promising use is in large-scale research or evaluation projects where data about individual clients are not required. However, for use at the client level (e.g., for IHP development), the instrument is weak because of its lack of behavioral detail and opportunities for the interviewer to insert narrative comments (which are very useful for client planning).

The proper interpretation of scores and understanding of procedures depends on the user's knowledge of the ABS. A user who is familiar with the ABS and who wishes to obtain an extensive data set at minimum cost could find the BDS convenient. However, the BDS cannot really be used or interpreted properly outside of the context of the ABS.

Bristol Social Adjustment Guides

Authors D.H. Stott and N.C. Marston	**Distributor** Educational and Industrial Testing Service San Diego, California 92107
Alternative Version None	**Date** 1956, 1970
Revisions in Progress None	**Test Manual** EITS Manual—Bristol Social Adjustment Guides, D.H. Stott, 1970, 1972

INTENDED PURPOSES

The 1970 edition of the Bristol Social Adjustment Guides (BSAG) is designed to detect and assess the type and extent of social maladjustment in children aged five to sixteen years within a school setting. The guides are concerned with identification of behavior disturbances as observed rather than inferred from projective techniques or self-reports from the child.

There are two test forms—Number 1 for boys and Number 2 for girls. The tests are identical except for pronoun changes to indicate the proper gender.

DOMAINS

According to the authors, the BSAG contains objective, nonevaluative descriptions of responses to situations that occur in school. On the diagnostic form, maladaptive behavior is grouped under two main scales—Unract and Ovract—which represent underreacting and overreacting styles of adjustment. Those scales comprising underreaction are three core syndromes—unforthcomingness, withdrawal, depression—and one associated grouping, nonsyndromic underreaction.

The overreaction scale includes two core syndromes—inconsequence and hostility—and two associated groupings—peer maladaptiveness and nonsyndromic overreaction. A neurological scale serves to identify behavior disturbances based on neurological malfunctioning. For ease of responding, the 116 items are grouped into seven areas: interaction with teacher, school work, games and play, attitude to other children, personal ways, physique, and school achievement. Summary scores are not produced for these areas.

PROCEDURES

Scoring the BSAG requires the use of a diagnostic template and a diagnostic form. Responses describing maladjusted behavior are recorded and coded according to syndrome (subdomain) and underreaction or overreaction (domain).

The BSAG assesses client behavior by observation of the child within the school setting. It is a checklist of phrases which describe the child's behavior or attitudes. The instrument should be administered by a trained professional (i.e., a teacher). The manual states that apart from general professional experience, no special training or psychological knowledge is required. Administration time is approximately 15 minutes.

COSTS

Specimen set	$ 3.50
(includes manual and one copy each of BSAG Child in School, boy form and girl form)	
BSAG forms, per 25	4.50
per 100	16.00
Diagnostic forms, per 25	2.00
per 100	7.50

REVIEW

CONTENT

The BSAG measures two domains of maladaptive behavior. Items included in each domain are derived from teacher observations of the student in a variety of school situations—with the teacher, with peers, at home, at play. The instrument requires that the teacher have sufficient contact with the student to be able to have formed certain impressions of the student. Some items imply a long time frame (e.g., "can never keep a friend long").

Without a template, it is impossible to know which item was placed on which scale. This is a benefit because raters cannot directly influence scores, thereby reducing the amount of error introduced by rater bias.

Many items are subjective and vague (e.g., "gets confused, inclined to be moody, cut off from people, remains aloof, poor spirited"). However, the parameters of each item could be defined in an instructional manual. Many items under the physique area are offensive and value-loaded: "babyish," "bulging eyes," "clumsy." Many other items also have a negative connotation. The authors of the BSAG, in an extensive book on the subject (Stott, Marston, and Neill, 1975), present empirical data supporting their concept, which is based on an ethological study of behavior and behavior disturbance. This review does not object to the constructs themselves, but rather to the lack of precise behavioral definitions of these concepts to guide raters. Without these definitions, items such as those described above present opportunities for a rater to make value-laden assessments of a client, even though the authors intend otherwise. The actions that seem "clumsy" for one client may not seem so for another, allowing rater bias to creep into the scores and thus reduce their validity.

ADMINISTRATION

The instrument is easy to administer and score, and it provides a useful way for a counselor to obtain teacher views of a student in a structured, standardized form, as opposed to the traditional informal, anecdotal comments usually included in student files. However, its content is very subjective. The main benefit of the instrument is its clear, simple format and its structuring of teacher subjective views. Although the author believes the instrument provides an "objective" view of the student, the instrument items, while structured into a clear format, are still very subjective in tone. This could lead to a biased assessment of a client.

The time to complete the instrument is minimal, and no special training is required, although it would be good if there were objective definitions of certain terms. The interpretation of scale scores to parents, service providers, juvenile court personnel, etc. is provided on a separate sheet. For example, unforthcomingness is defined as follows: "The child fears new tasks or strange situations, and is timid with people while maintaining a need for affection. As a relief from anxiety about school learning, the child may accept the role of being 'dull'." While this is very useful, the labels by themselves could be misleading or uninformative if presented improperly. Consequently, communication of scores requires a good deal of understanding and sensitivity.

INTERPRETABILITY

The instrument has no norms for developmentally disabled clients. Furthermore, the validity assessment of the instrument suggests that those clients with motor or multiple impairments, or ill health will score as more maladjusted than normal students, hence the instrument scores and norms must be used with extreme caution with such individuals.

The instrument has subscales that are intended to represent various aspects of maladjustment but the independence of these subscales is not established. The norms are for ages 5 to 14, a fairly broad age span considering that definitions of social adaptation are different at different ages (e.g., "invents silly ways of doing things"). The norms, particularly those of the subscales, are extremely skewed with half or more of the sample having zero scores. This means that having only three or four items may cause a student to be designated as showing "mild" maladjustment and a percentile rank of 30. In addition to the norms, there are cutoff scores for judging degrees of severity.

TEST DEVELOPMENT

In view of the extensive manipulations of the item responses by the authors, it is unfortunate that the 1970 version did not undergo further testing after the original version was cut from 150 to 116 items. Repeated readings of the manual only added to reviewer confusion regarding what information was obtained from earlier versions and what came from the 1970 version.

The items were originally selected based on descriptive phrases used by teachers with some attempt made by the authors to eliminate vague or subjective items. Items were also eliminated if they required teacher interpretation or attitudinal bias. Unfortunately, many items remain which are subjective, value-laden, or vague.

Items that were selected frequently for students with low total maladjustment scores were eliminated. Hence, the overall tone of the instrument is biased toward maladjustment. Of course, the scale is designed to measure maladjustment, so this may be appropriate.

The procedure used to assign items to scales and subscales is confusing and unorthodox. This problem could have been eliminated if the authors had given actual numeric findings or, even better, conducted a factor analysis of the items to verify that they are assigned to the most appropriate scale or subscale. Without more data and other confirmatory statistical analyses, it is difficult to establish the independence of the scales.

The instrument was field tested on normal students aged 5 to 14 in urban and rural public schools. No differences were found in the score patterns of students of different ages or socioeconomic status. No developmentally disabled or diagnosed emotionally disturbed students were said to be included in the field test. Maladjustment was inferred from the BSAG scores.

RELIABILITY

The reliability scores calculated in both the original version and in the 1970 revision were high for the major domain scores (underreact—.74, .83; overreact—.77, 91). Among the subscales, only inconsequence (.71, .83) and hostility (.68, .80) have satisfactory reliability coefficients. The other subscale average reliabilities range from .45 (neurological symptoms) to .68 (nonsyndromic underreact). There is some indication that scores are not stable over time; they tend to improve, possibly because teachers' response biases change—they become more accepting of behavior or recognize that it is not malicious. Thus, the instrument should not be used to measure change due to a treatment or habilitation therapy.

Reliability data are not available for developmentally disabled individuals.

VALIDITY

Validity was assessed by establishing that the scales represent important and independent manifestations of maladaptive behavior. The review is in agreement with the instrument's authors when they state that underreactions and overreactions are two distinct independent behavior syndromes. However, the differences in the subdomain scales seem somewhat arbitrary, and there is no psychometric evidence presented to establish their independence.

The fact that males and females have different scale score patterns supports the validity of the two domains. Validity studies also show that scores are related to physical health, motor impairment, and delinquency (overreaction scores only).

There is evidence of the predictive validity of the instrument, that is, that students identified as maladjusted by this instrument do in fact have serious emotional or school behavior adjustment problems. Although students with delinquency records have higher mean scores, there is no evidence in the manual suggesting that the scores can predict delinquent behavior. However, a study by Stott and Wilson (1978) does give ten-year follow-up data which is evidence for the predictive validity of the scale.

SUMMARY OF UTILITY

The BSAG could be used as a screening device for indicating those students who have serious school adjustment problems. However, those who use the instrument for this purpose should bear in mind that (1) the instrument has limited evidence of predictive validity, (2) the scores are expressed in terms of personality constructs that have no established construct validity (i.e., are not in general use in the profession) and are difficult to interpret and communicate, (3) the instrument provides no diagnostic cues regarding why the behavior problem exists or what to do about it, (4) the instrument has not been normed for developmentally disabled students, and they are likely to score differently than normal students, so it may be inappropriate for them, and (5) the instrument is very subjective and will reveal as much about teacher bias as student need.

Because the instrument has no norms for developmentally disabled students, many items are biased against them (e.g., gets confused and tongue-tied; makes aimless moves with hands), and students with poor health and motor impairments score as more maladjusted than do other students.

The instrument is appropriate only for the regular classroom but could be used for special class settings, although the norms will not be applicable.

The instrument might be used to determine whether the intervention or habilitation plan needs to focus on the social/emotional area. It could also be used to screen students for special counseling or more intensive evaluation. The authors suggest the use of the instrument for assessing the impact of a therapeutic intervention but the test-retest reliability studies suggest there is too much change due to teacher response bias to make the test useful for such a purpose.

The instrument may have value as a means of communicating with school counselors or psychologists in a standardized format rather than through anecdotal comments. However, more sensitive behavior assessment should be used to supplement and confirm this instrument.

Bruininks-Oseretsky Test of Motor Proficiency

Author Robert H. Bruininks	**Distributor** American Guidance Service, Inc. Circle Pines, Minnesota 55014
Alternative Version The Short Form of the Bruininks-Oseretsky Test of Motor Proficiency	**Date** 1978
Revisions in Progress None	**Test Manual** Examiner's Manual, Bruininks-Oseretsky Test of Motor Proficiency

INTENDED PURPOSES

The Bruininks-Oseretsky Test of Motor Proficiency was developed to provide educators, clinicians, and researchers with information to assist them in assessing the motor skills of individual students, in developing and evaluating motor training programs, and in assessing serious motor dysfunctions and developmental handicaps in children. The test is recommended as a screening tool for educational and other placements for individual children.

This test can be used in elementary or secondary schools or within the treatment environment for ambulatory handicapped and nonhandicapped children of either sex between 4½ and 14½ years old.

The short form can be used when evaluating large numbers of children in a limited time, or when only a brief survey of general motor proficiency is required.

DOMAINS

Forty-six items fall into three domains and eight subdomains. The three major domains are gross motor skills, gross and fine motor skills, and fine motor skills. The subdomains are running speed and agility, balance, bilateral coordination, strength, upper limb coordination, response speed, visual-motor control, and upper limb speed and dexterity.

PROCEDURES

Data are gathered by observation of the individual client under special conditions. Sufficient space for an 18-yard running course is required, and the setting should be free from major noises and other distractions. The test administrator observes the subject performing assigned tasks and records the time taken to complete a task and the number of successful attempts (or pass/fail, as called for by each item). While the test administrator does not need special training, he or she must become thoroughly familiar with the directions and practice giving the test in simulated situations before actual administration. Establishing good rapport with the subject is necessary. Estimated administration time is 45 minutes, 20 minutes for the short version.

The instrument is self-scoring; scores are obtained for each of the eight subdomains, the three domains, and the overall instrument.

COSTS

Examiner's manual	$ 12.00
Complete test kit	105.00

(includes examiner's manual, individual record forms—complete battery (25), short form (1 sample form), student booklet (25), and all equipment necessary to administer the test)

There is no quantity price. Additional forms (short and long) and booklets may be ordered separately.

REVIEW

CONTENT

The Bruininks-Oseretsky Test of Motor Proficiency was designed in a scholarly, painstaking manner. The conceptual framework is sound and the items are logical, well constructed, and tested extensions of the framework.

ADMINISTRATION

Proper administration of the test requires thorough knowledge of specific procedures for administration and scoring. While it appears that both the test and technical manuals could be simplified, overall, they are excellent. The author has included a short form which takes half the time to complete. Mastering the procedures for administering and scoring the test may take considerable time. However, it again seems worth the effort.

No special credentials are required of the administrator. It would be better to have someone familiar with the development of motor abilities, but this is not at all necessary. Also, if someone had testing or clinical experience, it would be helpful in establishing rapport and alleviating anxiety of the subjects.

INTERPRETABILITY

This assessment instrument is very easily scored and, therefore, interpreted. The word interpretation may not be appropriate since inferences appear to be involved rather than the mechanistic conversion of raw scores to normative or other indices. Performance can be converted into standard scores for different age groups, age development scores, or percentile ranks.

While the author does not stress interpretation, his conceptual schema and the resultant assessment tool obviously point out the deficits and gaps in motor skill development that need attention. These are not interpretations in and of themselves, but categorizations of problem areas. A skilled clinician, trained in the psychoneurological development area, should be able to use this tool for additional clinical interpretation.

TEST DEVELOPMENT

The author utilized the original Oseretsky test as the basis for this instrument and expanded and enriched the conceptual framework. Citing literature in the area, the author spent a great deal of time and effort devising the format of the testing procedures, items, scales, etc.

Field tests appear to have been extensive and thorough. Items were added, changed, dropped, and combined as a result of field testing and analysis. The testing was controlled and standardized, using many variables—age, sex, race, community size, and geographic region—and the field tests were conducted with mildly and moderately retarded as well as normal 4½ to 14½ year olds.

RELIABILITY

Reliability studies on this instrument are excellent. The test-retest reliability is high on the total test and subtests. Interrater reliability for items requiring extensive judgement in scoring is very high.

Reliability of the short form is quite high, closely approximating the levels obtained with the long form.

VALIDITY

The validation studies on this instrument were excellent; a continuing effort is needed in this area, and the author acknowledges this need.

Construct validity evidence is presented and supportive in the following areas:

1. the relationship of the test content to significant aspects of motor development;

2. relevant statistical properties of the test including the relationship of test score to chronological age; factor analysis of subtest items, lending some support to grouping of items into subtests; and internal consistency of subtests, with low correlation between item and subtests explained; and

3. the functioning of the test with contrasting groups of handicapped and normal children (mildly retarded with normal, moderately to severely retarded with normal, and learning disabled with normal).

SUMMARY OF UTILITY

This instrument is excellent for the assessment of motor skills of handicapped and nonhandicapped children. It is not suitable to assess the movement and motor behaviors of nonambulatory persons or those known to have severe motor disabilities.

The author, beginning with a sound theoretical and conceptual base, carries us through a test development procedure that attends to necessary detail in a scholarly fashion. Reliability and validity studies were done in an excellent fashion and the results will prove that this instrument will be a most valuable contribution to the area of assessment of motor proficiency. More extensive and cross-validation studies in this area are acknowledged as needed by the author. However, overall, this instrument deserves an exemplary rating.

What is of particular significance is the tie-in of the test to the conceptual scheme, as well as validation, in relation to the literature in the general area and other research instruments.

This test fulfills its goal in a maximum manner, that is, "to provide educators, clinicians, and researchers with useful information to assist them in assessing the motor skills of individual students; in developing and evaluating motor-training programs; and in assessing serious motor dysfunctions and developmental handicaps in children." The test will be useful to clinicians and researchers in evaluating children for a variety of purposes. Recommended uses of this test are primarily in the areas of making decisions about educational placement and assessing gross and fine motor skills.

Cain-Levine Social Competency Scale

Authors Leo F. Cain, Samuel Levine, and Freeman F. Elzey	**Distributor** Consulting Psychologists Press, Inc. 577 College Avenue Palo Alto, California 94306
Alternative Version None	**Dates** 1963, 1977
Revisions in Progress None	**Test Manual** Cain-Levine Competency Scale, Cain, Levine, and Elzey, 1963

INTENDED PURPOSES

The Cain-Levine Social Competency Scale was devloped to provide a method of measuring the social competence of the trainable mentally retarded children in institutions and in public school special education classes with a chronological age range of 5 to 12. The scale is intended to be of help in selecting children for school programs, determining placement within the program, and assessing the children's progress. According to the authors, the results obtained from administering the scale may be used as a basis for curriculum planning. The scale may also serve as a criterion measure for research or evaluation purposes to test the results of training, the relative effects of various teaching techniques, and the influence of different environmental conditions on the children's social competence.

DOMAINS

The Cain-Levine Social Competency Scale consists of 44 items divided into four domains: self-help, initiative, social skills, and communication. The items are intended to be a representative sample of behaviors that are important in evaluating the social competence of mentally retarded children.

PROCEDURES

The Cain-Levine Social Competency Scale is a rating scale which obtains information about an individual child by means of an interview with a person knowledgeable about that child. The descriptive statements within each item are ordered by difficulty level, with level one representing the least independent level of social competence and level five representing the most independent level.

A total score is reported for the instrument as well as one for each domain. Tables are provided for chronological ages 5 through 13 and permit the user to determine a child's percentile rank relative to his or her age group for each domain and for the total social competency scale.

Credentials necessary for administration of the scale and administration time are not stated.

COSTS

Specimen set	$7.50
Manual	1.50
Tests, package of 25	4.50

REVIEW

CONTENT

Many of the items in this scale do not translate well into behavioral objectives because they focus on deficits (e.g., "Makes brushing motions, but does not brush adequately"). Many items are difficult to score because they require a judgement on what is "occasionally," "frequently," or "nearly always." For example, such choices as "occasionally cleans nose," "frequently cleans nose," and "nearly always cleans nose," call for rater judgements. Given the unstructured interview method of data collection, this could be a problem if several raters/interviewers are involved.

The items in each of the four domains are representative of the domain under which each is subsumed.

ADMINISTRATION

The scale requires little training. Instructions are clear and the instrument's length is such that it could be administered in about 30 minutes.

INTERPRETABILITY

The conversion of the scores into percentile ranks provides a very useful procedure for interpreting relative standing with other trainable mentally retarded persons.

TEST DEVELOPMENT

The authors followed most of the standard procedures of scale development and revised the scale on the basis of the data collected. Selection of items drew upon all major curriculum guides for trainable mentally retarded children developed by public schools and institutions and through consultations with professionals, discussions with parents, and careful examination of existing scales.

The scale was field tested twice. The initial scale had 70 items and was used by six school districts (N = 188) and nine state institutions (N = 219). Ten items were deleted and a second field test was conducted in 23 public school districts (N = 556), 13 state institutions (N = 472), and 13 private and parent-operated schools (N = 212). An additional six items were deleted. All clients were classified as trainable mentally retarded.

Difficulty increasing independent performance was determined by rank order agreement of at least 70% by each group of judges. Items on which the judges could not agree sufficiently were either rewritten or deleted. Data on the internal consistency of the scale is presented in the form of odd-even correlation coefficients for each age group for the male and female samples. Further data includes the correlations for the 44 items with subscale and total social competency scores for the male and female samples. The correlations between the items and the total score indicate that each is contributing to the measurement of social competence.

The standardization sample consisted of 716 trainable mentally retarded children in the state of California of which 414 were males and 302 were females. They ranged in age from 5 years and 0 months through 13 years and 11 months.

RELIABILITY

The reliability data were very good on subtests and total score in terms of test-retest. It is doubtful that reliability on individual items would be as high due to the subjective judgments required on many items. However, Congdon (1969) obtained an interrater reliability of .94 with 23 institutionalized subjects.

Internal consistency was assessed by odd-even item correlations. Coefficients were high for self-help and communication compared to initiative and social skills. There was no report of interrater reliability. Test-retest reliability was assessed on 35 subjects randomly selected three weeks after the first rating. Total score reliability was .98. Reliability studies were quite adequate with the exception of interrater reliability which should have been assessed but apparently was not. This is a major deficiency, given the subjective value of the data collection procedure used by the scale.

VALIDITY

The items are commonly accepted indices of the social development of children. Therefore, the scale has strong face validity.

The authors did not report any validity studies in the manual. A study by Gardner and Giampa (1971) found use of the scale with severely and profoundly retarded children failed to distribute normally due to the large number of residents with minimal scores. However, the scale does discriminate severely and profoundly handicapped from trainable mentally retarded children. Congdon (1969) obtained correlations ranging from .58 to .77 between subtests on the Cain-Levine and the Vineland. All of these were significant at less than the .01 level. He also found a .81 correlation between the Stanford-Binet Forms L and M and the Cain-Levine, while the authors found only .26 correlation, which suggests a difference between institutionalized and community-based children. The factors causing this discrepancy need further examination.

SUMMARY OF UTILITY

It is doubtful that the Cain-Levine Social Competency Scale provides any new information to those who know a child well. Its best utility would probably be as a screening device to identify areas of deficit across a large number of children unknown to the examiner. It is not "sensitive" enough to change to permit evaluation of client progress or comprehensive enough for program implementation, monitoring, eligibility screening, or accreditation determination.

The scale has been purposely limited to the trainable mentally retarded and is not appropriate for more severely retarded clients or those with physical disabilities.

The use of the scale as a criterion measure to evaluate the results of training may be appropriate in some cases. A program designed to teach a few specific behaviors would produce gains on only those items on the scale measuring those behaviors. This would show only modest gains or no gain in percentile rank, thus lending the impression that the program was unsuccessful. The gaps between the items are quite large and, when this scale is compared with some others, it would be found less useful in evaluating progress with profoundly and severely handicapped individuals.

The scale appears to be a very useful device for making a rapid assessment of the relative standing of a particular trainable mentally retarded child in relation to other trainable mentally retarded children of the same age.

California Preschool Social Competency Scale

Authors Samuel Levine, Freeman Elzey, and Mary Lewis	**Distributor** Consulting Psychologists Press, Inc. 577 College Avenue Palo Alto, California 94306
Alternative Version None	**Dates** 1969
Revisions in Progress None	**Test Manual** California Preschool Social Competency Scale Manual, Levine, Elzey, and Lewis, 1969

INTENDED PURPOSES

According to the authors, the California Preschool Social Competency Scale is designed to measure the adequacy of preschool children's interpersonal behavior and the degree to which they assume social responsibility. Implicit in this definition is the concept of independence. Situational behaviors, selected in terms of common cultural expectations, represent basic competencies to be developed in the process of socialization. The instrument is intended for use by teachers within the preschool program context. The text is specific to $2\frac{1}{2}$ to $5\frac{1}{2}$ year-old children of all mental ages with no physical disabilities, but is best used for individuals of normal intelligence.

DOMAINS

The items cover a wide range of behaviors (subsumed under the construct of social competency) such as response to routine, response to the unfamiliar, following instructions, helping others, initiating activities, giving direction to activities, reaction to frustration, and accepting limits. No subdomains *per se* are defined.

PROCEDURES

Data are gathered by observation of the individual client in a typical preschool situation. The observer is generally the teacher or other staff person, and the behavior is observed in the context of routine daily activities. Each of the items is rated by checking incrementally ranked behavior statements describing levels of competence from 1 (lowest) to 4. Testing takes 15 to 30 minutes. There are 30 items which are combined into a total score for the instrument. No intermediate categorization is used.

COSTS

Specimen set	$1.50
Manual	2.75
Tests, package of 25	4.50

REVIEW

CONTENT

The items in the California Preschool Competency Scale reflect behaviors of importance to preschool programs and are detailed enough to be of valid and reliable use. For example, "identification" is broken into the following levels of detail:

a. can state first name only
b. can state full name
c. can state full name, age, and birthday
d. can state name, age, and address

ADMINISTRATION

The California Preschool Social Competency Scale is a very easy and efficient instrument to administer. However, the benefits of its use are not too far-reaching. The test manual instructions are sufficient with practice using the instrument. It requires no special training to administer, only that the rater be familiar with the child over time.

INTERPRETABILITY

The instrument and data produced need very little interpretation. Interpretive procedures are not presented in the manual but should not be a problem for classroom teachers.

TEST DEVELOPMENT

Original items were judged for face validity or content validity by preschool teachers and graduate students. Items were selected using eight criteria. Field tests were conducted in California with preschool children from both upper and lower socioeconomic families. Nine national sites were then used to provide a thorough set of national norms. Different norms were presented for children of "high and low occupational level" parents.

RELIABILITY

Reliability data presented are convincing. Reliability studies conducted in three sites established reliability between .75 and .79. Odd/even reliability coefficients ranged from .90 to .98. Individual items reflected a .50 correlation with overall scores. These data are more than adequate for this type of narrowly defined instrument.

VALIDITY

The instrument does have face validity but no empirical studies were cited to determine its content validity.

SUMMARY OF UTILITY

The California Preschool Competency Scale has acceptable utility for a classroom teacher who is identifying needs, screening, and perhaps program planning for an individual child. The scale is best used with a normal or heterogeneous population of children in classroom and group settings only. Its measurement properties and standardization procedures make the scale a potentially useful instrument for research or evaluation purposes involving a general population of young children (e.g., a Head Start program). There are not enough items at the lower range of functioning to make the instrument useful for the developmentally delayed or disruptive child. This is a serious deficiency if considering its possible use with a developmentally disabled client population.

Callier-Azusa Scale (F Edition)

Authors
Christy Battle, Carrol Boggess, Cleve Burton, Judy Burton, Stephanie Chambers, Patricia Spencer Day, Carmella Ficociello, Carol Gerber, Mary Ann Mariani, Cynthia L. Stone, Suzanne Tenison, and Jan Writer; Robert Stillman, editor

Alternative Version
None

Revisions in Progress
The G edition of the Callier-Azusa Scale will be available in late August, 1978. In this edition, the cognitive development subscale has been expanded to include higher cognitive levels. The socialization subscales have been reorganized into three subscales covering adult-child, peer, and environment interactions. Other less substantial additions and modifications have also been made in the language subscales.

Distributor
The University of Texas at Dallas
Callier Center for Communication Disorders
1966 Inwood Road
Dallas, Texas 75235

Date
1977

Test Manual
The Callier-Azusa Scale, Robert Stillman, editor, 1977

INTENDED PURPOSES

The Callier-Azusa Scale (F Edition) was designed specifically to aid in the assessment of deaf-blind and other severely and profoundly handicapped children. It is most comprehensive at the lower developmental levels. For children functioning at higher developmental levels, it should be used in conjunction with other assessment tools. Its three primary applications are (1) to assess the developmental level of children for whom other methods of assessment are inappropriate or inadequate; (2) to measure developmental progress by comparing the child against himself or herself rather than a norm, and thus to assess the overall effectiveness of the child's program; and (3) to provide a resource, but not a teaching program, for planning developmentally appropriate programs for individual children. The scale is intended for use within the classroom or training setting for all age groups falling within the developmental age range of zero to nine years (although the highest items are at the seven-year level and most are below the three-year level).

DOMAINS

The 249 instrument items are organized into 5 domains and 17 subdomains. The domains are motor development, perceptual development, daily living skills, cognition, communication and language, and socialization.

PROCEDURES

Administration of the Callier-Azusa Scale is based on observation of classroom behaviors. Test settings need not be artifically structured. Although the administrator needs no specialized testing expertise beyond good observational skills, he or she must be thoroughly familiar with the child's behavior. Thus, a minimum two-week classroom observation period is strongly suggested before the scale is completed. Most accurate results are obtained if several individuals having close contact with the child evaluate the child on a consensus basis. Items making up the 17 subdomains are arranged in sequential steps, although the behaviors within an item are not sequenced. The administrator's observations are converted directly to a developmental age for each subdomain by noting observed behaviors on the score sheet. For a single administrator, 45 minutes to 3 hours are required. A consensus evaluation would require more time.

COSTS

Instruments can be obtained at no cost by contacting the Callier Center for Communication Disorders. A paper (by Robert Stillman) on the scale's reliability is available for $.30 from the author.

REVIEW

CONTENT

The Callier-Azusa Scale does an excellent job of assessing the basic developmental levels of deaf-blind individuals. Very minute steps are identified in motor development, perceptual abilities, daily living skills, language, and socialization. The instrument does identify the very small steps in the sequence. The behavioral specification is extremely complete at the lowest developmental levels and weaker at the highest developmental levels.

The items are explained in detail and in most cases an example is given (e.g., Item A: voluntarily holds object; release is an unconscious relaxation of grasp. Example: when hand is placed on material, such as cloth, folded paper, hair, blanket, sleeve, will hold or pull).

ADMINISTRATION

Instructions for administration are provided in the test manual and are sufficient with practice. Although the administration of the instrument is simple and requires no training, the question of rater bias must be raised. Familiarity with the student is critical, but this familiarity also tends to encourage biases and to give the child the benefit of the doubt. The authors suggest the use of team assessments to help reduce observer bias and misinterpretation of behavior.

The items in the cognitive section are confusing; this may relate to the higher vocabulary level of these items. The authors are in the process of preparing papers describing the sequence of items included in the cognitive development and expressive and receptive language subscales, which should make the subscales easier to understand and use.

The manual emphasizes the need for good observational skills but fails to point out the problems of observing the minute behaviors (eye movement, slight head turning) of deaf-blind individuals for whom the instrument was designed. The manual also fails to point out the problems which may arise when the consensus evaluation approach is used.

109

INTERPRETABILITY

The instrument does give the teacher and trainer an easy and quick way to assess progress; the one-page summary and age equivalencies are extremely useful in that they allow them a quick look at where the child is and the growth on retesting. The authors are correct in stating that the age equivalencies for specific behaviors are subject to debate. Interpretation should be more concerned with the amount of development rather than the present level of functioning.

TEST DEVELOPMENT

The instrument should be considered in the developmental stage, but the authors are proceeding in a professional way. This instrument was designed specifically for assessment of deaf-blind children. Items were originally an outgrowth of the profile scales component of an educational program for multiply handicapped children. Occupational therapists, physical therapists, speech therapists, social workers, and teachers all contributed and changed the items of this instrument based on their experience with the deaf-blind. It has been field tested with 80 children and 95 teacher aides, parents, and specialists. Children in 13 centers throughout the south central United States are being used as the reference groups. The authors report continued refinement.

RELIABILITY

Interobservation correlation was calculated for both paired observers and individual observers. All correlations were significant, and ranged between .66 and .97. Higher reliability was found for motor scales than for social ability scales. Although individual rater correlation revealed no significant difference when compared with the correlations of paired observers, the authors recommend the use of paired observers as a means of obtaining higher reliability.

VALIDITY

One validity study of the Callier-Azusa Scale has been performed. This addressed the ordinality of the scales and found that the authors' proposed difficulty ordering of items was consistent with that suggested by two different analyses. However, additional validation research is in order.

SUMMARY OF UTILITY

The Callier-Azusa Scale is extremely useful for assessment of deaf-blind residents at the lower functioning level, suggesting areas of progress to emphasize. Although the instrument is designed basically for preschool age children, it can be used appropriately for school age and adult deaf-blind and profoundly and multiply handicapped persons. It is specifically appropriate for the deaf-blind in intensive school training programs. It is not appropriate for higher functioning deaf-blind persons, or any individual whose developmental level in most areas is above age nine. Because of its lack of normative data, it should generally not be used for group comparison but rather for individual program planning.

At present, the instrument is mimeographed and distributed free. If it was published, it would be very costly in its present form. An answer or rating sheet with space for comments could be developed and a single rating booklet could be used over again. The paired rater consensus procedure also is costly and assumes that at least two trainers or teachers will have opportunity to observe a child over time.

Camelot Behavioral Checklist

Author Ray Foster	**Distributor** Ray Foster Camelot Behavioral Systems P.O. Box 3447 Lawrence, Kansas 66044
Alternative Version None	**Dates** 1974, 1977
Revisions in Progress None	**Test Manual** Camelot Behavioral Checklist Manual, Ray Foster, 1974, 1977

INTENDED PURPOSES

The Camelot Behavioral Checklist is intended to identify specific training objectives for an individual and then to provide a summary or classification score which is directly based on these

111

objectives. Although the primary use of the checklist is to identify target behaviors for an individual, a composite score for a group of residents or students can be made for use in program planning decisions. The manual does not specify the population for whom the instrument is intended (e.g. types of disability, severity, level, age).

DOMAINS

Three hundred ninety-nine items are divided into 40 subdomains and 10 domains: self-help, physical development, home duties, vocational behavior, economic behavior, independent travel, numerical skills, communication skills, social behaviors, and responsibility.

PROCEDURES

The yes/no items on the checklist, arranged sequentially within subdomains in order of difficulty, are completed by a trained professional or other staff person, preferably by direct observation in a special testing setting. Information can also be obtained by interviewing a person familiar with the client. According to the author, the latter method, while less time-consuming, is also less reliable. Administration requires 20 to 40 minutes. A score is obtained for each of the 10 domains and for the total instrument.

COSTS

Not available.

REVIEW

CONTENT

The content of the Camelot Behavioral Checklist was generated primarily from a review of other similar instruments. Specific items were selected and/or written in behavioral terms, but only if they had clear implications for training. Item content is fairly comprehensive across 10 domains and 40 subdomains, although representation within subdomains is not even.

ADMINISTRATION

The administration of this instrument should not be difficult, given familiarity with the individual being evaluated.

INTERPRETABILITY

Most of the discussion in the manual is concerned with the interpretation of scores within the context of training. There is one scoring quirk that could lead to improper interpretations. If a subject is physically unable to perform a stipulated behavior, the administrator is instructed to score that behavior a "plus," indicating no need for training. Since a plus also carries the meaning of "can do," this scoring anomaly compromises the clarity of interpretation.

Empirically determined item difficulties help to provide a normative context for program planning by allowing the performance of the individual being assessed to be compared with a reference group. Norm referencing is a weak rationale for program planning, especially with severely retarded people whose current behavior frequently is a tremendous underestimate of potential. Program planning is more appropriately determined as a function of training resources available. The author of Camelot would probably be outraged at the use of his normative data as a constraint upon increased potential. Profile charts, at both item and domain score levels, have been developed in order to display relative strengths and weaknesses.

TEST DEVELOPMENT

After items were selected and/or constructed following literature reviews, revisions and modifications appear to be based upon data derived from a single sample of 624 institutionalized retarded people. Two other samples were also used to confirm the item sequencing along the dimension of difficulty. Only item difficulty statistics were calculated in order to guide test development. Internal consistency estimates would have also been appropriate.

RELIABILITY

Only interjudge reliabilities are reported at the domain and total score levels. Stability and internal consistency estimates, also relevant, are missing. Given the strong proclivity of the author to interpret at the item level, it would also be appropriate to somehow address the reliability of individual items.

VALIDITY

Only construct validity at the total scale level is presented; Camelot scores are correlated with other measures of intelligence and adaptive behavior. Surprisingly, the Adaptive Behavior Scale was not included in this study. Given the strong recommendations to use this scale for purposes of program planning, content and criterion validity should have also been explored.

SUMMARY OF UTILITY

A deliberate attempt was made to design the Camelot Behavioral Checklist in a way that would permit utilization at all levels of decision making. To an extent, this has been achieved, although program planning uses have been stressed more thoroughly than other administrative uses such as classification and program evaluation.

The manual does not make its population characteristics clear. The intended population probably includes mentally retarded people ranging in age from two years through adult, both sexes, and all degrees of retardation from profound to mild.

Task analyses at the lower end of functioning are not sufficiently discrete to permit goal setting for many profoundly retarded children and adolescents. Use of the checklist may have to be supplemented with other similar instruments.

The Child Behavior Rating Scale

Author Russell N. Cassel	**Distributor** Western Psychological Services 12031 Wilshire Boulevard Los Angeles, California 90025
Alternative Version None	**Dates** 1962, 1977
Revisions in Progress None	**Test Manual** The Child Behavior Rating Scale Manual, Russell N. Cassel

INTENDED PURPOSES

The Child Behavior Rating Scale (CBRS) is to be used for the objective assessment of personality adjustments of preschool and primary grade pupils, with a chronological age range of five to nine years. It is intended to measure children who are considered normal or emotionally handicapped as well as those who are handicapped in completing the conventional paper and pencil personality tests often used in school testing programs because of an inability to read or some other disability. The CBRS is designed to be administered in a school or home setting.

The CBRS is intended to be a means for making a periodic and objective assessment of personality adjustment and an aid to school personnel attempting to better understand the forces and circumstances operating in the life of the child.

According to the author, use of the CBRS over a period of time provides a frame of reference for evaluating long-term personality changes and adjustments of children, thus laying the groundwork for useful predictions of future behavior.

DOMAINS

The 78 CBRS items provide measures of adjustment in five domains: self-adjustment, home adjustment, social adjustment, school adjustment, and physical adjustment.

PROCEDURES

Data are collected about the individual child by observation techniques. Any literate person who has observed or knows the child to be assessed can complete the CBRS. On each CBRS item the child is rated on a six-point scale as to the degree a specific aspect of behavior is observed by the rater. The amount of time necessary to administer the instrument is not stated.

A score is reported for each domain as well as for the total instrument. The personality total adjustment score is designed by the author to provide a single meaningful score to indicate total adjustment.

COSTS

Record forms, 25 per package		$6.50
2 packages	(each package)	5.75
Specimen set		8.50
(manual & 25 record forms)		
Test manual		2.50

115

REVIEW

CONTENT

The content of the Child Behavior Rating Scale would not appear suitable for developmentally disabled clients since they were not included in the standardization study. Furthermore, many of the "deviant" items would probably be "normal" for a developmentally disabled population (i.e., "often appears to feel unwanted or disliked," "often seems to have little self-confidence," "often is very nervous and excited about things").

Many items on this scale that is intended to assess a child seem more related to parents. For example, domain of the home adjustment includes questions such as "parents are too strict" and "family lives in multiple-family dwelling." If a behavior has not been observed the rater checks "no." Thus, infrequent maladaptive behavior is assumed not to exist.

ADMINISTRATION

The test is well packaged and easy to administer and score. Minimum training is required and domain scores and total scores could be easily maintained in student files.

The manual is very short and although it includes the essentials, it gives very little detail about normative studies, selection of items, and interpretation of test scores. It is the reviewer's opinion that 25 minutes are required to complete this scale.

INTERPRETABILITY

The author suggests eight ways in which the test scores may be used. However, no data are provided as to the validity of such uses. T-scores of the "typical child" and presumed emotionally disturbed child are provided for comparison. Norms are based on "typical 5-9 year olds" and 200 children "referred for emotional problems." Other than the lower scores by the latter group and face validity of the items, no validation data are presented. Hence, interpretations should be made cautiously.

TEST DEVELOPMENT

Items were selected from the records of children referred for emotional problems. A panel of psychologists by majority vote selected and categorized the items. No empirical field testing was done to check item appropriateness or reliability. No factor analysis was done to evaluate meaningfulness of the five domains. There has been no further revision or refinement of the test.

RELIABILITY

Split-half reliability appears satisfactory. The author does report two studies, one with 50 parents with an r of .91, and one with 50 teachers with an r of .74. The details of these reliability studies are not given. This level of reliability is low for clinical purposes.

VALIDITY

The author argues for the "face validity" of his instrument. He does present T-scores of 200 children who were referred to a mental health clinic. These scores are significantly lower than the "typical child group." As Dunn (1972) points out, there is almost no discussion of the nature of the 200 emotionally disturbed sample. We do know they are a "referred" sample and not a "diagnosed" one.

No attempt is made to compare individual scores with children of the same age. The author groups the four age groups together although it is generally known that a younger child would show more immature emotional behavior.

The total score includes only three of the five subtests. Apparently two of the domains do not assist the test in discriminating between the maladjusted and the typical.

SUMMARY OF UTILITY

It would be most unwise to consider a child emotionally disturbed solely on the basis of this scale. It might be helpful as an aid in determining areas of stress for the child and in comparing parents' perception and teacher's perception of the child. Because the instrument deals only with emotional maladjustment, it does not have broad application. It might be a useful screening device for certain types of emotional disturbances, although there is no evidence of predictive validity offered for the instrument. Use of the instrument with a developmentally disabled population must be approached with caution, as the function of interest in the author's mind was "personality adjustment."

Client-Centered Evaluation Model

Author Arne T. Bjaanes	**Distributor** Center for the Study of Community Perspectives P.O. Box 66 Patton, California 92362
Alternative Version Short Form CCEM and the complete CCEM	**Dates** 1975, 1977
Revisions in Progress Completed by the end of 1978	**Test Manual** Client-Centered Evaluation Model Field Manual (2nd edition), Arne T. Bjaanes, 1975

INTENDED PURPOSES

The Client-Centered Evaluation Model (CCEM) is a client performance measure responding to the requirements of both the Developmental Disability Council and the Developmental Disability Service Network. It is intended to be responsive to evaluation requirements in both state and federal legislation. At present, the CCEM is being used as part of an evaluation system by the California Department of Health which also includes the ANDI, (a Normalization and Development Instrument.)*

The CCEM consists of three major parts: a tracking system, a comprehensive process assessment instrument, and a service description plan. Data collected by the CCEM is used to provide reports to service level staff, program management, statewide management, departments, area boards, the Developmental Disability Council, and the legislature.

The short form is designed to be used as a survey and census instrument and the complete CCEM is to be used as a comprehensive process evaluation instrument. According to the manual, clients exhibiting any developmental or other disabilities,

---

*ANDI is also reviewed in this report.

with a chronological age range of one year to adult, can be evaluated with this instrument in a residential or day care setting.

DOMAINS

Both forms of the CCEM assess the individual along seven domains: motor, independent living, social, emotional, cognitive, communication, and vocational. The short form contains 32 items, the complete form, 126.

PROCEDURES

The CCEM is a rating scale to be completed by a person familiar with the client's behavior. For clients receiving multiple services, the domains are best filled out by those providing the services with which each domain coincides. According to this manual, this instrument can be administered by a trained professional or other staff person with a minimum of training. The short form requires a half hour to administer, the long form, approximately two hours.

Scoring information provided in the manual is not explicit about types of scoring. The author does state that "After the completion of each section (domain) they are brought together to form a comprehensive evaluation package for each client."

COSTS

Specimen set	$5.00
Test manual	3.50
Tests, per 100	1.70

REVIEW

CONTENT

The CCEM domains and items are very appropriate for the proposed use of this instrument. However, individual ratings on each item could be suspect relative to reliability.

It is assumed that the various people reporting have had an opportunity to observe all behaviors required. This is most likely a faulty assumption and could lead to inaccuracies and lack of reliability.

The scales are comprehensive in range but not in depth. Items are based on behavioral observation but require judgements about actions.

ADMINISTRATION

While the CCEM is relatively simple to use and rate, it requires a very responsible rater who has had extensive contact with the client to make the necessary discriminations. The short form provides a better cost/efficiency ratio and could serve in most instances for monitoring and planning service programs.

INTERPRETABILITY

The results require relatively little interpretation and reveal a useful profile of a person's abilities. No information is given relative to interpretation but it should be relatively straightforward in that behavioral levels are presented.

TEST DEVELOPMENT

The procedures are not presented, but judging from the product they are acceptable.

RELIABILITY

No data were presented and, therefore, unreliability could be a problem. The author, in personal communication, reports high reliability coefficients (.89 and above) for all scales except emotional (.61). However, no details of the nature of these coefficients is available. This information does suggest some potential for the instrument to have acceptable reliability.

VALIDITY

No information on validity was presented, but the instrument does have face validity. Also, in personal communication, the author reports coefficients for "domain validity" for the scales. Most are high (ranging from .80 to .92), except emotional (.37).

SUMMARY OF UTILITY

The information presented by the CCEM is very useful in developing an individual service plan and monitoring program effectiveness for developmentally disabled and otherwise handicapped persons.

At the client level, the instrument is most promising for screening and program planning. Data are also useful at the local administrative and state levels for determining range and severity of handicapping conditions for program planning and evaluation. The instrument appears to be useful for the purposes intended.

Perhaps it collects more data than needed at the administrative and planning levels but the more client-oriented data are helpful at the direct service levels.

The CCEM provides excellent coverage of the behavioral domains important to providing services for the developmentally disabled. Unfortunately, not enough information is presented regarding construction, reliability, and validity to pass a final judgement on its usefulness. However, it does appear to be a more than adequate system for providing information for client assessment and providing data to be used by service planners. The long form data would be most useful at the service level and the short form data at the administrative and planning levels.

Community Adjustment Scale

Authors Marsha Mailick Seltzer and Gary Seltzer	**Distributor** Educational Projects, Inc. 22 Hillard Street Cambridge, Massachusetts 02138
Alternative Version None	**Date** Not Specified
Revisions in Progress None	**Test Manual** Instructions for Community Adjustment Scale in *Context for Competence*, by Marsha Mailick Seltzer and Gary Seltzer, Educational Projects, Inc., Cambridge, Massachusetts, 1978

INTENDED PURPOSES

The purpose of the Community Adjustment Scale is to assess how well a retarded adult is adjusting to life in the community. The components of community adjustment assessed are whether a person has the skills to act independently, whether a person actually uses his or her skills, whether the physical and social environment promotes the acquisition and performance of skills, and whether a person seems to be motivated to acquire and perform skills. A major goal of the scale is to allow the user to distinguish between a client's skills and his or her demonstrated performance.

DOMAINS

The Community Adjustment Scale measures skills along eight domains within the four basic dimensions of skills, performance, environmental opportunity, and motivation. The domains include advanced personal care, housekeeping, communication, social adjustment, community participation, economic management, work, and agency utilization. There are a total of 452 items.

PROCEDURES

The Community Adjustment Scale collects data by obtaining information from a person knowledgeable about the client. The instrument contains open-ended (impressionistic) and fact-gathering questions, binary (yes/no) choices, and rating scales. The authors give no information about administration credentials or administration time.

No scores are reported. It is intended that an assessment of the individual's performance on scale items enables the evaluator to assess the person's skills along the four dimensions and to record and plan for remediation where deficits exist.

COSTS

Not available.

REVIEW

CONTENT

The content of the scale is quite good in covering eight areas of community adjustment which appear to possess a high degree of construct and content validity. The content of the scale is not appropriate for assessing the community adjustment of persons with severe to profound developmental handicaps. It is intended primarily to assess persons who are capable of placement in the typical group home setting. For the most part, the items are stated clearly and appear relatively simple to administer and interpret.

The underlying assumption upon which this scale is based is that the retarded client's capability to perform a wide range of skills associated with successful community adjustment will be strongly influenced by the motivation of the client and the opportunities to perform provided by his or her environment. The scale, therefore, considers the dimensions of skill mastery, performance, motivation, and environmental opportunity in assessing the client's capabilities in each of the eight content areas outlined above.

While the scale offers a unique approach to reviewing the client's adaptation to community living, it also has the following inherent shortcomings:

Subjectivity. Many of the items used in the scale do not lend themselves to a completely objective response. For example, under house cleaning (II-E), the respondent is asked: "Does he/she regularly clean own bedroom and other rooms in the house, so that they usually look neat and well-cared for?" Obviously, standards of neatness and cleanliness vary from person to person, depending on their cultural background and upbringing, Thus, responses to this and many similar questions are open to cultural bias which could distort the results. The authors offer no data on interrater reliability and it seems unlikely that acceptable scores could be obtained if such studies were conducted.

Distortion. The authors point out in the manual that "the interview format may not be the most advantageous method for assessing environmental opportunity," since the respondents (facility staff) "might have an investment in presenting the setting in the best possible light." They suggest that the effects of such response bias might be minimized by directly observing the environment or conducting reliability checks on the staff's responses. Such reliability checks might be of some assistance but they wouldn't obviate the subjective nature of the process. It might be added that some level of response bias can be anticipated in answers to questions concerning skill mastery, performance, and motivation as well, although, perhaps, this phenomenon will not be as pronounced in these latter areas. Unlike reliability checks on the environment, it will not be nearly as simple to validate the respondent's answers in these other dimensions of the scale.

Binary choice. The authors have generally been successful in structuring the items so they lend themselves to either/or responses. However, in some instances, what the authors refer to as the "fixed alternative method" of responding does not offer the respondent a means of reflecting nuances in the client's capabilities or performance. For example, under clothing care

123

(item I-D-1), the question is: "Does he/she know how to fold clothing and hang clothing upon hangers?" It is possible that a client may have mastered some simple folding tasks (e.g., folding socks) but not more complex tasks (e.g., folding long sleeved shirts). To cite another example (item I-E-2), a client may have mastered sweeping the floor and vacuuming the rug but may be unable to wash the floor effectively.

Sequencing. For the most part, the items are developmentally sequenced within each of the subdomains. However, there are a few instances where the existing sequence seems questionable. For example, in the subdomain dealing with finding a job, it would seem more appropriate if the question about asking friends and acquaintances preceded the more complex tasks of contacting an employment agency and filling out an application. Similarly, the questions under the subdomain of banking should be reordered so that cashing a paycheck appears first, maintaining a savings account is the second question, and maintaining a checking account comes third.

One year performance criteria. The authors' criterion for mastery of any particular skill is that the client "has independently (without prompts) used the skill at least once in the last year." While this criterion may be appropriate for certain types of skills, it is questionable that such a rate is sufficient to demonstrate the mastery of all skills. For example, given the difficulty in defining what constitutes interest, is a display of "interest in reading for pleasure" sufficient to demonstrate that a client has mastered the skill (item IV-A-2)? Or, looking at the opposite side of the question (i.e., performance), must a resident read a book, magazine, or newspaper for pleasure once a week in order to establish the fact that he can perform the task? Many normal adults would fail to meet that performance criterion.

Availability of Training Programs. Throughout the instrument, questions are raised about whether the residential facility offers its clients who lack particular skills a training program which will assist them in acquiring those skills. Yet, nowhere do the authors define their concept of a training program. Given the possibility of response bias, some attempt should be made to specify the minimum elements of a structured training program; otherwise, the responses to this question are likely to be less than helpful.

One of the unique aspects of this scale is its direct assessment of the individual's opportunity to perform various tasks. There is a separate environmental opportunity subscale which measures, in terms of each content domain, the extent to which individuals have the opportunity to perform the various skills and behaviors.

There is some question as to whether the domains of the test which assess skills, performance, environmental opportunity, and motivation to perform are really independent of one another. The authors were quite sensitive to this issue in the preliminary development of the scale, but there is still some question as to whether the information obtained through additional items in these four areas justifies the required time and cost. There may be considerable redundancy in the skills and performance sections of the scale, for example. Future research should establish whether the additional time needed to gather information in these areas is beneficial.

ADMINISTRATION

One of the scale's most serious deficiencies is in the area of administration. While the instructions for administration are relatively simple, the proper use of the scale requires that essentially parallel items be administered in four separate areas: skills, consistency of performance, environmental opportunity or the opportunity to perform, and motivation. In the preliminary development of the test, an effort was made to reduce the redundancy in content across these four areas of assessment, but an inspection of the skills content shows a good deal of overlap, especially between the skills and performance areas of the test. In its present form, the amount of information gained from assessing environmental opportunity and motivation may not be sufficient to justify the time required to complete the instrument. The present version of the tests appears, therefore, to represent considerable costs in terms of the time required for assessment in relationship to the information that can be used for program planning and evaluation of client progress.

Compared with many other assessment tools, this scale would appear to be relatively costly and time-consuming to administer. However, the results may be worth the additional cost and time if the resident staff gains insights into the client's motivation and/or the impact of his or her environment. The need for such data should be a crucial determinant of the user's decision to employ this scale.

INTERPRETABILITY

The scale would appear to yield relatively imprecise data in behavioral terms, that is, there are no normative scores provided in the test manual, only general behavioral statements that allow the examiner to assess the extent of the person's community adjustment. Nonetheless, the instrument might be useful in gaining information about the interaction between the client's skills acquisition, performance, motivation, and the surrounding environment.

The authors suggest that the instrument may be used as either a research tool or as a clinical tool. In program settings, the authors claim that the CAS "can be used to generate a clinical profile of a resident." This profile can be used to determine "the resident's present level of functioning and prescriptively (identify) environmental and motivational interventions that would improve independent performance." Since no provision is made for scoring the scale, norms, percentiles, and graphic displays are not provided. The authors, however, do provide a form which may be used in developing a clinical profile from the CAS.

Few instructions are given in the available manual for interpretation and use of information gained from the administration of the Community Adjustment Scale. Further work should be undertaken to translate the measures of performance more easily into suggestions for training and environmental modification. With some additional investment, the interpretability of performance from the scale could be substantively improved.

TEST DEVELOPMENT

Items from other adaptive behavior scales (AAMD Adaptive Behavior Scale, Progress Assessment Chart, and others) were included in the initial draft of the CAS because "it was felt that the *content* of the other scales of adaptive behavior was fairly inclusive." The draft instrument was field tested with a sample of 34 retarded adults residing in group homes, institutions, or in their family homes. The results of the field test were subject to a correlation analysis, a factor analysis, and a path analysis. Based on these analyses and face validity review by 14 experienced and knowledgeable professionals, the draft instrument was extensively revised.

While it is clear from the manual that considerable time and effort went into the development of the scale, the original field sample of clients was small (N=34) and selected primarily on the basis of accessibility rather than on any statistical sampling basis. Under the circumstances, further validation studies appear to be necessary before the validity and reliability of the instrument are fully established. While other means were used in test development (e.g., the use of an expert panel to rate the value of test items), there is insufficient detail provided in the manual to indicate clearly all the possible procedures that were used in developing test items. For example, very little information is provided on the source of possible items and the extent to which existing scales contributed to the content of the scale. Two of the most positive aspects of the scale were the use of path analysis and factor analyses to make modifications in the design of items and in the test structure. Such procedures represent a very promising approach to test development and, with further cross-validation of results, may yield a very useful scale to assess the community adjustment skills of mentally retarded people.

RELIABILITY

Only one form of reliability is reported in the test manual, a measure of internal consistency. Measures of internal consistency using alpha coefficients are reported for the different content areas and domains of the test. The alpha coefficients for these various content areas and domains appear to fall generally into an acceptable range, with somewhat lower reliabilities obtained for the areas of environmental assessment and motivation. The alpha reliabilities for the skills and performance sections appear particularly strong. However, the coefficients were run on a very small sample of subjects (N=32) and no cross-validation was used in computing reliability statistics for the final Community Adjustment Scale subscale scores (i.e., alpha reliabilities were run on the preliminary sample and then repeated again on the same sample in assessing internal consistency reliabilities for the final subscale scores). The American Psychological Association's manual of standards for test construction clearly regards this approach as an unacceptable practice; an independent sample should have been selected to establish the reliability of scores.

There are other forms of reliability which should be considered in establishing the stability of the Community Adjustment Scale. It would seem to be of some advantage to use test-retest reliabilities to establish the stability of the scale and to determine whether different respondents would produce relatively similar information for the same individuals (i.e., interrespondent agreement).

VALIDITY

The Community Adjustment Scale appears to possess minimally acceptable validity, although the manual reviewed was clearly inadequate in its presentation of information related to this area. There is some evidence of construct validity for the concept of community adjustment and the content of the scale, as well as empirical support for the construct of community adjustment obtained through factor analysis and path analysis studies. Unfortunately, the data for these analyses are derived from an extremely small sample of subjects who may not represent in general the community adjustment status of mildly retarded adults. Therefore, construct validity of the scale should await more detailed cross-validation studies on larger samples of subjects.

There is one additional source of validity used in the development of the Community Adjustment Scale. A panel of 18 persons with expertise in the area of mental retardation was asked to rate each of the scale items for its appropriateness as a measure of community adjustment. Apparently, decisions regarding the final content of the scale were based, in part, on these ratings of knowledgeable professionals.

Another possible measure of the scale's validity is the differences in performances found in a study of approximately 150 adults living in institutions or less restrictive living arrangements. It was a general finding that persons living in less restrictive settings achieved generally higher scores on the Community Adjustment Scale than did those living in more restrictive settings. These results could be construed as an indirect measure of predictive validity.

Further work should be conducted to establish the validity of the Community Adjustment Scale. Additional work on larger samples of subjects, assessments of the relationship between the Community Adjustment Scale and other measures of adaptive behavior and community adjustment, and predictive studies of later adjustment and work performance would seem advisable.

SUMMARY OF UTILITY

The Community Adjustment Scale would appear to be useful in helping supervisors and direct care staff in community residences understand the complex interaction between skills development, skills utilization, motivation, and the programming environment. It also should assist such staff in preparing for more sophisticated and targeted intervention strategies.

With the resolution of certain issues of reliability, validity, and interpretability, the CAS can be useful in assessing the community adjustment status of mildly retarded adults. However, it can be of only limited use with more severely retarded and multiply handicapped clients in community settings. Since there is some evidence that such clients are likely to make up an increasing proportion of community placements in the years ahead (as states make further reductions in their institutional populations), consideration should be given to either revising the items so they are more applicable to severely retarded and multiply handicapped clients living in community facilities or developing a subscale applicable to this group.

The CAS should be regarded as a promising experimental measure rather than a finished product. Considerable work must be done to establish clearly the validity and value of the scale as a measure of community adjustment. There is also the need for further work to determine the extent to which the scale yields consistent and reliable measurement. In addition, potential users should be provided with information and suggestions regarding the interpretation and application of test results and evaluating client progress and designing needed training programs.

Denver Developmental Screening Test

Authors
William Frankenburg and
Josiah Dodds
	Distributor
	LADOCA Project and
	  Publishing Foundation
	East 51st Avenue and
	  Lincoln Street
	Denver, Colorado 80216

Alternative Version None	**Dates** 1967, 1970, 1975
Revisions in Progress None	**Test Manual** Denver Developmental Screening Test, William K. Frankenburg et al., 1975

INTENDED PURPOSES

Developmental deviations in young children are difficult if not impossible to detect through a routine physical examination. The Denver Developmental Screening Test was designed and standardized to aid the health provider in detecting potential problems. The test is administered to children to sort out those who have a high probability of being developmentally impaired. Its intended applications are thus (a) to screen asymptomatic children for possible problems; (b) to confirm intuitive suspicions with an objective measure; and (c) to monitor high-risk children such as those who have experienced prenatal difficulties. According to the authors, the screening test can be used for male and female children from birth to six years. It is intended for well or apparently well children rather than the physically handicapped or disabled.

DOMAINS

One hundred and five test items provide information about four domains: personal-social, fine motor-adaptive, language, and gross motor.

PROCEDURES

Each performance of a specific behavior is given a pass/fail designation. Information is obtained by direct client observation and from a person familiar with the child's everyday behaviors. According to the authors, the test is administered by professionals or paraprofessionals, and the test manual instructions are sufficient preparation with some practice. The instrument takes 10 to 20 minutes to administer.

The self-scoring test yields an overall interpretation of the client compared to the normal range for the particular age of the client tested. Categories are normal, questionable, abnormal, and untestable.

The authors stress that only the total DDST performance of a child should be considered in evaluating a child's apparent developmental status since the four individual sectors of the DDST do not constitute separate tests and none has been validated individually against any outside criterion measure. The authors encourage periodic developmental screening and suggest that care should be taken not to consider a child normal merely because he or she passes a developmental screen. All supplementary information, including intuition of the examiner or parent, should be considered important.

COSTS

Test kit (without forms and manual) $7.00

Test forms, per 100	2.00
Reference manual	4.00
Manual/workbook	6.00
Manual in Spanish	4.50
Test forms in Spanish, per 100	2.00

REVIEW

CONTENT

Although areas of concern reflected by the items in the Denver Developmental Screening Test are not comprehensive, and many items are not behavioral, the content is very good, considering the DDST's intended use as a screening instrument. However, in the personal-social domain, interpersonal and self-help items are insufficiently related and appear to belong in separate domains. Another problem is that there are too few sequential items within the personal-social domain accounting for the age range from two and one half to six years and in general at the upper age ranges. Item examples appearing to belong in separate domains are "initially shy with strangers," "feeds self cracker" (for babies), and "washes and dries hands" and "plays interactive games" (for children a bit older).

ADMINISTRATION

The major difficulty in administering the DDST is the lack of behavioral specificity which also, then, requires examiners to be highly trained and practiced (although health aides can be trained as examiners). Otherwise, administering and interpreting the test is straightforward and logical, as are manual instructions. The major costs of the test appear to be requirements for testing space, trained personnel, and 10 to 30 minutes to screen each child. The benefits are that it (1) has high reliability and validity, (2) encompasses the entire age range from infancy through preschool years, and (3) can be administered by health aides and other professionals and paraprofessionals with proper training.

INTERPRETABILITY

Due to very clear instructions and computations which are limited to counting passes and failures, the DDST has exemplary interpretability for its intended use.

TEST DEVELOPMENT

Especially commendable development procedures were (1) the large number of children (1,036) to which the test was standardized; (2) efforts to reflect the Denver population in the sampling procedures; (3) high standards in determining reliability and validity; and (4) efforts to ensure ease of administration and interpretation. The weakest development aspects are that there was no field testing conducted and thus no revision of items or domains based on content. There was also no random sampling.

RELIABILITY

Reliability of the DDST is very high—given a test-retest reliability at 95.8 percent, interrater reliability at 90 percent, and the cautionary procedures within the reliability design itself. However, there could have been more children included in the procedures for obtaining interrater reliability.

VALIDITY

The validity is very high. In a study of 18 children (4 to 68 months) the Denver correlated .97 with the Revised Yale Developmental Scale (Frankenburg and Dodds, 1967). Of greater importance is that no child with a Yale Development Quotient (DQ) of less than 89 was judged normal by the DDST and that all children judged by the DDST as having serious developmental delay were found to have a Yale DQ of less than 90. These same relationships held, although they were less strong, when comparisons among subsections were made. A second study (Frankenburg, 1976) reports that well trained aides were able to identify 92 percent of the children who subsequently obtained a Bayley Infant Scale or Stanford Binet DQ or IQ below 70 and 97 percent of those with DQ or IQ of 70 or above. Other studies confirm that the DDST has strong predictive validity when used as a screening device.

Although the instrument seems valid in its ability to predict a child's need for comprehensive assessment, it is unfortunate that attempts were not made to obtain content and construct validity.

SUMMARY OF UTILITY

The DDST is excellent for its intended use as a screening instrument for children from birth to six years. It provides more than sufficient information to determine if a child should be referred for a comprehensive assessment. It also provides gross data to facilitate some program planning, especially at the local level.

The reviewer's primary problems with the instrument concern items contained in the personal-social domain and insufficient items for older children, especially in the personal-social domain. However, it should be noted that both of these points were addressed by the individuals who developed the instrument. More items were included for children of younger ages because developmental changes occur faster. Readers were also warned that "many seemingly unrelated items which would appear to be related (such as two language items) have strong common factors..."

Although the above points are valid ones, the addition of several more items to the existing personal-social domain are warranted and attempts should be made to reconceptualize this domain.

THE FAIRVIEW SCALES

The Fairview Scales are a battery of five different instruments intended to be a "modular" system of measurement which corresponds to phases of development in institutionalized mentally retarded persons. The scales are intended for use with the mildly,

Fairview Self-Help Scale

Author Robert T. Ross	**Distributor** Currently not available Inquire to: Alan Boroskin Center for Dynamic Therapy 14120 Beach Blvd., #202 Westminster, California 92683
Alternative Versions Language Evaluation Scale, Problem Behavior Record, Development Scale, Social Skills Scale	**Date** 1970
Revisions in Progress None	**Test Manual** Manual for the Fairview Self- Help Scale, Robert T. Ross, 1970

moderately, severely, and profoundly retarded. According to the manual, the scales can be filled in by parents, caretakers, or ward personnel, as well as teachers, psychologists, and other professionals. The review section covers all five scales.

INTENDED PURPOSES

The Fairview Self-Help Scale (FSHS) is adapted for use primarily with institutionalized, severely and profoundly retarded individuals. According to the manual, the FSHS can be used with an individual of any age, although it is recommended for use when the behaviors of the person are in the nine-year mental age range. It is intended to assess various aspects of adaptive behavior so that change can be detected.

DOMAINS

This scale consists of 34 items which provide measures of motor dexterity, self-help skills, communication, social interaction, and self-direction.

PROCEDURES

Data on the Self-Help Scale is gathered by obtaining information from a person knowledgeable about the client. However, in some cases direct observation of the client may be necessary to provide complete information. According to the manual, special credentials are required to administer this rating scale. The author makes no statement about expected completion time.

   In addition to a total score for the scale, a score for each domain, and for each of the following subdomains is reported: ambulation, toilet training, dressing, eating, and grooming. These scores are used to compute behavioral age (in months), behavioral quotient, and behavioral level. Medical status, mechanical aids, and behavior problems are also recorded, but not scored.

COSTS

Test, per 100	$10.00
Manual	.50
Specimen set	3.00

   (includes one each of the five scales and five manuals)

Fairview Language Evaluation Scale

Author Alan Boroskin	**Distributor** Center for Dynamic Therapy 14120 Beach Blvd., #202 Westminster, California 92683
Alternative Versions Self-Help Scale, Problem Behavior Record, Development Scale, Social Skills Scale	**Date** 1971
Revisions in Progress None	**Manual** Manual for the Fairview Language Evaluation Scale Alan Boroskin, 1971

INTENDED PURPOSES

The Fairview Language Evaluation Scale (FLES) is designed for use primarily with institutionalized, severely and profoundly retarded individuals. The scale's intent is to assess various levels of verbal and nonverbal language so that change can be detected. This scale measures language age from 0 to 72 months, based on the chronological age of "normal" children.

DOMAINS

The FLES contains 68 items which measure language age. The language skills are grouped into ten sequence levels.

PROCEDURES

The FLES is a checklist of language-related behavior. Data are collected from an individual familiar with the client's behavior.

135

Information can also be gathered by direct observation of the client when necessary. According to the manual, special credentials are required to administer this scale. The author gives no indication of expected administration time.

A total score for the FLES and a total point score at each level is recorded. These scores are converted to language age (in months), language quotient, and language level. Speech-related handicaps are recorded but not scored.

COSTS

Test, per 100	$10.00
Manual	.50
Specimen set	3.00

(includes one each of the five scales and five manuals)

Fairview Problem Behavior Record

Author	**Distributor**
Robert T. Ross	Currently not available
	Inquire to:
	Alan Boroskin
	Center for Dynamic
	Therapy
	14120 Beach Blvd., #202
	Westminster, California
	92683
Alternative Versions	**Date**
Self-Help Scale, Language Evaluation Scale, Development Scale, Social Skills Scale	1971
Revisions in Progress	**Test Manual**
None	None

INTENDED PURPOSES

The Fairview Problem Behavior Record (FPBR) was devised to establish a baseline against which changes in behavior and affective status can be measured. It is intended for use with mentally retarded individuals of all ages. According to the author, this scale pinpoints those behaviors which might interfere with the client's independent functioning.

DOMAINS

The first part of this record contains 29 items or problem behaviors grouped into five categories: aggressive, hyperactive, sexual, covert, and inappropriate. The second part is an adjective checklist of 99 items which gives an index of prevailing mood.

PROCEDURES

The FPBR collects data about the individual client. Information may be gathered totally from a person knowledgeable about the client, although in some cases direct observation may be necessary to provide complete information. This instrument consists of two parts; Part I contains binary choice items (yes/no) which indicate the presence or absence of a behavior, and multiple choice items to describe the frequency severity, and control of present behaviors. Part II is a checklist of problem behaviors. No special credentials are required of the administrator other than that he or she be thoroughly familiar with the client's behavior. The author gives no information about administration time. Only Part I, the actual problem behavior record, is scored. A total score, a score for each domain, and a score for each item within domains is recorded.

COSTS

Test, per 100	$10.00
Manual	.50
Specimen set	3.00

(includes one each of the five scales and five manuals)

Fairview Development Scale

Authors Robert T. Ross and Alan Boroskin	**Distributor** Currently not available Inquire to: Alan Boroskin Center for Dynamic Therapy 14120 Beach Blvd., #202 Westminster, California 92683
Alternative Versions Self-Help Scale, Language Evaluation Scale, Problem Behavior Record, Social Skills Scale	**Date** 1971
Revisions in Progress None	**Test Manual** Manual for the Fairview Development Scale, James S. Giampiccolo and Alan Boroskin, 1974

INTENDED PURPOSES

The Fairview Development Scale (FDS) is a behavior-rating instrument designed for use primarily with institutionalized, severely and profoundly retarded individuals. The FDS is intended to measure the behavior of individuals who function at a level at or below the lower limit of the Fairview Self-Help Scale and to assess their development, which typically occurs in small and often subtle increments. The manual states that although FDS can be used with individuals of all ages, it is especially recommended for use where sensitive measurements below the two-year level are required.

DOMAINS

This scale consists of 26 items which provide measures of perceptual and motor skills, self-help skills, language, social interaction, and self-direction.

PROCEDURES

The FDS rates the individual's behavior in terms of developmental level. According to the authors, the items proceed by small increments so that the scores can reflect subtle changes in behavior. Data are collected from a person knowledgeable about the client's behavior. When necessary, this information may be supplemented by direct observation of the client. This scale is intended to be administered and scored by ward personnel, parents, or caretakers, as well as by social workers, psychologists, and teachers. The authors make no statement about administration time.

Scores are recorded for the total instrument, for each domain, and for each subdomain. A score is also recorded for the ambulation item within the perceptual and motor skills domain. Developmental age (in months), developmental quotient, and developmental level are derived from the above scores. Medical status and mechanical aids are recorded, not scored.

Fairview Social Skills Scale

Authors James S. Giampiccolo and Robert T. Ross	**Distributor** Currently not available Inquire to: Alan Boroskin Center for Dynamic Therapy 14120 Beach Blvd., #202 Westminster, California 92683
Alternative Versions Self-Help Scale, Language Evaluation Scale, Problem Behavior Record, Development Scale	**Date** 1971
Revisions in Progress None	**Test Manual** Manual for the Fairview Social Skills Scale, James S. Giampiccolo, 1974

INTENDED PURPOSES

The Fairview Social Skills Scale (FSSS) is a behavior-rating instrument adapted for use primarily with the mildly and moderately retarded. It is recommended for use in cases where the behaviors of the individual seem to be at, or above, the ten-year age level. The FSSS was developed on and intended for use with institutionalized mentally retarded persons.

DOMAINS

This scale consists of 36 items which provide measures of self-help skills, communication, social interaction, occupation, and self-direction.

PROCEDURES

The primary source of information is a person familiar with the client's behavior. In some cases it may be necessary to directly observe the individual in order to complete the data. No special credentials are required of the administrator. The authors give no information about administration time.

Scores are reported for each subdomain (five), and for the total instrument. Social age (in months), social quotient, and social level are derived from these scores. Medical status and mechanical aids are also recorded, but not scored.

COSTS

Test, per 100	$10.00
Manual	.50
Specimen set	3.00

(includes one each of the five scales and five manuals)

REVIEW

CONTENT

The Self-Help Scale and the Development Scale are the most adequate of the entire battery. These two break steps into finer segments than the others. The only limitation of the Self-Help Scale is that the items are not explained or qualified in a manual. The Language Evaluation Scale seems to be more complete at its lower end, including more items per level. Therefore, short-term change may be shown in these age ranges.

The Language Evaluation Scale and Problem Behavior Record contain items not appropriate for their respective scales. At the higher age levels the language scale includes numerical concepts not usually dealt with in language sections. The Problem Behavior Record inappropriately includes sexual preferences, treating homosexuality as a problem behavior.

On all of the Fairview Scales residents are referred to as patients, which implies a predetermined medical model of services. Contemporary forms of address refer to developmentally disabled persons who are recipients of services as clients, residents, or simply individuals, rather than the no longer acceptable terms of patients, inmates or retardates.

ADMINISTRATION

The Fairview Scales obtain a lot of information on the behavior of institutionalized, retarded clients with minimal training time for raters.

INTERPRETABILITY

The interpretability of individual items is good. Interpretation of each scale is straightforward, yielding two scores (e.g., Language Age (LA) and Language Quotient (LQ); Social Age (SA) and Social Quotient (SQ); and similarly for the Self-Help and Development Scales). The Problem Behavior Record is merely a record of client activities and does not yield a score. General use of these scores by untrained evaluators may be subject to misinterpretation.

TEST DEVELOPMENT

Items were primarily chosen from already established scales (e.g., Bayley, Gesell). Only the Fairview Development and Self-Help scales used item analysis or any revision from the original format. Items do have good face validity and correlate well with other tests.

RELIABILITY

SELF-HELP SCALE

Interrater and test-retest reliability were calculated on two wards (70 residents). Each worker rated two residents; three months later the same workers rated the same residents again.

The average correlation was .91 for interrater reliability for the same time. Across this three-months time span the average correlation was .87.

LANGUAGE EVALUATION SCALE

Test-retest and interrater reliability tests yielded coefficients of .85 to .90 (for 114 residents). Items are descriptive enough to show that the reliability aspect was adequately investigated. The high reliability coefficient reported is rather surprising due to the lack of definition of items in the manual and the inconsistent specification of items on the scale itself.

PROBLEM BEHAVIOR RECORD

No data are reported by the author in the manual.

DEVELOPMENT SCALE

Interrater reliability tests involved ratings provided by morning staff compared with those completed by evening staff. Correlation coefficients averaged from .71 to .94. Test-retest reliability involved ratings of morning and evening staff compared to ratings two months later. Correlation coefficients averaged from .85 to .97 (N=163).

SOCIAL SKILLS SCALE

Both interrater and test-retest reliability coefficients were determined on an institutionalized population of 105 individuals. Measures were obtained on two wards by morning and evening shifts and repeated two months later. The tests yielded correlation coefficients of .64 to .87 (interrater) and .71 to .93 (test-retest).

VALIDITY

SELF-HELP SCALE

Two validation tests were performed by the author.
The scale was administered to a group of 155 normal children aged one month to ten years to develop the standards for age equivalents used to calculate a behavioral age. The

distribution of scores derived in this study was consistent with the author's expectation that calendar age is related to scale scores in a curvilinear manner.

A second study (population undefined, but it is assumed that it was institutionalized retarded individuals) examined the correlations between the Fairview and both the Vineland and Cain-Levine scales. Very high correlations were observed for subscales and total scores. The total FSHS score correlated .965 with the Vineland total score and .937 with the Cain-Levine total. It is argued by the author that, although the FSHS is intended for a different population than these other scales, this study is concurrent validation of the ability of the FSHS to assess self-help.

LANGUAGE EVALUATION SCALE

Construct validity tests correlated language age (LA) of mentally retarded individuals with mental age (MA) of mentally retarded individuals and with chronological age (CA) of normals. The tests found a one-to-one correspondence between LA and MA (or CA for normals), with a constant error of four months (212 residents at Fairview; 45 normal children of various chronological ages, 4 to 72 months).

Other validity tests correlated LA performance on the Language Evaluation Scale with a simple rating scale comprised of speech and understanding; there was a correlation of .755 with understanding and .804 with speech.

These studies were conducted by the author. Content validity was not measured; it was assumed in the selection of items from other tests. In terms of face validity, the items generally seem appropriately operationalized for evaluation.

PROBLEM BEHAVIOR RECORD

No validation studies are reported by the author in the manual.

DEVELOPMENT SCALE

The test was administered to 127 normal children (4 to 71 months). The relationship of chronological age to total score was nonlinear and consistent with the authors' expectations.

SOCIAL SKILLS SCALE

Two validation studies were performed by the authors. One test assessed the relationship between the FSSS and Vineland social quotients. For a sample of 105 residents, the correlation was .53. This is not a very strong association, given correlations reported for other of the Fairview scales.

The second study was similar to the procedure followed for the Fairview Self-Help Scale. A group of 259 normal children were tested with the Fairview Social Skills Scale. Age and Social Skills Scale score were found to be related in a curvilinear manner. Data from this study were used to develop the table of social age equivalents reported in the manual and used to interpret scores of retarded clients.

SUMMARY OF UTILITY

It should be noted that the Fairview battery is intended to be a "modular" system of measurement which presents the advantage of a holistic approach to the measurement of adaptive behavior in the case of the mentally retarded, institutionalized individual. To further clarify the integration of five different yet interrelated scales, see the summary table (3.3).

Three authors developed the system. Four of the scales are more or less developed and presented as measurement scales, and authors claim development and utilization in a legitimate manner. The fifth (Problem Behavior Record) is presented as an adjective checklist which "gives an index of prevailing mood." As such, it claims little objectivity and it is neither confimed nor validated as an objective measurement tool.

The Development, Self-Help, and Social Skills scales are presented as the first three modules and cover the chronological age span of 0 to 10+ years (CA: 0—2, 2—9, and 10+, respectively). The language scale aims at lower age skills (0—72 months) and the Problem Behavior Record is not age-specific. Some general characteristics of the scales are mentioned by the authors and justifications for development, results of confirmation, and claims for utilization are stated. The following table summarizes these statements. The terms used in the manual need some revision, particularly rewording the term patient to read resident so that the hospital/medical model is avoided. Also, the section on sexual

Table 3.3 Fairview Scales Summary Tables

Author's Claims	SCALE				
	Problem Behavior	Development	Self-Help	Social Skills	Language Evaluation
Specifically designed to be used with mentally retarded	X	X	X	X	X
Used with mildly and moderately retarded				X	
Applies to severly and profoundly re-tarded institution-alized	X	X	X		X
Client mental age at which scale is applicable	any age	0-2 yrs	2-9 yrs	10+	0-72 mos.
Records progress in small increments of change		X	X	X	X
Focuses on basic skills		X	X		Language skills only
Measures from low on age scale to mastery		X	X	X	X
Expresses results in terms of "does" and not of "can do."		X		X	X
Expresses results in numerical equivalents of behavioral status		X	X	X	X
Easily scorable and filled out by parents and caretakers	X	X	X	X	X
Is short	X	X	X	X	X
Contains general instructions for rating and scoring	X	X	X	X	X
Offers both summary scores and individual skill scores		X	X	X	X
Vineland and Cain Levine correlation high but do not match in other respects			X	X	
Reason for development: no similar scale available at the time		X	X	X	X

activity in the Problem Behavior Scale should be entirely revised and brought closer to contemporary views on sexuality and acceptable sexual behavior.

The Fairview Scales give caretakers an organized way of recording the behavior of ward residents. They give valuable information for screening, needs assessment, and initial program planning at the case management level. Some of the scales also show client change over varying periods of time.

The attempt to develop a system of measurement out of several modules corresponding to several phases of development in the adaptation of the mentally retarded to his or her environment is commendable and should be encouraged. The restriction of the system to an institutionalized population is not contemporary or congruent with the current philosophy of service. Further research using reference groups living outside of the institution may serve well to extend the utility of these scales.

Learning Accomplishment Profile

Author Anne R. Sanford	**Distributor** Chapel Hill Training- Outreach Project Lincoln Center Chapel Hill, North Carolina 27514
Alternative Version None	**Date** 1974
Revisions in Progress None	**Test Manual** A Manual for Use of the Learning Accomplishment Profile, Anne R. Sanford (ed.), with Donald Bailey, Judith Leonard, and Peter D. O'Connor, 1974

INTENDED PURPOSES

The Learning Accomplishment Profile (LAP) is designed to provide the teacher of the young handicapped child with a simple criterion-referenced record of the child's existing skills. According to the author, use of the LAP enables the teacher to identify developmentally appropriate learning objectives for each individual child, measure progress through changes in rate of development, and provide specific information relevant to pupil learning. The LAP is intended to provide the teacher or paraprofessional with a comprehensive file of the handicapped child's developmental accomplishments. The manual states that the instrument is appropriate for use with males and females from birth to age six. It is intended to be used in preschools and day care centers for the developmentally delayed.

DOMAINS

The LAP assesses skills along six domains—gross motor, fine motor (including writing), social self-help, cognitive, and language. There are a total of 481 items.

PROCEDURES

Data is collected by observation of and interview with the individual client. Items in the LAP are age sequenced. A child is rated as either able or unable to perform each task. The teacher is usually the administrator of this instrument although it may also be administered by a parent. The author does not indicate how much time is required for administering the profile. A score which equals the developmental age is reported for each domain. These scores are then plotted graphically to form a developmental profile.

COSTS

Not available

REVIEW

CONTENT

Items are mostly given in behavioral terms, making the scale very useful for assessment of child progress, and thus helping teachers to plan educational programs.

Each domain seems appropriately comprehensive, relative to other developmental scales of this type. Practically all items are written behaviorally, although there are a few exceptions (e.g., "enjoys finger painting," "enjoys short walks"). Items are sequenced. Because this is a criterion-reinforced developmental scale, correct sequencing is very important. The scale seems to be quite adequate.

ADMINISTRATION

Instructions are clear. Test administration is simple for adequately trained teachers. Aides and parents can be trained to use the scale at relatively low cost.

The manual includes a very adequate description of administration, scoring procedures, and the purposes and applications of the scale. The manual is written in language requiring the reader to be familiar with educational terms, however, so it seems likely that persons without some training in education or special education may have difficulty understanding some of the instructions.

INTERPRETABILITY

Test results are directly useful in the development of educational plans for a child in that behavioral items not passed can become instructional objectives for the child's Individual Education Plan or Individual Habilitation Plan.

If a child cannot pass four out of five development tasks, his or her "ceiling" is established. Viewed in this way, interpretation is simple, direct, and very useful to the teacher.

TEST DEVELOPMENT

There is no information in the manual about test development, except the statement that the items in each scale were selected from a variety of other similar scales. The theoretical basis is probably derived from task-sequencing, child development theory, and experience.

There is no information in the manual on field testing, item analysis, or refinement.

RELIABILITY

No information is provided.

VALIDITY

The LAP seems to have reasonable face validity. It seems likely that validity problems, if present, can be overcome since the scale is so closely associated with the child's educational programs.

SUMMARY OF UTILITY

As previously stated, the LAP is very useful in developing an Individual Education Plan for a child. The instrument is also useful for monitoring the progress of Individual Habilitation Plan implementation relative to achieving behavioral objectives. It is most appropriate for normal preschoolers and developmentally delayed children. Although the manual states that the instrument is intended for children from birth to six years, the LAP could be used from birth to 14 or 15 years if the older client has severe developmental delays.

The LAP comes as a system which includes a diagnostic tool, a prescriptive tool, and a curriculum document. As such, it becomes more attractive than a simple behavioral assessment tool.

The Lexington Developmental Scales (Long Form)

Authors United Cerebral Palsy of the Bluegrass, John V. Irwin, Consultant-Evaluator, et al.	**Distributor** The UCPB Child Development Centers P.O. Box 8003 465 Springfield Drive Lexington, Kentucky 40503
Alternative Version The Lexington Developmental Scales (short form) The short form of the Lexington Scales has half the number of items of the long form and is designed as a screening tool for teachers, nurses, social workers, and homemakers to assess children individually during a 30-minute clinic or home visit.	**Dates** 1973, 1977
Revisions in Progress None	**Test Manual** The Lexington Developmental Scales United Cerebral Palsy of the Bluegrass 1973, 1977

INTENDED PURPOSES

The Lexington Development Scales (LDS) are intended to provide meaningful profiles of attainment levels of children from birth to six years of age. The scales are designed as a tool to assess the behavior of children at the beginning and end of the school year or as a curriculum guide during the year for use by parent-infant workers and preschool, special education, and first grade teachers. The manual states that the scales are appropriate for cerebral palsied and multiply handicapped children. The LDS is intended to be administered in early childhood centers, Head Start offices, kindergartens, schools, and cerebral palsy clinics.

DOMAINS

Forty-seven subdomains, including 424 items, are organized into four developmental domains of motor, language, cognitive, and personal-social development.

PROCEDURES

Two types of items appear on the LDS: behavioral and experiential. Behavioral items are assessed by direct observation. Experiential items rely on anecdotal records or parental observation over a period of time. Items involve a 10-increment ranking scale from 0 to 72 months, with descriptions of normative behavior for each increment. The scale is designed for administration by a teacher or someone with training or experience in the service delivery field. Familiarity with the test items and practice with the instrument are requried. The LDS may be administered over a three-week period for children over two years of age, although more compressed schedules may be followed for these children.

Scoring of the LDS is in the form of a profile for each domain on which the pertinent subdomain ratings are charted. An individual graph depicts the child's developmental age level according to age norms for each of the four areas. A summary page contains annual hearing and visual screening test results and blocks for comments concerning strengths, weaknesses, and recommendations. The child's developmental age and developmental quotient, which summarize results for the instrument as a whole, can be computed by hand or obtained in a computerized printout from United Cerebral Palsy of the Bluegrass.

The Lexington Computerized Evaluation Program requires entry of each subject's code number, birth date, test dates, and behavior on each item. The program automatically gives for any group (as one classroom) and/or any combinations of groups (as one school or one school system) the mean change in developmental age scores for each of the four test areas and an F-test of the statistical significance of the difference for each area. Both the mean pretest and posttest developmental ages and developmental quotients for each item are then tabulated. In addition, a before and after graph for the group (and/or combination of groups) is printed. Finally, the before and after rankings of each child within the appropriate group by each test area on each test item are given. With the use of optical coded data forms, the authors claim that turnaround time can be virtually overnight.

COSTS

Manual (long form)	$5.00
Manual (short form)	1.50
Long form scale	.30
Short form scale	.25

REVIEW

CONTENT

Although the Lexington Scales are developmental, they lack the fine developmental steps along the continuum. Furthermore, it is limited to developmental stages zero to six years of age and only identifies certain developmental high points along the continuum. Some items such as sharing are too global and their ratings are dependent on the subjective feelings of parents and teachers.

ADMINISTRATION

The cost-beneficial nature of the LDS cannot be calculated since the assessment is incorporated as part of two to three weeks of the child's curriculum. The amount of time spent in administration yields very little specific data for training purposes.

The manual and the instructions for administration of the instrument are extensive, but there is a statement regarding the need for more highly refined formal testing procedures and referral to specialists in different areas which is not clarified.

The instrument is designed for use by a teacher who has developed rapport with the child and who administers the instrument piecemeal over a three-week period. Extensive familiarity with the instrument is required.

INTERPRETABILITY

Since items were chosen from the literature of existing developmental scales, it yields an adequate measure of developmental age and developmental quotient. The authors state that deviations from age level are the bases for training and planning activities. The instrument does measure in-depth causative factors (e.g., perceptual vs. visual difficulties resulting in motor deviations).

TEST DEVELOPMENT

Extensive studies were conducted in developing this instrument. Its greatest value is that it was teacher-developed and thus it might be more readily accepted for use. Items were assigned from basic developmental literature.

The LDS was developed by one teacher who felt a need for a measuring tool which would give meaningful profiles of attainment levels of individual children. After using it for two years, reliability studies with 40 infants and 33 children (two to six years old) were conducted. Reliability was calculated on interrater comparisons. A short form was also developed and reliability again was measured using 40 infants and 33 children (two to six years old). Both forms yielded high reliability.

RELIABILITY

The authors state that the LDS is useful as a tool for assessing selected behaviors of children, but it only reports where the child is on the continuum; it does not yield any in-depth assessment of strengths and weaknesses in a particular area. It appears to be reliable in motor areas, but weak in the personal-social areas.

Reliability was calculated for each of the four domains and each item within the domains. Correlation coefficients were consistently above .90. The lowest correlations were found in the personal-social domains, although subsequent studies (not cited in the manual) report correlations of over .85. Independent evaluations were made and interjudge reliability was calculated. The percentage of variability between judges that accounted for the correlation was also calculated. The correlations for the infant group were consistently higher than the two to six years group.

VALIDITY

Validity was measured by content and criterion-related studies. Of the 424 items, 414 have been described and assigned a developmental age by at least one or more citations from basic literature. There was disagreement as to age level placement by different authors, and in several instances disparity between books by the same author. Thirty-six Head Start teachers and 37 United Cerebral Palsy of the Bluegrass staff made a major effort to refine the items.

In an attempt to measure criterion-related validity, the relationship between developmental age as measured by the LDS and chronological age was studied. Five males and five females were drawn from nine age intervals and a mean developmental quotient was calculated. The developmental quotients were generally close to 100, which suggests that items are correctly placed with respect to chronological age.

In another study (involving 33 children), the Stanford-Binet was compared with the LDS cognitive area. A correlation of .84 was calculated. In another study the LDS scores of 33 children were compared with language measurement instruments. The correlation of the LDS language scale with the Illinois Test of Psycholinguistic Abilities was .74.

SUMMARY OF UTILITY

The most promising use of the LDS is the measurement and monitoring of progress over a one- or two-year period. It also suggests areas where training should be emphasized. It appears that this instrument would be particularly appropriate for use in early childhood development centers. Overall, the content and criterion-related validity of the LDS is acceptable, but it does not assess selected behaviors of children in depth. The instrument can be used to evaluate the progress of each child and can serve as a basis for referring children for evaluation and diagnosis. The LDS does not, however, appear to have sufficient depth for prescriptive teaching plans. It is not good for Individualized Habilitation Plan development, as the steps are too global and the gaps between stages are too great. This instrument is not suitable for use with the profoundly handicapped, whether they be mentally retarded or physically, visually, or auditorally impaired.

MDC Behavior Identification Form

Authors Arnold B. Sax, Tom Allen, and Tom Esser	**Distributor** Materials Development Center The Dept. of Rehabilitation and Manpower Services School of Education, University of Wisconsin Stout-Menomonie, Wisconsin 54751
Alternative Version None	**Dates** 1972, 1974
Revisions in Progress None	**Test Manual** Recommended Procedure MDC Behavior Identification Format

INTENDED PURPOSES

The MDC Behavior Identification Form was developed as an aid to the observation, identification, and recording of work and work-related client behaviors which may limit or enhance employment opportunities. According to the authors, it is helpful in determining job placement or training objectives, in providing specificity and structure to work adjustment training and treatment programming, and in measuring progress or change within treatment/training programs. This form can also be used as a resource for in-service training of staff members and as an aid in report writing and communication with individuals and agencies concerned with the client's program.

The MDC Form is intended for use in assessing job behaviors of developmentally disabled and mentally handicapped adolescents and adults. It may be administered in both regular and sheltered work settings.

DOMAINS

The MDC Behavior Identification Form assesses client characteristics along one domain—behaviors related to employment. It consists of 22 items or behavior categories in which a client is evaluated.

PROCEDURES

The MDC Form is a rating scale which collects data by observation of the individual client. The manual does not specify administrator qualifications or administration time.

The behavior ratings reflect the rater's judgments and opinions as to the appropriateness of the client's work behaviors and how they relate to his or her job goals. The ratings are not intended for use in deriving a score or series of scores.

COSTS

Form, per copy $2.00

REVIEW

CONTENT

The MDC Behavior Identification Form, although functional, is not totally objective. It is functional because it compares client behavior to the unique characteristics of the job and job environment, it rates over time to determine change and importance of the behavior, and it provides fairly comprehensive items, including item definitions, examples, and sample descriptions. However, the objectivity is left to the rater because of the lack of precise behavioral specification for ratings.

ADMINISTRATION

The administration and training time are cost-beneficial if (1) raters provide objective data and follow examples, (2) the client is readily available in the work environment, and (3) the work environment provides full opportunity for exhibiting behaviors. Instructions are general and support materials are included in the appendix. Although information for administration is more than adequate for a professional involved in testing and evaluation, these instructions may not be adequate for a paraprofessional or professional without a related background. Still, such persons could be trained fairly easily. Administration is expected to require about one hour per client for each observation. Several observations are used over time.

INTERPRETABILITY

Each item is interpreted in three major areas, with each of these major areas divided into two minor areas. There is no composite interpretation mechanism (i.e., no total score is generated). On an item-by-item basis, the interpretation procedure is "good" if the rater has been objective and can communicate information.

No graphs or charts are used, only the MDC Behavior Identification Form. Specific behaviors are to be identified and rated over time. Item-related behavioral information and change ratings by item are easily obtained.

TEST DEVELOPMENT

Not enough information is provided on test development. The developers do state that the information was field tested in 1972 but no additional information is furnished on the methods of design and development utilized by the authors.

RELIABILITY AND VALIDITY

The authors do not provide enough information on the reliability or validity of the MDC; it appears that the instrument is marginally acceptable on face value.

SUMMARY OF UTILITY

The instrument is fairly simple and deals with assessment of the client's work in work behavior and the unique requirements of the environment. Its utility is high because it is simple and can deal with the problem at hand. It is particularly useful for teaching the progress of clients in normal or sheltered work settings, and identifying behaviors that can be used to place clients in jobs with a higher degree of success. Its utility for other purposes is limited.

Mid-Nebraska Mental Retardation Services
Three-Track System

The Mid-Nebraska Three-Track System is a set of three articulated scales designed for use in assessing the different stages of a client's developmental functioning. Each track or level is concerned with a particular set of behaviors of interest in the assessment of a client and the delivery of habilitative services at these different functional levels.

Clients are expected to progress over time from the lowest level (basic skills) to the highest level (competitive employment). The content of their habilitative programs should reflect this change. Only one of the three tracks is appropriate for a given client at any particular point in time. The content of each track is presented separately below, although the review considers the system as a whole.

Basic Skills Screening Test

Authors Robert L. Schalock, Barbara E. Ross, and Irwin Ross	**Distributor** Mid-Nebraska Mental Retardation Services 518 Eastside Boulevard Hastings, Nebraska 68901
Alternative Version None	**Dates** 1972, 1976
Revisions in Progress None	**Test Manual** Basic Skills Screening Test, Robert L. Schalock, Barbara E. Ross, and Irwin Ross, 1976. Used in conjunction with: Basic Skills Remediation Manual, Schalock, Ross, and Ross, 1976 (second edition)

INTENDED PURPOSES

The Basic Skills Screening Test (BSST) is geared toward lower functioning clients who need remediation in the basic behavioral domains of sensory motor functioning, auditory and visual processing, language, symbolic operations, and social-emotional behavior.

DOMAINS

One hundred seven items and 26 subdomains form the components of the seven domains of sensory motor functioning, visual processing, auditory processing, language, symbolic operations, social-emotional development, and work skills.

PROCEDURES

The individual is tested in a room free from extraneous noise or other distractions. Other items are completed after observation of the client performing typical activities within a clinical setting. Items include response to stimuli, sentence completion, and responding to tasks like writing numbers in sequence. Item completion is rated by a specified pass/fail criterion. The test administrator should be familiar with the client and the instrument prior to screening. Each component of an individual's total behavior is depicted on a circle graph, where each target behavior is represented on a mastery/nonmastery basis. The criterion for attaining mastery is "passing" 80 to 90 percent of the attempted trials or possible correct responses for an area. As remediation successfully produces behavioral progress, it is indicated on the circle graph.

COSTS

Remediation manual and screening test $22.00

Independent Living Screening Test

Author Robert L. Schalock	**Distributor** Mid-Nebraska Mental Retardation Services 518 Eastside Boulevard Hastings, Nebraska 68901
Alternative Version None	**Date** 1975
Revisions in Progress Revision currently being field tested	**Test Manual** Independent Living Screening Test, Robert L. Schalock, 1975. Used in conjunction with the Independent Living Teaching Manual, Robert L. Schalock, 1975

INTENDED PURPOSES

The Independent Living Screening Test (ILST) and its teaching manual are geared to those individuals who are currently being trained in independent living. The ILST tests target behaviors such as cooking, cleaning, community awareness utilization, functional academics, and leisure time.

DOMAINS

Eighty-eight items in twenty-six subdomains measure behavior attainment in the nine domains of personal maintenance, clothing care and use, home maintenance, food preparation, time management, social behavior, community utilization, communication, and functional academics.

PROCEDURES

The individual is tested in a room free from extraneous noise or other distractions. Other items are completed after observation of the client performing typical activities within a clinical setting. Items include response to stimuli, sentence completion, and responding to tasks like writing numbers in sequence. Item completion is rated by a specified pass/fail criterion. The test administrator should be familiar with the client and the instrument prior to screening. Each component of an individual's total behavior is depicted on a circle graph, with each target behavior represented on a mastery/nonmastery basis. The mastery criterion is "passing" 80 to 90 percent of the attempted trials or possible correct responses for an area. As remediation successfully produces behavioral progress, it is indicated on the circle graph.

In addition to containing the types of items which are included in the Basic Skills Screening Test, this instrument includes an open-ended evaluation of the client's general self-maintenance level and role playing situations. Specific tasks observed include items like preparing a meal or replacing a light bulb.

COSTS

Teaching manual and screening test $9.00

Competitive Employment Screening Test

Author Robert L. Schalock	**Distributor** Mid-Nebraska Mental Retardation Services 518 Eastside Boulevard Hastings, Nebraska 68901
Alternative Version None	**Dates** 1976, 1978
Revisions in Progress Just revised. Updated version was not available in time to be included in this review. For further information, see the Competitive Employment Screening Test, Robert L. Schalock, 1978 (used in conjunction with Competitive Employment Teaching Manual, 1978)	**Test Manual** Competitive Employment Screening Test, Robert L. Schalock, 1976, used in conjunction with Competitive Employment Teaching Manual, Robert L. Schalock, 1976

INTENDED PURPOSES

The Competitive Employment Screening Test (CEST) and teaching manual are job training related, and include such target behaviors as punctuality, interview skills, job stamina, and eye-hand coordination skills.

DOMAINS

Sixty-three items in twenty subdomains measure behavior in the five domains of job-related skills, responsibility toward work, work performance, behavior in the job situation, and personal appearance.

PROCEDURES

The individual is tested in a room free from extraneous noise or other distractions. Other items are completed after observation of the client performing typical activities within a clinical setting. Items tested include response to stimuli, sentence completion, and responding to tasks like writing numbers in sequence. Item completion is rated by a specified pass/fail criterion. The test administrator should be familiar with the client and the instrument prior to screening. Each component of an individual's total behavior is depicted on a circle graph, and each target behavior is represented on a mastery/nonmastery basis; mastery is achieved by "passing" 80 to 90 percent of the attempted trials or possible correct responses for an area. As remediation successfully produces behavioral progress, it is indicated on the circle graph.

In addition to containing the types of items which are included in the Basic Skills Screening Test, this instrument includes open-ended evaluation of job-readiness and role playing situations that are job-related.

COSTS

Teaching manual and screening test $9.00

Composite Review of Mid-Nebraska Three-Track System

CONTENT

Each of the three screening tests described above (Basic Skills, Independent Living, Competitive Employment) can be used independently or as the three-track system for which they were originally designed. Each component or track is intended to have its own staff, program components (including screening test and remediation-teaching manual), and location. According to an article written by Schalock and Harper, when all three components are used as part of a systematic programming effort, adult clients could move in the following sequence:

Entry→Basic Skills→Independent Living→Competitive Employment→Exit

This Adult Developmental Model, which underlies the three-track system, assumes that all persons are capable of learning productive behaviors which will lead to increased self-reliance and independence. This concept led to the development of a general remediation-development component (Basic Skills) and two application-exit components (Independent Living and Competitive Employment).

The primary domains addressed by the Basic Skills Screening Test are those related to learning and problem-solving abilities. The test's manual is geared to remedy response deficits in these areas. The Independent Living component concentrates on skill development, primarily within the domains of self-care and independent living skills. The Competitive Employment Screening Test focuses on work habits and work adjustment.

The items are placed appropriately within the domains of each assessment tool. Each instrument contains several subareas within each of the major skill areas. Target behaviors are stated within each subarea of the tests. For example, in the Competitive Employment Screening Test, Area II, is "Responsibility Toward Work," Subarea C. "Will Follow Directions" contains the target behaviors of C.1, "Indicates will follow specific requests;" C.2, "Carries out supervisor's requests without unnecessary delay;" and C-3, "Remembers directions."

The items are criterion-referenced on each of the screening tests. An explicit evaluation procedure for target behavior and pass criteria are stated for every target behavior in each of the three assessments. The procedures and criteria seem very appropriate for assessment of the target behaviors.

Each instrument is developmentally sequenced. Furthermore, each of the components (and respective screening tests) is intended to follow the sequence of development presented above (from basic skills to competitive employment).

The tests contain no sensitive stereotypes or biases and, in fact, are built on very contemporary concepts. The instruments were developed to assess training needs and have the technology available to deal with the individual's identified needs. Thus, the effort was put into generating test manuals which would contain training and remediation techniques for the same set of target behaviors found in each screening test.

Each screening test seems very thorough in covering its respective domain(s); however, the tests do not claim to be comprehensive. In fact, throughout the tests other diagnostic tools, such as a specific in-depth audiology or language instrument, are referenced for the user should further testing of a trainee be necessary.

ADMINISTRATION

Instructions for test administration accompany each of the screening tests. In essence, the evaluation procedure outlined for each target behavior is the administration procedure for measuring that respective behavior. No scoring or numerical ratings are involved in using any of the tests. Pass criteria must be attained for each behavior, using the indicated evaluation procedure; otherwise, the behavior is considered to be a training need requiring remediation. Test results are recorded on a circle graph (Baseline and Skill Acquisition Record) which corresponds to the areas and subareas of each of the three tracks and screening tests. Once programming has occured, the target behavior should be reevaluated using the original evaluation procedure. If the client meets the criterion for a particular behavior, the circle graph should indicate this so that training/remediation can focus on another target behavior.

The evaluation procedures and pass criteria in the tests are very specific and are clearly stated. It is important to note here that the evaluation procedures cover a wide array of measurement techniques which are performance-based, that is, clients are involved in skill demonstration, role play, simulation exercises, and on-site observation. In addition, materials for the evaluation procedures are also required, but not supplied by the authors or publishers of the test. These materials may be pictures, a flashlight, word cards, etc., or particular settings or opportunities requisite to observe and evaluate particular target behaviors. While this circumstance can be an advantage in that materials can be developed which are meaningful to the client, it also means that time must be invested in developing these materials before test administration can begin.

The nature of the evaluation procedures, which may include a skill demonstration taking only a few minutes or a two-week observation of behavior or appearance, also makes it difficult to offer an estimate of the actual administration time for any of the tests. No time estimates for overall test administration are included in the remediation manuals or supporting materials. Mid-Nebraska Mental Retardation Services may be able to provide this information based on their years of experience, but administration time is not readily apparent (and would seem to vary among individuals tested) in the materials reviewed.

The manuals and supporting materials are also not explicit regarding professional credentials required for test administration. From language found in supporting materials related to the purpose and development of the tests and remediation manuals, it seems that test administrators should have training or experience in the service delivery field (e.g., teaching).

Training and practice relative to administration of these screening tests does, however, seem necessary for successful use of the instruments. In describing application of the system in Mid-Nebraska, the statement was made that "all program staff are trained to assess and remediate." Test instructions state the need for familiarity with the client and test evaluation procedures before administration.

INTERPRETATION

One of the most attractive features of the screening tests in this three-track system is their interpretability. This is due in large part to the remediation manual which accompanies each screening test. A second factor enhancing the system's attractiveness is its emphasis on systematic programming as a result of the assessment results and corresponding training techniques found in the remediation manuals. Prescriptive programming, modeled after Ogden R. Lindsley's technique, is suggested, and a form for use in the system is provided in each manual. The circle graph depicting assessment results, provided for each screening test, is simple to read and use, and is the system's third attractive feature.

The remediation manuals are an obvious strength of this assessment-training approach. They include: (1) the target behaviors that correspond with those found in the screening test, (2) specific teaching objectives for each behavior, (3) remediation activities and teaching techniques to accomplish the objectives, and (4) materials needed for each activity or technique. The BSST Manual has a fifth component for each assessment target behavior—a suggested movement cycle for each teaching objective.

Although the activities found in the manuals are suggested activities only, they would provide the trainer with a base from which to devise supplemental activities which are meaningful to the client. In addition, the manuals provide general guidelines for conducting training sessions.

TEST DEVELOPMENT

The screening tests, manuals, and supporting materials did not include much detail about the actual phases of the instruments' construction. The information that could be gleaned was that each test has had one or two editions over four years and has been developed "with input from program staff, literature searches, and outside consultants." Specific references can be found in each remediation manual. The references and resource materials which are cited in each manual provide excellent bibliographies in each area tapped by the screening tests and remediation manuals. However, the actual procedure for the generation and selection of items is not described.

According to the authors, field tests were conducted for each of the screening tests. However, only the characteristics of clients used in the reliability studies and norming studies were provided in the *Description of Mid-Nebraska Programs, Materials, and Program Evaluation Data*. The population used (N = 127) in the Basic Skills Screening Test norming study (conducted at baseline, baseline + 6 months, and baseline + 12 months) was between 18 and 52 years of age, with a tested IQ of 19 (or not testable) to 69. The Independent Living Screening Test was normed on a population (N = 48) with tested IQ levels of 40 to 79 and chronological age of 18 to 52. For the Competitive Employment Screening Test the study was conducted using a population (N = 44) ranging from 50 to 80 in tested IQ and between 18 and 52 chronological years of age. The norming studies indicate the average number of target behaviors passed for each area of each screening test, according to tested intelligence level and chronological age at the 6-month intervals stated above.

RELIABILITY

Interrater reliability studies were conducted on each of three screening tests. Results for the basic skills test showed reliability coefficients significant at the .05 level between raters for all areas of the test. The high interrater agreement across skill areas for each intellectual level is indicative of the high structure and specificity of the target behaviors, evaluation procedures, and pass criteria of the test.

Independent Living Screening Test results were not as high as those of the Basic Skills Screening Test. The individuals tested were at moderate, mild, and borderline intellectual levels. The interrater agreements across ILST areas ranged in reliability coefficients from .31 to .77. No reliability coefficients were statistically significant. The lower agreement coefficients fell in the areas of community utilization (.31), personal maintenance (.46), and communication (.49), whereas the highest agreement between raters was attained in the area of functional academics (.77).

The Competitive Employment Screening Test showed higher interrater agreement coefficients than the ILST, but not as high overall as those on the BSST. The study was done with individuals having mild and borderline level IQs. Two of the five areas tapped by the CEST achieved significance at the .05 level, and attained a significant interrater reliability coefficient (.88) for the overall test results. Reliability coefficients ranged from .53 in the area of behavior in the job situation to .98 in the area of responsibility toward work.

The design of these studies seems less than adequate due to the small number of subjects involved (six to eight clients). In addition, varying the training and background of the raters in order to examine the variable of credentials and training of raters might prove interesting as well. Finally, reliability studies to examine test-retest coefficients would seem appropriate for the screening tests.

VALIDITY

Validity studies were conducted to measure content validity and criterion-related or predictive validity. The content validity study used screening test and the Weschler Adult Intelligence Scale (WAIS) scores from 73 clients who had been evaluated on theWAIS by the same licensed psychologist. The results were used to determine the relationship(s) between screening test area scores and WAIS verbal/performance scores. Significant intercorrelations were obtained between WAIS subscales and about half of the areas screened by the Basic Skills and Independent Living screening tests. Low correlations were obtained in the competitive employment area. These correlations are lower than is typical for such measures, and indicate that something in addition to "intelligence" is being assessed.

The criterion-oriented validity study examined the validity of the screening tests for placement decisions. A two-year follow-up study was conducted regarding clients placed from either the Independent Living (N = 79) or Competitive Employment (N = 52) tracks. The criteria included in the study were (1) pre- and post-Independent Living and/or Competitive Employment data; (2) placement for six months or longer (success criterion); and (3) return to training track anytime after placement (criterion for being judged unsuccessful). Of placements made from both the IL and CE tracks, 87 percent were successfully placed by the criterion stated above for success.

SUMMARY OF UTILITY

The three screening tests are intended for use with adults 18 years of age and older. The tested intelligence levels of individuals for whom the tests were most appropriate varied. Individuals with borderline (70-79 IQ), mild (55-70 IQ), moderate (40-54 IQ), and severe (39 IQ) levels of mental retardation were successfully tested by the BSST. The ILST seemed most appropriate for individuals with moderate, mild, and borderline mental retardation; and the CEST is most appropriate for the mild and borderline mentally retarded.

The screening tests are not discriminatory, relative to attention to physically handicapped conditions. An individual could be evaluated if he or she were nonambulatory. Individuals who are blind or deaf could not easily be evaluated using the screening tests; modifications and adaptations would be necessary for successful administration. However, the tests could be used for the most part if individuals were nonverbal. This is particularly true with the BSST.

This three-track system was designed for use in community-based programs for the mentally retarded. The Independent Living track would prove exceptionally useful in the setting of community residences and the Competitive Employment component would be useful at a job training center or on the job. In addition, these tests and target behavior-based programs could be useful in institutional settings where the program effort and concern is toward community integration of clients.

The format and approach followed in the three screening tests, remediation manuals, monitoring graphs, and prescriptive programming form are very good to excellent for application to Individual Habilitation Plan development.

The remediation manual states the teaching objective, materials needed, and suggested techniques for achievement of a respective unattained target behavior. The test itself states the evaluation procedures and passing criteria for measuring successful accomplishment of the behaviors. The inclusion of these elements and the thorough nature of the procedures and suggestions make each of these tools, and the three together as a system, very successful efforts to bridge the gap between assessment and training.

The screening tests would also be very useful for screening/ eligibility determination, needs assessment at the individual level, program monitoring, and monitoring of client progress. Each of the track components also has utility as a basis for staff development and in-service training.

Minnesota Developmental Programming System— Behavioral Scales

Authors
Warren H. Bock and Richard F. Weatherman

Distributor
Outreach Training Project
301 Health Service Building
St. Paul, Minnesota 55108

Alternative Version
None

Dates
1972, 1976

Revisions in Progress
Yes

Test Manual
MDPS Technical Manual and MDPS User Manual, Warren H. Bock and Richard F. Weatherman, 1976
The Behavioral Scales-Revised: A User's Guide and Technical Reference Manual for the MDPS, Warren H. Bock & Richard F. Weatherman (forthcoming, 1978)

INTENDED PURPOSES

The Minnesota Developmental Programming System (MDPS) Behavioral Scales is a package of materials, procedures and training, the purpose of which is to enable individualized developmental programs to be designed for mentally retarded persons and persons with similar service needs. The behavioral scales are designed to provide initial behavior assessment of individuals as well as to provide a means for measuring the subsequent client status and progress of program management according to the authors. The MDPS is designed for developmentally impaired persons and focuses on a broad midrange of age ability within this population. The MDPS materials state that the assessment instrument can be used in all service settings within the mental retardation system to assess most individuals of either sex, excluding the very young, the very old, the totally dependent, and the near normal. According to the authors, two areas of testing pay close attention to physiclly handicapped persons.

DOMAINS

The MDPS Behavioral Scales assess behavior across 18 domains. Each domain contains 20 items; the entire instrument contains 360 items. The domains are gross motor development, fine motor development, eating, dressing, grooming, toileting, receptive language, expressive language, social interaction, readiness and reading, writing, numbers, time, money, domestic behavior, community orientation, recreation/leisure time activities, and vocational.

PROCEDURES

The MDPS Behavioral Scales collect data about the individual client by use of a rating scale describing the frequency with which a person performs the specified behaviors. Information is obtained by observation of the client in typical settings. When necessary, this data is supplemented with information from a person who has directly observed the person's behavior. According to the authors, no special credentials are required of the test administrator, and the test manual provides instructions which do not require extensive training. The authors do not specify the time required to administer the scales. A score is reported for each domain.

COSTS

Behavioral scales	$1.75
User's manual	1.00
Response form, per client	2.00
(includes data processing)	
Priority goal statement forms, tablets of 50	1.50
Individual program plan forms, tablets of 50	1.50
Problem behavior assessment forms, tablets of 50	1.50
Quarterly Program Plan Forms, tablets of 50	1.50
Technical manual	1.75

REVIEW

CONTENT

The content of the MDPS Behavioral Scales suffers overall from its attempt to be wide-ranging in terms of domains. Nonetheless, the authors do not claim comprehensiveness: "It does not represent all the possible kinds of decisions...aid(s) planners in arriving at a relatively comprehensive picture." Items within the scales are occasionally not appropriate because of the wide breadth of scales (e.g., vocational, community orientation). One author stated to the reviewer that the tool is used for rough screening. Unfortunately, this more modest claim is not made in the printed materials; if it were, the materials would be judged more favorably.

Sequencing occasionally appears arbitrary. Many of the sequences appear to discriminate against the physically handicapped, and some appear to be most age-appropriate for children. For example:

Scale: Domestic Behavior

Basal: Picks up household trash or litter and places it in a wastebasket upon request

Ceiling: Prepares and serves a meal, including one hot dish

The difficulty of this item (and other items in the test) for physically handicapped persons should be noted. Also, the sequencing of many items is puzzling. In this case, is the implication that one begins with trash to learn meal preparation?

The authors state that the 20 items in each domain are intended to represent the infinite set of possible behaviors that constitute the domain; they are a sample from that universe. They are explicitly not intended to represent any underlying trait or behavioral construct. Rather, they were selected by behavior analysis with inputs from a variety of experts. Despite these caveats, however, it must be realized that users select and use a test based on its stated content and the implicit domains it assesses. Consequently, potential users of the MDPS would be well advised to examine the detailed item content carefully to assure that it is consistent with their assessment needs since the domains being measured are not necessarily consistent with the user's conceptualization of the constructs embodied by the labels of the scales.

ADMINISTRATION

Training materials, user manual, and other materials in the specimen set provide clear, simple, and rational directions and guidance on use. One of the great strengths of the system is that the scales can be used by attendants, presumably with ease. Moreover, the scales do not appear to require a great deal of time in training or administration.

INTERPRETABILITY

A very helpful aid to interpretation (and scoring) is a computerized reporting service available from the distributors of the MDPS. This report provides information on each individual in bar graph format (showing item performance for each scale as well as total scores), summary group or facility statistics for each data element and scale, and pre/post change data at the item and scale level for both individuals and groups. This format is especially clear and detailed.

Although the printout is an effective means of communicating the raw data about a client's (or group's) performance, no useful performance standards (i.e., norms) are provided to allow the user to see how a client's performance compares to expectations for his or her age or developmental level. However, the data can be useful for monitoring the progress of individual clients over time and for making decisions about specific skills which should be addressed in an individualized program.

TEST DEVELOPMENT

The authors do not have a strong theoretical basis for the development of their scales. Rather, rationales were pragmatic ones, including the need for data for devising Individual Program Plans and the desire to encourage least restrictive programming. Scales and items were originally generated through expert opinion. Subsequently, at least five revisions of the scales and items have been undertaken, some based upon expert judgement and others upon extensive statistical tests with comparison groups.

RELIABILITY

Extensive reliability and related psychometric studies have been performed for the MDPS. While early versions of the instrument contained some domains with unacceptable reliabilities, the most recent revision (1978) has been improved significantly. This revision contains very few scales with either internal consistency or interrater reliabilities below .90. The authors claim that items are behaviorally sequenced, suggesting both the need for high internal consistency and scaling properties best assessed by a Guttman Scalogram analysis. Data from these assessments supports the authors' claims of sequencing.

VALIDITY

The revised MDPS manual contains an extensive validity section. However, little empirical or theoretical support for the validity of the scales is contained therein. The content validity of the scale is high because of the procedures followed to identify behaviors and the expert input (and item analysis) which went into refining the scale. However, the specific content validity for a local program must be determined by individual users. The items appear to be a reasonable sample of something, but whether that something is appropriate for a particular program's needs cannot be determined except by their own inspection of the items.

The authors make no claim for construct validity, stating that the scale does not assess any underlying psychological trait. However, data about the correlation of scale scores with measures of known constructs (reported for an earlier edition of the scale) suggest that there is a moderate degree of intercorrelation among the 18 domains and that scores correlate more highly with IQ than age. While certain scales (e.g., reading) should correlate with IQ, others (e.g., gross motor development) should be more correlated with age. The conclusions reached from reviewing these sketchy data are that the MDPS measures a single construct that is correlated with IQ and that the differentiation among domains claimed by the authors may be weaker than presented. A factor analysis of the entire instrument may shed some light on these issues.

Criterion validity is addressed in a few studies. The primary study cited in the revised manual is, in essence, a computer simulation of the relationship betwen MDPS scores and program admission/release decisions based on analysis of existing data on residents. No primary data collection employing analysis of the use of MDPS data for placement or programming are reported.

Overall, empirical evidence presented for validity is weak. It is ultimately up to the potential user to investigate the content of the MDPS to determine its specific validity for his or her purposes.

SUMMARY OF UTILITY

The MDPS is most appropriate for use with mentally retarded young people. It also has greater utility as a gross screening device in a statewide evaluation or management information system than as a primary instrument in individual client assessment. By admission, it is not appropriate for use with the very young or very old, and it excludes the near normal and the totally dependent. The MDPS is not necessarily appropriate for the full range of adults. Persons 20 to 61 years of age are considered equal. This seems inappropriate, given that many persons who are retarded may at age 20 be functioning at a childlike level, although many who are 40 will be functioning very differently from those who are 61. The weakest feature vis-a-vis population is the rather extensive discrimination which the scales are likely to provide against the physically handicapped. This discrimination occurs despite the fact that the claim is made that the materials were developed for the developmentally disabled population (a possible requirement of the funding stream). The MDPS would not be useful for fine assessment in specialized settings. While appropriate for screening behavior for broad goal development, it would not be useful for developing prescriptive programs in, for instance, the areas of vocational preparation and community adjustment.

Intended uses of the scales and the system are generally valid ones which are possible to attain. The most exciting use has always been that for which the MDPS was originally intended—a baseline for Individualized Habilitation Plan development quite closely linked to IHP processes and products. Uses in program management and evaluation are not outlined in the materials.

The MDPS is a widely used system, and appropriately so, because it has some very strong practical applications at the service delivery level. Authors have responsibly attempted to revise the system, test its reliability and validity, and communicate basic uses and methods. However, as noted above, the authors should be advised to communicate the system's limitations as well as its strengths.

O'Berry Developmental Tests:
Behavior Maturity Checklist II

Authors Don Soule, Jim Bell, and Dave Smith	**Distributor** O'Berry Center — Psychology Research and Evaluation Section P.O. Box 247 Goldsboro, North Carolina 27503
Alternative Version None	**Dates** 1970, 1977
Revisions in Progress None	**Test Manual** O'Berry Developmental Tests: Behavior Maturity Check- list II Manual, Don Soule, Jim Bell, and Dave Smith, 1978

INTENDED PURPOSES

The O'Berry Behavior Maturity Checklist (BMCL) is a measure of behavior development intended for use with mentally retarded persons. The original instrument (BMCL I) was constructed for use with severely and profoundly retarded individuals. The manual claims that the revised instrument (BMCL II) can be used with more moderately retarded persons as well; both instruments were designed for use with individuals in institutional settings. There are no chronological age restrictions on the use of the BMCL II. According to the manual, the BMCL is particularly useful with persons with mental age levels from one month to eight years, although it may also be used as a screening instrument for persons outside of this mental age range.

DOMAINS

The BMCL has 8 domains, 11 subdomains, and a total of 15 items. The domains are dressing, grooming, eating, toileting, communication, social interaction, ambulation, and supported mobility.

PROCEDURES

Data, gathered by obtaining information from a person knowledgeable about the individual client, are recorded on a rating scale with seven to nine increments. According to the authors, the BMCL should be administered by a person who is familiar with the instructions in the manual and has some basic knowledge of testing, that is, "a teacher, cottage parent, or aide who has been given instruction in the administration of the BMCL." Testing time is approximately 15 minutes.

Procedures for scoring involve converting the total raw score (which excludes Ambulation and Mobility scores) to a behavior age (BA), which is then used to compute a behavior quotient (BQ). For persons 16 years of age and older, 16 years is used as the devisor to compute BQ. Raw scores for individual domains and the total instrument may also be converetd to BMCL Levels, ranging from Level 1 (functions independently) to level 5 (completely dependent and makes no active attempts to perform).

COSTS

Specimen set $3.00
    (includes one manual, 5 test booklets, and 25 profiles)

REVIEW

CONTENT

The major content deficit of the O'Berry Behavior Maturity Checklist is in its item sequencing. The last behavior (the highest order) of some items is quantum leaps away from the mini-incremental nature of the previous six or eight items. Some of these items appear to be "tacked on" in an effort to extend utility of the overall scale to the more normal. For example, in the "Use of Money" item, Level 7, "knows absolute value of all money," jumps to Level 8, "independently uses a checking and/or savings account," rather than to a more incremental step such as "makes change."

ADMINISTRATION

No special credentials or training are required to administer the O'Berry BMCL. Instructions and ratings are simple and clear.

However, a problem appears to exist in the ordering of topics within the manual itself. First, there are several specific instructions that appear in the manual which should more properly precede discussions of the item or the test itself, since these cover special cases. Secondly, the example relating how to assign a score falls short since there is no discussion of what a "correct" or "good" score is.

INTERPRETABILITY

To provide a normative basis for interpreting scores, raw scores may be converted to an equivalent behavior age (BA). These, in turn, may be converted to a Behavioral Quotient (BQ) which is directly comparable to an IQ score. As a second guide to interpretation, raw score ranges for each domain are divided into five BMCL functioning levels.

These two sets of standards are based on a study of 731 institutionalized retarded clients. A standardized intelligence test was used to derive the BA scores because of the very high correlation (.93) between the BMCL total score and IQ. Consequently, it is possible to treat BQ scores as if they were IQ scores.

TEST DEVELOPMENT

This instrument needs more work in the area of test development. The authors do not discuss generation and selection of items, initial item analysis, and refinement. In regard to field testing, only standardization tests, and one reliability and one validity test are mentioned.

RELIABILITY

One test-retest reliability study was conducted with a small number of subjects (N=30), and yielded a high correlation (r=.88) for a one-month interval. However, authors noted that a weakness in the study's design could have led to an inflated estimate of reliability. A second study (Clements and DuBois 1978a) used 103 subjects and a one-year test-retest interval. This study obtained r=.87. Internal consistency reliability of the total score was calculated in a split-half study to be .96.

VALIDITY

In the validation studies reported, the BMCL II and one of two other intelligence measures were given to the same residents in an institution. This resulted in moderate correlation coefficients (.76 and .62). This correlation with standardized intelligence tests leads one to conclude that the BMCL is, in effect, a rough measure of the same general construct, although there is evidence of the existence of some additional constructs in the scale. Further, relatively high intercorrelations among subtests suggest that they do not measure items which are very different than the total score.

SUMMARY OF UTILITY

It is the authors' claim that the BMCL is appropriately used in institutional settings with severely and profoundly retarded children of all ages. They also suggest that it is useful with younger, trainable or educable retarded children.

This instrument cannot cover appropriately all the groups claimed by the authors. It appears that, in the revision, the scale attempts to extend behaviors toward the normal to cover less retarded individuals. The BMCL is, however, particularly appropriate for use in institutional settings for the profoundly or severely retarded.

Although preliminary findings are positive for both reliability and validity, more field testing is needed. There are several problems in item construction, with sequencing of behaviors appearing to be inappropriate (e.g., several items list behaviors in ascending order of proficiency, with the final behavior suddenly many ratings higher). This problem makes the item a two-level scale—the first level using six ratings and the second level using one. This is a major problem with the scale.

However, the scale is easy to administer and costs of doing so will probably remain low. Probably best used for self-help assessment, the test can be used for the development of IHPs, needs assessment, and, in some cases, screening.

Ohio Performance Scale

Authors Norman Niesen, Maxine Mays, Kay Hardesty, and Carol Pranitch	**Distributor** Office of Habilitation Services Div. of Mental Retardation and Developmental Disabilities Ohio Dept. of Mental Health and Mental Retardation State Office Tower/Rm. 1236 30 East Broad Street Columbus, Ohio 43215
Alternative Version None	**Date** 1976
Revisions in Progress Expected to be available in 1978	**Test Manual** How to Use the Ohio Performance Scale

INTENDED PURPOSES

The Ohio Performance Scale (OPS) is a behavior-rating scale used to evaluate a person's development in several areas of functioning. The OPS is administered when a person enters an institution and every 90 days thereafter (or more frequently if necessary) to assist his or her progress. It is designed for use with institutionalized mentally retarded individuals at all levels of severity.

Scores on the scale, along with the results of other kinds of evaluations, are intended to help determine a person's placement in an appropriate program unit in the institution. Performance on the scale also provides a guideline to help staff develop Individual Habilitation Plans based on each individual's strengths and weaknesses.

DOMAINS

The basic performance scale contains five domains, 20 mandatory subdomains, and another 63 items in four additional optional subdomains. The basic domains are caring for self, motor development, social interaction, communication, and self-maintenance. The optional domains are nonverbal communication, mobility, wheelchair, and behavior.

178

A score is reported for each subdomain or item. These scores are used to develop Individual Habilitation Plans and Program Implementation Plans.

PROCEDURES

Data on the OPS is gathered by observation of the individual client. A rating scale is used to describe the client's current level of performance and also the amount of assistance required to complete a behavior. The scale administrator should have some training or experience in the service delivery field. The authors provide no information about administration time.

In using the scale, the rater selects the individual client's current level of performance in each of 20 subdomains (plus four optional subdomains), each of which is arranged in nine sequential steps according to developmental level. Once the appropriate level is determined, the rater also indicates the degree of assistance the client requires by checking A (total assistance), B (some assistance), or C (no assistance). The completed ratings are then transferred to a profile sheet which is used to develop the resident's Individual Habilitation Plan.

COSTS

Not available.

REVIEW

CONTENT

The instrument covers a reasonably wide range of behavioral characteristics and rates the client according to skill level and degree of assistance required. Although the selected behavioral domains and subdomains are quite similar to other more widely used adaptive behavior scales, no evidence is provided by the authors that the client's performance in these particular areas will be predictive of his or her performance of other developmental tasks.

For the most part, the items appear to be appropriately organized by domain. At a few points, however, the authors' adherence to the nine-step gradation of skill levels within each subdomain led to forced and unnecessary duplication (e.g., Level 8 in "toileting skills" is "uses public restrooms" while Level 9 is "uses public facilities"). By and large, items are stated in measurable behavioral terms. However, differences in rater perceptions of the same items appear to be possible. The developmental sequencing is uneven and better defined at the lower range of abilities. In some cases an individual item contains more than one aspect of behavior.

ADMINISTRATION

The OPS is intended for use by people familiar with the client on a daily basis. The instrument could be relatively time-consuming and costly to complete, depending on the resident's functional level and the rater's prior knowledge of the resident. It would appear to require two to three hours of a knowledgeable staff member's time to complete. The manual does not provide sufficient instructions for use by people not familiar with the client.

INTERPRETABILITY

The results of this scale are intended to provide the interdisciplinary team with sufficient data on a client's developmental functioning level to prepare an Individual Habilitation Plan and Program Implementation Plan. Since no aggregate score is calculated, the manual does not include norms, percentiles, or other interpretive aids.

While the instrument manual does not include a scoring system per se, it does provide what appear to be workable forms for preparing a profile sheet for an IHP and a PIP. However, "by-the-numbers" approach used to develop IHPs is disturbing.

TEST DEVELOPMENT

The manual contains very little information on how the scale was developed. Nor is there information on the type of field test conducted, if any. Although the authors provide no information on how the scale items were selected, it seems apparent that other widely used behavioral assessment instruments were heavily relied on. A shortcoming in the current manual and instrument is that no careful development studies have been conducted to justify selection of items, organization of items by domain, sequencing of items, and reliability and validity of the item domains and the scale as a whole.

RELIABILITY

No information is provided. A particularly important omission is the lack of available data establishing consistency among different raters in evaluating the same behavior.

VALIDITY

No information is provided.

SUMMARY OF UTILITY

The scale was designed primarily for use with severely to profoundly retarded children and adults in Ohio's institutional system. Although it is intended to cover a broad developmental range, it is considerably less appropriate for mildly and moderately retarded people. There appears to be nothing in the scale which would limit its application in other noninstitutional care and training settings.

The scale has a fourfold purpose: (a) to assist in grouping institutional residents into appropriate program units: (b) to aid in establishing unit-by-unit program goals; (c) to help in developing an Individual Habilitation Plan for each resident; and (d) to facilitate statewide communication about resident needs and to share information about effective programming techniques. This review of the instrument suggests that these general purposes are appropriate. However, the information derived from this scale should be supplemented by data gathered through other behavioral assessment tools for many residents. Such information would be especially useful for mildly and moderately retarded residents since the scale is aimed primarily at severely and profoundly retarded persons. The authors recognize this point in the manual and note that the OPS "should be used in conjunction with other formal and informal assessment devices...to get a full and accurate picture of a person's current abilities and educational needs."

Properly applied, the OPS should be most helpful in pinpointing the severely and profoundly retarded client's developmental strengths and weaknesses in the process of developing his or her IHP. The authors' warning against using only this instrument to assess the resident's developmental level and programming needs should be underscored. Aggregated data could be useful in facility or program-wide evaluation as well, and might provide guidance for statewide program needs or priorities.

While the system for assessing the resident's developmental level and current programmatic needs appears workable, this "by-the-numbers" approach to preparing habilitation plans could stifle the local initiative and imagination so essential to the individualization of program services and, thereby, undermine the habilitation planning process.

The system for administering the scale could be quite time-consuming and costly if the rater is unfamiliar with the residents and conscientiously follows the procedures outlined. Thus, for example, in those areas where the rater is not aware of the resident's capabilities, he or she is instructed to observe the resident's behavior and performance directly to establish the appropriate developmental level.

The OPS manual provides almost no information on how the instrument was developed. In addition, there is no indication that reliability and validity tests have been conducted. While the scale would appear to be applicable to the assessment of similar clients in other states, the fact that the authors offer no evidence that reliability and validity studies have been conducted must be considered a strong argument against wider application of the scale.

Pinecrest Behavior Meters of Primary Functioning

Author Robert H. Cassel	**Distributor** Robert H. Cassel N.W. State School Box 5519 Bossier City, Louisiana 71010
Alternative Version None	**Date** 1967
Revisions in Progress None	**Test Manual** Pinecrest Behavior Meters of Primary Functioning Manual of Instructions, Experimental Form V, Robert H. Cassel, Margaret E. Cassel, and Gary Milford

INTENDED PURPOSES

The Pinecrest Behavior Meters of Primary Functioning (PBM) was developed to fill a perceived need to measure the acquisition of skills by the severely and profoundly retarded in smaller increments than available assessment tools provided. The scale is intended for use with institutionalized clients of mental age 0 to 6.9 years. It is appropriate for all chronological ages.

DOMAINS

The 138 test items fall into 21 subdomains. These are organized into the eight domains of locomotion, eating, self-cleaning, self-drying, evacuation (wetting and soiling), communication, dressing, undressing, and dressing and undressing motivation.

PROCEDURES

The instrument uses the informed report of a person with direct knowledge of the client to collect yes/no responses to descriptive behavior statements. If the rater knows the behavior of the client, he or she can omit the informant and rate the behavior directly. The test is administered by a person with some professional training who has had general experience with instruments of this nature. The test manual instructions are sufficient training for this instrument. With practice, administration requires 25 minutes.

Scores are obtained for each subdomain, domain, and the instrument overall.

COSTS

Not available

REVIEW

CONTENT

The content of the Pinecrest Behavior Meters is restricted, dealing mainly with self-care. Although the items are not behaviorally defined, examples are given to help clarify the level of proficiency required for a pass. For example, "Person holds bottle or cup or training cup with assistance and drinks." If he or she spills, it does not count. The point here is that the person does something to help in his or her own feeding but still needs outside help. The person is given a zero score even if the failure is due to a physical impairment such as a paralysis. If no information is available as to whether he or she can or can't perform an item, it is scored NI and if the person hasn't had an opportunity to perform the item, it is scored NC for no chance. These do not count toward the total score but might be credited if the client scored at a much higher level on other items in the same domain.

ADMINISTRATION

The rater can be a psychologist, teacher, or cottage supervisor who has had some training and familiarity with the instrument. This person interviews someone (referred to as the informant) who is familiar with the child or adult in the self-care areas. Several suggestions are given to encourage the informant to answer honestly and objectively.

INTERPRETABILITY

There are no norms presented and the author does not attempt to weight the scores for different degrees of importance or different distances between items. The items are scored pass/fail and the scores used for interpretation are the total raw scores in each domain. No information on interpretation is given.

TEST DEVELOPMENT

This instrument is an expansion of the Vineland Social Maturity Scale* and was developed because of the need to measure smaller steps in the skills acquisition of the severely and profoundly retarded. Some early training programs for the profoundly retarded at the Pinecrest State School in Louisiana indicated that the Vineland Social Maturity Scale did not reflect client improvement in self-care behaviors because of the wide gaps which existed between one scored level and the next (e.g., appropriate use of the fork to appropriate use of the knife).

The test was published in 1967 and apparently little or no work has been done on the scale since.

RELIABILITY

Unfortunately, the authors did not compute a reliability coefficient. It was given to 163 residents in the age range of 0 to 40 years. A test-retest reliability check was done with 34 cases on 19 of the 22 subareas and total agreement was obtained in 75 to 100 percent of the cases. Two rater/informant pairs were compared on 28 cases and total agreement ranged from 85 to 100 percent.

*The Vineland Social Maturity Scale is also reviewed in this text.

VALIDITY

No validity studies were done with the instrument. However, "clinical experience" and known developmental sequences were used to select and order items.

SUMMARY OF UTILITY

This scale is clearly geared to an institutional setting and tends to give major attention to those skills which would make the client easier to manage (i.e., toileting behavior, eating, dressing, etc.). The author indicates that the scale is useful in determining levels of client progress and being of aid in program placement and planning. He feels that it provides a quantitative measure which reflects client progress and the effectiveness of programming. He admits that the items were selected to fit the Pinecrest State School and may not be as relevant for other facilities. The most promising use of the instrument is to plan programs for profoundly retarded persons who lack self-care skills.

Preschool Attainment Record

Authors Edgar A. Doll and Geraldine Doll	**Distributor** American Guidance Service, Inc. Publishers' Building Circle Pines, Minnesota 55014
Alternative Version None	**Dates** 1966, 1967
Revisions in Progress None	**Test Manual** Preschool Attainment Record Manual, Edgar A. Doll

INTENDED PURPOSES

According to the authors, the purpose of the Preschool Attainment Record (PAR) is to provide an assessment of children of preschool years, with or without handicaps, who are not readily accessible to direct examination because of sensory impairments, speech or language difficulties, emotional disturbances, neuromuscular embarrassments, resistance to examination, and cultural problems. The instrument is intended to be a downward extension and expansion of the Vineland Social Maturity Scale.* The assessment is intended to provide a measure not only of what the child can do but of what he or she actually does in his or her usual state.

DOMAINS

The PAR assesses the child's behavior along three domains: physical, social, and intellectual. There is a total of 8 subdomains and 112 items within these domains.

PROCEDURES

The primary method of obtaining data for the PAR is by interview with an informant who is familiar with the child's usual behavior. In addition, the examiner may observe samples of the performances that are reported. The examiner assigns a rating of "passed," "marginal," or "unsatisfactory" to each behavior item.

A score is reported for each subdomain (i.e., items passed by category). A similar score is reported for items passed by age periods. The total raw score for the instrument is computed and then converted to attainment age and attainment quotient.

COSTS

Not available

REVIEW

CONTENT

The content of the Preschool Attainment Record appears quite good in that it contains many of the significant developmental milestones of early childhood. There is some question, however, as to whether the items are appropriately placed by domain and are accurately placed in terms of developmental sequence. The content does not appear, however, to be dated in any important way.

Each domain includes approximately 12 items that are representative of early childhood development within the age range of less than one year to seven years. The skills appear to be representative of those developed by children during this period of life. The items are generally appropriately assigned by domain,

---

*The Vineland Social Maturity Scale is also reviewed in this text.

with a few exceptions. Ambiguity in the placement of items is noted in the review by Collard in the *Seventh Mental Measurements Yearbook* (Buros 1972). In some cases, numerical items are included under communication (e.g., adds to ten). There are a few other examples of items that may not be appropriately placed. Placement of items, however, is generally good. The items seem to be specific in nature, and further definition of each item is contined in the examiner's manual.

The scale provides special scores for individual behaviors which have not been performed because there was no opportunity to do so. Items can be scored positively if the individual could perform the behavior at one time but currently does not because of lack of opportunity. There is also provision to score items positively when there is no opportunity or occasion to exhibit the behavior, but the respondent clearly believes the individual can perform the behavior in question.

ADMINISTRATION

It takes considerable time (2 hours) and formal training to administer and interpret the PAR. Instructions for administration are reasonably clear but the manual does not meet accepted technical standards. Administration of the PAR requires extensive formal training in test construction and test interpretation. It is particularly useful for the clinician skilled in personal interviewing and quite knowledgeable about the normal development of children and adults. It is not an instrument that can be administered properly by a layman and should not be used without formal training and experience in individual test administration.

INTERPRETABILITY

Interpretation of performance on the Preschool Attainment Record is assessed primarily through means of an age score and an attainment quotient. Performance on the test in age terms is displayed graphically on a summary profile which gives an indication of performance by specific domain and broad groupings of domains. Despite known statistical limitations, these scores are relatively easy to interpret and communicate. However, the lack of statistical data to justify such scores makes their usage at present inadvisable.

The use of the summary profile and age scores results is very direct and easy to communicate, although differences in age scores across subtests, of course, are not comparable. Profile analyses involving computation of differences in performance across subtests should be avoided due to the lack of substantiated reliability for the subscales and normative justification for the age placements of items. Use of the PAR as a substitute for conventional intelligence testing does not seem warranted at present since the experimental version of the instrument and test manual includes no data to justify this use. Finally, there are no actual data to support the placement and grading of items by age. Therefore, little credence can be placed in the age or quotient scores.

TEST DEVELOPMENT

The PAR appears not to have been subjected to the normal procedures of test development and standardization. There are no data presented in the manual on item development and no information is provided relative to the reliability and validity of the scale. Until such information is available, the scale should be used quite cautiously. There does seem to be logic to the placement of items in developmental sequence and in the domains included in the instrument.

The PAR is an experimental research edition. It does not include any norms based on performances of a representative sample of children. Initial placement of items for the PAR was based upon a review of research and theory regarding the development of children during the preschool years. There are some practice tryouts of items but no data are provided in the manual to justify placement of items. The manual states: "We prefer to use this Record for the time being as a developmental inventory which is speculatively developmental but not statistically verified. Actually, any misplacement of items on a progressional basis causes no real difficulty except on the order of nuisance, in that such an instrument is less 'neat' than is desirable. As an unstandardized inventory, comparative studies can be made with normative standardization." This statement is not plausible, however; the problem is more severe because of the confusion which can result from misplaced items and the tendency of practitioners to make unwarranted use of instruments.

RELIABILITY

No reliability data are reported in the manual.

VALIDITY

The validity of the PAR has not been clearly established. There are no specific validity studies recorded in the examiner's manual. The arrangement of items clearly possesses some content and face validity in relationship to normative studies of children's development and existing theory regarding the early development of skills and abilities in young children. Since its publication, a factor analysis of the Preschool Attainment Record has been conducted on a population of institutionalized mentally retarded children between the ages of $2\frac{1}{2}$ to $12\frac{1}{2}$ years by Owens and Bowling (1970). This analysis resulted in two general dimensions of adaptive behavior: a physical-developmental factor and a social-intellectual factor. The physical-developmental factor included the subtests of ambulation and manipulation.

SUMMARY OF UTILITY

The usefulness of information gathered from the administration of the Preschool Attainment Record is quite good and should be rated acceptable. Its most useful application is the assessment of individual clients. The use of this scale, pending further development and standardization, would be particularly warranted in early screening programs as part of a more comprehensive assessment of a child's early development. It provides rather good information on pertinent social and motor behaviors of young children on a clinical basis, but lack of important developmental work and the absence of a norming sample limit its widespread usage.

The instrument could be quite useful in determining whether children exhibit serious developmental handicaps and are therefore eligible for program services. It could also be used to plan general individual programs and as a device to monitor client progress. The PAR is not a highly prescriptive device which includes a great many detailed behaviors that can be converted into precise instructional objectives. Therefore, it is not particularly appropriate as a measure for determining precise instructional objectives within a teaching program or as a means for local administrative, statewide, or national planning and program evaluation.

Progress Assessment Chart
of Social and Personal Development

Author
H.C. Gunzburg

Distributor
Aux Chandelles
PAC Department
P.O. Box 398
Bristol, Indiana 46507

Alternative Versions
P (Primary) P-A-C is concerned with the development of the very young normal child and is suitable for mentally handicapped children up to approximately 7 years of age and sometimes older.

P-A-C 1 assesses a selection of skills particularly relevant to the development of school age children. This is the standard form suitable for mentally handicapped children aged 6 to 16 years, but can also be used for older age groups.

P-A-C 2 was designed for the adolescent and adult mentally handicapped and assesses combinations of various skills useful to help the mentally handicapped in his or her social adjustment.

M/P-A-C 1 is an adaptation of the P-A-C 1 particularly suitable for children with Down's syndrome, aged 6 to 15+.

P-A-C 1A is an extension of P-A-C 1 and tests additional social skills particularly relevant to the social education of the mentally handicapped.

Dates
P-P-A-C: 1966, 1973
P-A-C 1: 1963, 1975
P-A-C 2: 1963, 1974
M/P-A-C 1: 1973
P-A-C 1A: 1972, 1974
S/P-A-C: 1976

Progress Assessment Chart (continued)

The S/P-A-C 2 was designed for the severely mentally handicapped adult.

Revisions in Progress
Yes, available in 1978: A/P-A-C 1, a slightly revised second edition of the P-A-C 1A and two more forms of the S/P-A-C designed for use with the severely handicapped.

Test Manual
P-A-C Manual, Volume I: The Three Basic Forms (P-P-A-C, P-A-C 1, and P-A-C 2) H.C. Gunzburg, 1972, 1974, 1976, 1977
P-A-C Manual, Volume II: The Special P-A-C Forms (P-A-C 1A, M/P-A-C, and S/P-A-C), H.C. Gunzburg, 1972, 1974, 1976, 1977

INTENDED PURPOSES

The Progress Assessment Chart (P-A-C) was designed to give a fairly comprehensive picture of an individual's social functioning by assessing the presence or absence of selected social skills and information. This assessment, in the various forms outlined above, can be used with mentally handicapped young children, adolescents, and adults. The P-A-C allows the charting of an individual's weaknesses and strengths and can form the basis for teaching emphasis decisions and, through later assessments, recording of social functioning progress.

DOMAINS

In each of its six forms, the P-A-C covers four domains: self-help, communication, socialization, and occupation. The number of items and subdomains varies as indicated in the table below.

TEST	P-P-A-C	P-A-C 1	P-A-C 2	M/P-A-C 1	P-A-C 1A	S/P-A-C
SUBDOMAINS	8	12	18	12	16	18
ITEMS	130	120	108	120	160	180

PROCEDURES

Data are gathered for sequenced checklist items primarily by direct observation of the individual client in a typical setting. These data are augmented by interviewing a person knowledgeable about the client, and in some cases by directly observing the client in a special setting. No special credentials are required of the test administrator. However, the rating criteria presented in the manual must be adhered to in a consistent fashion for results to be meaningful. The author gives no information about administration time.

Assessment for each item is represented in a circular graph, which is organized so that performance level within a domain is easy to see. A Progress Evaluation Index is available for each of three basic forms [P (Primary) P-A-C, P-A-C 1, and P-A-C 2] and there is also a male and female version accompanying the M/P-A-C 1. The P-E-I compares the individual's assessment records with the average achievement levels of his peers, and collects the P-A-C records over time.

COSTS

Specimen set $22.00
    (includes manual vols. 1 and 2, a set of assessment
    charts and a set of evaluation indices)

REVIEW

CONTENT

The P-A-C scales are designed primarily to assess a client's social functioning. Areas such as physical and emotional development, learning and problem solving are included. A checklist of 39 items is provided which evaluates the normalization of the residential living environment. Although the items themselves are not always stated in explicit behavioral terms, the manual includes detailed instructions on how to rate each item. By and large, the items seem appropriate to the domains in which they have been placed. On the whole, the scale items seem appropriate to the overall purpose of the scales—to provide "a fairly comprehensive picture" of the social functioning of mentally handicapped persons.

ADMINISTRATION

The scales appear as though they would be reasonably easy to administer and cost-beneficial in nature. Approximately one hour would be required to administer the test to a client, with an additional 30 minutes for scoring.

INTERPRETABILITY

The chart form of presenting the results of the assessment avoids the obvious pitfalls of a numerical score and also makes the results immediately apparent to the skilled reader. Although formal test norms are not provided, the author does offer average levels of performance by age in every domain of the P P-A-C, P-A-C 1 and M/P-A-C 1, and by intelligence grouping in the domains of the P-A-C 2 to assist agency programmers in establishing reasonable client goals. These average achievement levels are useful for determining where a client stands—or should stand—in relationship to peers. The population bases from which these averages were derived appear to be of adequate size and composition, although the authors claim that no statistical procedures to "safeguard against sampling errors" were followed. Consequently, these averages should be treated as rough guidelines and levels of expectation for minimal achievement.

TEST DEVELOPMENT

There is some circumstantial evidence in the manuals which indicates that considerable time and effort went into the development of the P-A-C scales. Unfortunately, its developmental procedures are not clearly documented in the manuals. While the author tells us that many of the P-A-C items were taken from other behavioral assessment instruments, the manuals contain only scant information about the field tests, the item analysis which was conducted, and the subsequent refinement of scale items, if any.

RELIABILITY

Again, while there is some evidence in the manuals that reliability studies have been conducted on at least some of the scales, the reliability of the instruments is not fully established in the manuals.

VALIDITY

Validation studies of the P-A-C 1 conducted by Marshall (1967) as well as Elliott and MacKay (1971) related P-A-C domains to the Stanford-Binet and the Peabody scales. Only moderate correlations with these two IQ scales were observed (in the vicinity of .50), suggesting that the P-A-C is not entirely a measure of general intelligence. Also, the intercorrelations among domains are of a magnitude which suggests the domains are somewhat independent.

A similar study of the M/P-A-C was conducted by the authors and results similar to those reported above were obtained.

No validity data for any other versions are presented.

SUMMARY OF UTILITY

In general, the P-A-C scales appear to be appropriate for the purposes for which they were designed. The scales provide a means of systematically observing the social behavior of mentally handicapped individuals by comparing the records made at different times. It is possible to assess the extent of progress during that time span. Unfortunately, the lack of documentation of the measurement properties of the scale (development procedures, reliability, and validity) must somewhat erode the reviewer's confidence in the utility of the scale for widespread applications. However, the P-A-C is in use in several states for large-scale, routine assessments of retarded clients being served by agencies within those states, indicating that it does indeed have some potential for extensive use.

San Francisco Vocational Competency Scale

Authors	**Distributor**
Samuel Levine and Freeman	The Psychological Corp.
F. Elzey	757 Third Avenue
	New York, New York 10017
Alternative Version	**Date**
None	1968
Revisions in Progress	**Test Manual**
None	Manual—San Francisco Vo-
	cational Competency Scale,
	Samuel Levine and Freeman
	F. Elzey, 1968

INTENDED PURPOSES

The San Francisco Vocational Competency Scale was designed to provide an assessment of the mentally retarded adult based on observation of his or her characteristic performance within a work discussion of social development and the concept of social maturity situation. Its uses include (1) selection of mentally retarded individuals for training in semi-independent or sheltered situations; (2) assessment of an individual's status at a particular time; (3) judgement of growth in vocational competence over time; (4) measurement of the relative efficacy of different training methods; and (5) screening of mentally retarded individuals for placement in independent work situations. The scale is best administered in a workshop setting to adults of chronological age 18 and older. According to the authors, it is suitable for use with mentally retarded individuals with mild to severe disability.

DOMAINS

Thirty items are divided into four domains: motor skills, cognition, responsibility, and social-emotional behavior.

PROCEDURES

Information is obtained from an interview with a person knowledgeable about the client by a trained professional or other staff person familiar with similar instruments and with the individual being tested. Scale items contain four to five sequential options to check, ranging from a low to a high level of competence for that item. The vocational competency score is the sum of all selected level numbers. Administration time is approximately 15 minutes.

A total score, converted to a percentile, is obtained for the instrument.

COSTS

Scale booklet and manual, package of 25	$ 3.40
package of 100	11.55
Specimen set	1.10
(includes scale booklet and manual)	

REVIEW

CONTENT

The 30 items in the final version of the San Francisco Vocational Competency Scale are presumed to tap the four domains of motor skills, cognition, responsibility, and social-emotional behavior in a work setting. Each item is scaled according to ascending levels of competency. The items themselves are not sequenced in any particular order, nor are they administered, scored, and/or interpreted according to domains. Many items are better than average in terms of their clarity and behavioral orientation. Although the scale is not fully comprehensive in scope, it does an adequate job of covering the domains that are addressed.

ADMINISTRATION

The administration of this scale should be fairly easy for anyone who is acquainted with the vocational behavior of the person rated.

INTERPRETABILITY

Raw scores are converted to percentiles that were derived from the performance of a normative sample. The authors, however, provide no guidelines for interpreting such scores, nor are there any validity studies presented that would provide a foundation for interpretations.

TEST DEVELOPMENT

Test development was generally good, involving the following four discrete stages:

1. item generation and professional review;
2. first pilot study;
3. second pilot study; and
4. final revision, including norm gathering.

The samples for the last three stages were national in scope, and seemed to be fairly adequate. Care was taken to scale each item according to ascending levels of subject competency. Item analyses, however, were not presented, making it impossible to evaluate the psychometric outcomes of this carefully designed and implemented set of developmental procedures.

RELIABILITY

Reported internal consistency and test-retest reliabilities over a one-month interval are good (.95 and .85, respectively), although the number of subjects involved in test-retest was small (N = 54). Since this instrument involves ratings, the estimation of inter-judge reliability would also have been appropriate.

VALIDITY

No validity studies are reported in the manual. A subsequent study, however, reports the outcomes of a factor analysis which produced four factors that were labeled cognitive competence, cognitive interpersonal flexibility, cognitive-motor ability, and initiative-dependability. These factors appear to be similar, but not identical, to the *a priori* domains that were used to initially define the content of the instrument.

SUMMARY OF UTILITY

The scale has the greatest *potential* utility in the areas of screening and eligibility determination, as well as program evaluation. The realization of this potential application is dependent upon the implementation of future validity studies. Since the scale yields only one global score, its utility is very low for specific needs assessment or program planning.

Vocational settings are the only ones for which this instrument is appropriate. It is conceivable that other nonretarded adults in vocational settings could be evaluated with this instrument.

Santa Cruz Behavioral Characteristics Progression

Authors	**Distributor**
Santa Cruz County Office of Education, Richard Fickel, Superintendent	VORT Corporation P.O. Box 11132 Palo Alto, California 94306
Alternative Version	**Date**
None	1973
Revisions in Progress	**Test Manual**
None	BCP Binder Office of the Santa Cruz County Superintendent of Schools, 1973

INTENDED PURPOSES

The Behavioral Characteristics Progression (BCP) is part of Santa Cruz County's Special Education Management Project. Within this project, the BCP is intended to serve as the major assessment, instructional, and communication tool. As an assessment tool, the BCP provides the teacher and/or diagnostician with a comprehensive chart of pupil behaviors to assist in identifying which behavioral characteristics pupils display and which they do not. As an instructional tool, the BCP aids the special education teacher in developing individualized and appropriate learner objectives for each pupil. As a communication tool, the BCP offers a historical recording device which can be used throughout the schooling of pupils to display their progress and to help communicate this information to all those concerned with their educational program.

The BCP materials state that the instrument is appropriate for use with all disability types. It is designed primarily for school age children, 3 to 18 years. It may be administered either in the school or at home.

DOMAINS

The BCP contains 2,400 observable traits referred to as behavioral characteristics. Age and label have been discarded and behavioral characteristics have been grouped into categories called behavior strands.

PROCEDURES

The BCP is a checklist of specific behaviors. A simple rating scale is used to describe the presence or absence of behaviors. Data are collected by observation of the individual client and by direct interview. The teacher is the principal administrator of this instrument. According to the manual, a teacher is capable of conducting the BCP assessment alone, but it is suggested that speech, physical, and occupational therapists, school nurses, and school psychologists be consulted in their respective areas of expertise.

Training or experience in the service delivery field (e.g., as an educator or therapist) is necessary to administer this instrument.

From three to eight hours are required to complete this checklist for an individual client.

An individual is assessed on each behavior item with the BCP Charts. By looking at all the items within each strand it is possible to get a more complete picture of an individual's behavior skills.

COSTS

BCP observation booklet	$ 9.85
BCP charts	4.35
BCP binder	10.95

REVIEW

CONTENT

The BCP is one of the most comprehensive scales on the market. The items are behaviorally defined and very appropriate for all handicapped, particularly the young and severely retarded. The items are sequenced in a developmental order. Although this is not essential since this is not a normed scale, it does make it more efficient. If an individual has had no opportunity to perform a particular measured behavior(s), the examiner sets up the situation for the child to perform.

ADMINISTRATION

Administration of the BCP is described by clear instructions. Although the BCP yields substantial detail on an individual's abilities and is easy to score, it is expensive to use given the time and personnel required for administration. It is best administered in an interdisciplinary setting where several professionals can take responsibility for sections of the scales; in this case, administration should take three to eight hours. Otherwise, it would take a day or more to test and plan lessons for each child. An examiner's training or experience in the service delivery field is also important to reduce administration time.

The authors make no claim for standardization or use of scores for comparison of children. Performance on the strands are used for individual education plan development and for setting educational objectives.

INTERPRETABILITY

The child's performance is used to decide educational objectives and to select teaching strategies. No norms are provided. Lesson plans are available for each strand in BCP Method Books. The teacher and/or therapist relates performance on the BCP to lesson plan selection.

TEST DEVELOPMENT

This test is not standardized and does not provide test scores. Trained professionals apparently selected and arranged the items. No information is provided that indicates any data were collected on its use.

The items were selected from a wide number of existing scales and tests that relate to development and skills in areas the authors considered to be important. The initially published scale items were not well defined behaviorally; the instrument has been revised to correct this fault. The sequencing seems to have been based on the clinical experience of the authors as well as the norms of those tests from which the items were selected.

RELIABILITY

No reliability data are provided. However, one would guess that reliability is high and acceptable because the instrument's items are clear, behaviorally defined, and criterion-referenced.

VALIDITY

The BCP has high face validity. No validation tests are provided.

SUMMARY OF UTILITY

The BCP is a nonstandardized continuum of behaviors in chart form which can be used in schools or in homes with all handicapped populations, particularly with the young and severely handicapped. It is geared toward a comprehensive special education program. It is particularly appropriate for IEP and lesson plan selection, not for comparison of pupils or program evaluation. The lack of reliability studies and a scoring system reduces its utility. Because of the unusual length of the BCP (2,400 traits), there is some question as to whether it should be considered a scale or a tool of client training objectives.

This is a complex and comprehensive scale but is designed only to assess an individual child and plan his or her treatment program. At least two state agencies, the Arkansas Division of Mental Retardation and Developmental Disabilities and the Texas Department of Mental Health and Retardation, have adapted the scale and developed a scoring system in order to compare student progress, class placement, state planning, etc. This increases its utility considerably.

School Behavior Profile

Authors	**Distributor**
Bruce Balow and Rosalyn A. Rubin	Educational Follow-Up Study Department of Special Education University of Minnesota Minneapolis, Minnesota 55455
Alternative Version	**Dates**
None	1965, 1973
Revisions in Progress	**Test Manual**
None	Manual of Directions for the School Behavior Profile (Draft), Bruce Balow, 1974

INTENDED PURPOSES

The School Behavior Profile (SBP) was designed for use by school personnel to aid in identifying those children with a high probability of needing special attention, such as placement in special classes or special programs, retention at current grade level, referral to the school psychologist or social worker, remedial reading instruction, or individual tutorial help.

According to the manual, the School Behavior Profile can be used to provide information to special service personnel, parents, and external authorities regarding the child's classroom behavior. It can also be used to assess improvement in disruptive behavior following the types of interventions noted above.

The profile is designed for classroom administration to children of both sexes between five and nine years of age who have mild to moderate physical, intellectual and/or emotional impairments. A mental age range within one standard deviation of the average is recommended.

DOMAINS

Fifty-eight items are used to assess control, developmental immaturity, and anxious-neurotic aspects of the child's in-school behavior.

PROCEDURES

The classroom teacher observes the individual in the course of routine school activities and records observations on rating scales describing the frequency with which the child shows the particular behavior. According to the manual, the profile takes five to ten minutes to complete.

A score for the instrument is obtained, but responses within each of the three subscales can be evaluated to gain more specific information about the individual's particular problem type.

COSTS

Not available

REVIEW

CONTENT

The content of the SBP reflects three dimensions of school behavior: poor control, developmental immaturity and anxious/neurotic. The items listed under poor control appear consistent with that construct. Several items under developmental immaturity do not seem related to that construct (e.g., rapid thinking, dislikes school work, social withdrawal, inattentive to others, self assertive). Perhaps this factor scale should be renamed to reflect its item content more accurately. Many items do not have a clear behavioral referent (sluggish, clumsy, depressed, anxious, daydreamer, jealous) and a few items have double meanings (passivity, suggestibility).

There is no attempt to sequence items developmentally even though one subscale is termed "developmental" immaturity.

ADMINISTRATION

The authors provide evidence for their view that the classroom teacher can provide valid ratings of student behavior. Although it is assumed the rater will be a teacher, anyone familiar with the child in social situations could probably also provide useful ratings (e.g., parents, aides, therapists). This instrument has a satisfactory manual and is easy to administer and score.

The rater indicates the frequency with which a behavior occurs and then sums the frequency ratings. All behaviors on the scale are presumably negative since all are scored the same way. However, the direction of the scoring on certain items (self-assertive, shows rapid thinking, talkative) must be questioned.

INTERPRETATION

The normative data consist only of means and standard deviations for males and females by grade (one to five). No frequency distributions or percentile ranks are provided. Normative data are available only for the instrument total scores, not for the subscales. The normative population differs from the general U.S. population in ethnic characteristics; 96.5 percent are white. There are no norms available for developmentally disabled populations. The authors suggest as cutoff scores ±1 standard deviation from the mean (168 and 217).

One minor but annoying feature of the instrument is that a high score represents more adaptive behavior. Thus a high score does not imply more behavior of the type represented by the scale name, and hence is a departure from common psychometric procedure.

The interpretability of the subscales, particularly developmental immaturity, is open to question since several items on the scale have little to do with development or immaturity.

TEST DEVELOPMENT

Items were selected from checklists and scales assessing deviant behavior. The original 200-item pool was reduced by eliminating redundant, inappropriate, ambiguous, and nonobservable items. Teachers then reviewed a set of 73 items and used these items to rate students. Changes were made based on these teacher reviews and subsequent experience so that the present scale consists of 58 items.

The instrument was field tested on 1,613 children in Minnesota who are part of a large-scale longitudinal study of infants.

Items were assigned to subscales based on factor analysis, although for some unexplained reason three items are assigned to two different subscales, and some items are not assigned to any scale.

RELIABILITY

The split-half reliability coefficient corrected by the Spearman-Brown formula for the full test is .96 stability over time. Coefficients for the same student at two different grade levels ranged from .42 to .50. Stability coefficients over a three-year period for the subscales range from .47 to .55 for poor control, .38 to .48 for developmental immaturity, and .09 to .19 for anxious-neurotic.

Stability coefficients for the subscales are probably too low for individual comparison or interpretation. The extremely low reliability for the anxious-neurotic subscale raises questions of whether interpretation of these items by subscale is even warranted.

VALIDITY

All validity studies have been conducted on the field test population by the authors. Predictive validity was assessed by comparing first grade SBP scores with fourth grade teacher ratings on two general questions reflecting behavior and attitude problems, and with the number of special service referrals and placements received. Of those students with poor behavior profile scores (≤ 168) in the first grade, 24 percent were judged to have severe behavior problems and 29 percent to have severe attitude problems by their fourth grade teachers; 56 percent had had at least one special service referral. These data provide only moderate evidence for predictive validity.

Concurrent validity is suggested by differences in the scores of males and females in the predicted direction.

SUMMARY OF UTILITY

This instrument has potential as a gross screening instrument for indicating students who may be exhibiting problem behaviors. Even when used as a screening device, further professional diagnostic evaluations are necessary. The predictive validity of the instrument is not adequate to support its use for determining eligibility, diagnostic classification, or individual program planning.

Because the instrument was normed on normal children in public school settings, the use of the instrument with developmentally disabled populations in special classes or schools should proceed with caution, particularly with regard to the use of the cutoff scores suggested in the manual.

Although the subscales have intuitive meaning, great caution should be exercised before using them. Subscale interpretation is not recommended for the following reasons: (1) there are no internal consistency data available for these subscales; (2) the validity evidence for them is not strong; (3) the construct names selected for at least one of the scales do not accurately reflect the item content; and (4) stability coefficients are too low to make such interpretations with any degree of confidence.

Although the instrument may be used as a structured form for communicating to parents, counselors, or psychologists, interpretations based on individual items are not recommended. Many individual items are ambiguous or subjective and none of them have psychometric properties that suggest their independent use.

Social and Prevocational Information Battery

Authors Andrew Halpern, Paul Raffeld, Larry K. Irvin, and Robert Link	**Distributor** CTB/McGraw-Hill Del Monte Research Park Monterey, California 93940
Alternative Version Social and Prevocational Information Battery, Form T	**Date** 1975
Revisions in Progress None	**Test Manual** Social and Prevocational Information Battery, Examiner's Manual Andrew Halpern, Paul Raffeld, Larry K. Irvin, and Robert Link, 1975

Social and Prevocational Information Battery-Form T

Authors	**Distributor**
Larry K. Irvin, Andrew S. Halpern, and William M. Reynolds	CTB/McGraw-Hill Del Monte Research Park Monterey, California 93940
Alternative Version Social and Prevocational Information Battery	**Date** 1977
Revisions in Progress None	**Test Manual** Social and Prevocational Information Battery, T Edition Larry Irvin, Andrew Halpern, and William Reynolds, 1977

INTENDED PURPOSES

The Social and Prevocational Information Battery (SPIB) contains nine tests designed to assess knowledge of certain skills and competencies regarded as important for the community adjustment of educable mentally retarded students. It is intended primarily for junior and senior high school students whose IQs are in the approximate range of 55 to 75. The areas measured by the SPIB reflect five long-range educational goals that are considered to be important for successful postschool adaptation of mildly retarded adolescents and young adults: employability, economic self-sufficiency, family living, personal habits, and communication.

According to the authors, because knowledge measured by SPIB tests is also needed by the trainable mentally retarded if they are to function successfully in a community setting, the SPIB-Form T was developed for administration to both educable and trainable mentally retarded individuals. The SPIB-Form T edition also reflects the five long-range goals of the original SPIB.

Both editions of the SPIB are intended for use in community residences, schools, and other training settings (prevocational, social, and community programs). According to the authors, information from both editions can be used on an individual level to identify areas of student needs and to program specific remedial instruction, as well as on an administrative level to plan and evaluate programming that emphasizes instruction in areas of potential concern on a schoolwide or districtwide basis.

DOMAINS

The SPIB contains 277 items across nine domains; each domain is measured by a separate test. The domains are purchasing habits, budgeting, banking, job-related behaviors, job search skills, home management, physical health, personal hygiene and grooming, and functional signs.

The SPIB-Form T contains 291 items across the same nine domains. However, for test administration purposes, the order of the domains has been changed in this edition. Modifications were also made in some of the items in order to increase clarity and reduce word difficulty.

PROCEDURES

The SPIB consists mostly of true/false, orally administered items. A few items require the student to select pictures offered as alternatives to an orally presented item. The tests vary in length from 26 to 36 items. The test administrator needs no special credentials other than a thorough knowledge of the test material.

Each test in the SPIB should take from 15 to 25 minutes. The tests can be administered to a group of not more than ten students. The nine tests should normally be given in three sessions of three tests each. Whenever possible, the entire battery should be completed within one week.

Three scores are derived for each of the nine tests within the SPIB and for the total battery: raw score, percentage correct, and percentile rank. Tests can be hand scored or machine scored. Machine scoring is available through the distributor.

The SPIB-Form T includes two pretests which should be administered to all examinees prior to administration of any of the nine tests. These pretests determine whether or not an individual can respond to the yes/no type format required by the Form T. Individuals who demonstrate an inability to understand the format presented in the pretest cannot be further tested on any SPIB-Form T tests.

Every item on the Form T of the SPIB is constructed in either the yes/no or picture selection format. The test is presented orally by the examiner and may be presented to a group of individuals at one time. As in the case of the original SPIB, the test administrator of the Form T needs no special credentials other than a thorough knowledge of the test material.

Administration time for each test in Form T should range between 10 and 20 minutes; the total battery can be administered in one and one half to two and one half hours. Most examinees can take three to five tests on any one day. Each individual should complete the battery within a week.

Unlike the original SPIB, only hand scoring is available for the SPIB-Form T. Raw scores and percentage correct scores are derived for each test and for the total battery.

COSTS (SPIB)

Specimen set	$ 5.00
(includes a machine and hand scorable test book, examiner's manual, user's guide, and class record sheet)	
Machine scorable test book, per 20	21.00
(includes examiner's manual, answer key, and user's guide)	
Hand scorable test book, per 20	16.00
(includes examiner's manual, answer key, user's guide, and class record sheet)	
Examiner's manual	2.00
User's guide	2.00
Class record sheet	.25
(for hand scoring)	
Technical report	3.00
Scoring services	
basic service, per student	.60
(includes original plus two copies of class record sheet)	
Optional services	
additional class record sheet, per student	.08
individual test record, per student	.10

COSTS (SPIB-Form T)

Not available

REVIEW*

CONTENT

Both editions of the SPIB adequately measure work and social skills needed for community adaptation. In the Form T version, the content is appropriately revised downward and reworded in order to make it possible to evaluate trainable or mildly retarded individuals. However, the pretest of the Form T will probably eliminate about 25 to 50 percent of trainable mentally retarded persons because of their inability to respond to the content and format of the items.

ADMINISTRATION

Since the SPIB is a true/false orally administered test, it is very cost-beneficial and easy to administer. The manuals and materials for both tests are very complete. Administration time is not extensive. The scoring procedures are simple. The instruments can be administered by anyone with some background in test administration; no extensive training is required.

Similarly, the yes/no format and pretests of the Form T version make it very simple to administer.

INTERPRETABILITY

The authors have gone to great lengths to make this instrument interpretable. Several scoring reports are available: (1) class record sheet, (2) individual test record, and (3) administrator's summary. The use of these reports in planning and evaluating programs is discussed in the user's guide.

In the examiner's manuals for both forms of the test, procedures are outlined for interpreting raw scores, percentage correct scores, and percentile ranks. The limitations of the different kinds of scores are discussed. Two main methods of interpretation are discussed in the Form T examiner's manual—comparing individual scores to performance of a similar group of persons and comparing individual's percentage correct score to a standard set by the educator or trainer. Since the first method provides no guidelines for training (i.e., it only tells you if the client or groups of clients compare with other known groups of the same age and IQ, etc.), the

---

*This Review covers information on both the original Social and Prevocational Information Battery (SPIB) and the Form T edition.

authors recommend that the second method of interpretation be used for education or training decisions. In interpreting data from Form T, users must constantly remember that they are comparing the results only with moderately retarded individuals who were *not* eliminated from being tested by the pretest.

In addition to the information contained in the examiner's manuals, the user's guide is very beneficial, providing information which links interpretation to the next essential step—implementation. The user's guide provides methods and graphic procedures to assess student needs, monitor program progress, and evaluate outcomes.

TEST DEVELOPMENT

The SPIB was originally constructed for use with educable mentally retarded persons. Twenty-six secondary teachers of EMR students identified the skills and competencies thought to be essential for a student's postschool community adaptation. A review of current curriculum guides and research studies was also utilized to identify these competencies. Eight long-range and 54 short-range objectives emerged which were then rated in terms of relative importance. This yielded five long-range and nine short-range objectives which serve as the foundation for construction of the instrument.

Initial item pools of 80 to 100 items per test were created and sent to the 26 participating teachers who were asked to rank the relevance of items. Final selection of items was based upon the following considerations: degree of internal consistency, difficulty level of each item, and preservation of content integrity.

The instrument was then intensively field tested. A proportionate random sample of Oregon secondary schools containing EMR classes was used to obtain reference group data. The samples consisted of approximately 30 percent of all junior high schools and 30 percent of all senior high schools in Oregon.

The SPIB-Form T, based on modifications of the original SPIB, was developed to use with trainable mentally retarded persons. Changes were made in the original SPIB's administration directions, item response format, and some of the items in order to increase clarity and reduce word difficulty. The SPIB-Form T was field tested on 186 residents of 25 group homes in six northwestern states and on 128 individuals in 20 TMR classes in Pennsylvania.

Since the criteria for community adaptation remained the same in both versions of the test, trainable mentally retarded individuals are expected to adapt at the same level as educable mentally retarded persons and slow learners.

RELIABILITY

Initial and follow-up reliability studies of the original SPIB indicate internal consistency, as well as stability. Reliability was found to be internally consistent with the Kuder-Richardson formula 20 range of .78 to .82 in the various nine tests and .94 for the total battery. Reliability was also found to be stable by the Pearson Product coefficients ranging from .70 to .79 for junior high and .62 to .78 for senior high students.

In 1977 a brief report in the American Journal of Mental Deficiency used four samples to reassess reliability and found it continued to be adequate.

The Form T instrument has excellent reliability and internal consistency. Reported reliability studies show internal consistency (coefficient alpha) reliability estimates range from .78 to .87 for the group homes sampled and .68 to .82 for the Pennsylvania TMR sample. The average interitem correlation is from .10 to .18 for the group homes sample and from .07 to .12 for the school TMR sample. The prospective user must realize, however, that based on the data presented, approximately 50 percent of moderately retarded persons cannot be assessed by this instrument because of their inability to be tested successfully using the SPIB-T yes/no format.

VALIDITY

Although predictive validity is difficult to assess, the authors have attempted a number of studies. One hundred thirty students tested with the experimental SPIB version in 1972-73 were evaluated by vocational rehabilitation counselors one year after graduation, based on five subscales of the criterion instrument. A first order canonical correlation of .58 indicated a moderate relationship between the SPIB tests and the five criterion subscales over a one-year period. The authors state, however:

> Although some support for a relationship between SPIB and postschool adaptation has been found, these results must be considered tentative since the published version of SPIB (1975) was not used in the initial study of predictive validity.

Concurrent validity of the original SPIB was determined by comparing scores of 103 vocational rehabilitation clients with counselors' ratings. The data from this study yielded findings similar to those of the predictive validity study.

The AJMD brief report (1977) of four new samples reassessed the validity of the original SPIB and provided additional support for the appropriateness of the instrument.

SUMMARY OF UTILITY

The major value of the SPIB is its ability to evaluate slow learners and educable mentally retarded persons for training in prevocational adult activity settings, social skills, and community skills orientation programs. The SPIB-Form T is extremely useful when making decisions about the placement of high trainable and low educable mentally retarded persons in community alternative settings. As discussed previously in this review, Form T appears inappropriate for low level trainable mentally retarded persons because of their inability to respond to the yes/no format of the pretest. Both instruments would also present difficulties for those with auditory, visual, or perceptual difficulties.

The most promising use of both instruments is to measure social and prevocational skills necessary to succeed in group home, semi-independent, and independent living arrangements as well as in sheltered or semi-supervised work situations. The instruments can be utilized in EMR and TMR classes to select and train individuals for group home and community adaptation. They can also identify specific areas or domains of weaknesses which can be emphasized in training programs.

One of the important strengths of the SPIB is its supporting materials which help the user bridge the gap between assessment and implementation. Four uses of the instruments are identified in the user's guide: (1) assessing student needs, (2) planning and implementing programs, (3) monitoring program progress, and (4) evaluating outcomes. The user's guide offers concrete suggestions about how to use the SPIB in each of these areas.

The TARC Assessment System

Authors	**Distributor**
Wayne Sailor and Bonnie Jean Mix	H & H Enterprises, Inc. P.O. Box 3342 Lawrence, Kansas 66044
Alternative Version	**Date**
None	1975
Revisions in Progress	**Test Manual**
None	The TARC Assessment System User's Instructions Wayne Sailor and Bonnie Jean Mix, 1975

INTENDED PURPOSES

The Topeka, Kansas, Association for Retarded Citizens (TARC) Assessment Inventory for Severely Handicapped Children is intended to provide a short form educational assessment and accountability tool by selectively tapping observable self-help, motor, communication, and social behaviors in children 3 to 16 years of age with severe and profound mental retardation, autism, or celebral palsy. It thus is an alternative to, but not a replacement of, more extensive assessment batteries. According to the authors, the TARC Assessment Inventory can be used specifically to assess instructional objectives for individual children or a class, to evaluate the effects of a particular educational strategy or curriculum, or to demonstrate accountability for education or rehabilitation by repeated testings over time. This instrument is not reliable for the mildly or borderline retarded. Administration can be carried out in a residential or day care setting.

DOMAINS

Twenty-six items are presented in 12 subdomains within the four domains of self-help skills, motor skills, communication skills, and social behavior.

PROCEDURES

Data are gathered by obtaining information from a person who has been able to observe the child in a group or class setting for a minimum of three weeks and knows his or her average existing capabilities. Some items are scales with 4 to 6 choices of appropriate descriptive statements. Other items are categorical checklists. The inventory is administered by a teacher or other staff person. Reading the instructions provided in the test manual are sufficient preparation for administration of the instrument with practice. The rating process itself requires minimal time—a quarter of an hour—but observation of three weeks or more is a necessity. Scores are obtained for each subdomain and domain and are entered on a profile sheet. The sum of the four domain scores yields an inventory total score.

COSTS

Specimen set $6.25
    (includes 1 instruction manual and 10 assessment
    inventories)

213

REVIEW

CONTENT

The TARC Assessment Inventory purports to tap selectively a few representative skills in each domain, but items sometimes do not fit the domain. For example, it has a measure of maladaptive behavior within a motor area: "plays in sand without eating it" is an item in the subdomain of large muscle coordination.

Items are not behaviorally defined and could lead to much unreliability in scoring. The author states that the instrument is sensitive to small increments of progress, which suggests sequencing. However, items are not only unsequenced but sometimes unrelated behaviors are listed in an item.

ADMINISTRATION

Training or experience in the service delivery field is necessary to administer the instrument. Three weeks of observation plus 15 minutes to complete the assessment are required.

INTERPRETABILITY

Interpretation of a client's score is to be accomplished by comparison against a set of standard scores available for each subdomain, domain total, and scale total. The standardization sample consisted of 283 severely handicapped children of ages 3 to 16. Most children were mentally retarded (ranging from profound to moderate). Further information about the setting of the clients (residential or day program), the location of the sample (Kansas, presumably) and so on, is lacking, and limits the generalizability of the standard scores. Also, becuase of the range of ages included in the sample, the usefulness of the standard scores is extremely limited. Norms for a more narrow age range would be preferable.

TEST DEVELOPMENT

The instrument was developed through a collaborative effort between a mental retardation research psychologist and a teacher with years of experience in educating severely handicapped individuals. There is no description of the procedures for the selection of items. And, as stated earlier, the instrument was standardized on 283 severely handicapped children 3 to 16 years of age.

RELIABILITY

Sixty-six severely handicapped children were used to study interrater reliability; fifty were institutionalized, 16 were from day care centers. Interrater reliability coefficients for each domain were acceptable: self-help, .95; motor, .63; communication, .72; social, .78; and total, .85. Test-retest reliability was studied with the same sample. Correlations of more than .80 were obtained after a six-month interval.

VALIDITY

Validity studies are in progress. No other information is provided.

SUMMARY OF UTILITY

The TARC Assessment Inventory is a short, efficient instrument for assessing the functioning of severely and profoundly retarded clients in an educational program. However, to achieve this efficiency the instrument must be administered by a rater who is very familiar with the client and his or her behaviors. Consequently, the most promising uses of the scale are for program planning and the monitoring of client progress over time. Its use as a screening tool with unfamiliar clients is not recommended.

The Test of Social Inference

Authors Barbara Edmonson, John de Jung, Henry Leland, and Ethel Leach	**Distributor** Educational Activities Inc. P.O. Box 392 Freeport, New York 11520
Alternative Versions Full-length version and short version; a modified version is being developed for use with young children.	**Dates** 1964, 1974
Revisions in Progress None	**Test Manual** The Test of Social Inference Teacher's Guide

INTENDED PURPOSES

The Test of Social Inference (TSI) was developed to demonstrate the remediability of the social comprehension deficit of retarded persons. The instrument itself was devised to assess the differences with which individuals make social interpretations, and the relevance of social interpretations to behavior. The authors recommend use of the long form, except for purely exploratory investigations.

The test's range of item difficulty permits its use with mildly retarded pupils as young as 9 or 10, presumably with no upward limits for age. Its most useful range for the moderately retarded is from the age of 12 or 13 and upward. The TSI can also be used to test individuals who are not retarded, the useful range being from about 7 years to 13. The TSI could be used investigatively with other populations, ruling out only those subjects who have impaired vision and/or are unable to give responses which could be equated with the examples in the scoring guide.

DOMAINS

Individuals are evaluated along one domain—social perception. The long form contains 30 items and each of the short forms contains 14.

PROCEDURES

This instrument collects data through interview of the individual client. It consists of a set of pictures of diverse situations accompanied by standard questions verbally presented by the examiner to elicit client interpretations. The authors make no specifications regarding administrator qualifications, although they do recommend that examiners familiarize themselves with both the test administration procedures and with the classification and scoring of the types of responses they will receive. Test administration should take 45 minutes.

A total score for the individual is derived from his or her verbal responses. This score is compared with normative scores (provided in the manual's tables) in relation to the client's age, level of measured intelligence, and place of residence.

COSTS

Complete kit	$29.95
Extra recording forms	5.95

REVIEW

CONTENT

The content of the Test of Social Inference as a measure of social inferential abilities seems generally adequate. The only significant criticism that might be made relates to the dated quality of the pictures. They clearly appear to represent situations of a much earlier era. More contemporary art work seems desirable if further technical studies indicate that the test should receive more widespread usage.

ADMINISTRATION

Skilled interpretation and judgement is required to administer and score this test, similar to skills needed for acceptable administration of WISC vocabulary. Examiners who wish to use the test should probably have completed courses on test and measurements, preferably training in individual test administration and interpretation.

INTERPRETABILITY

The standards and recommendations contained in the manual for interpreting scores are most inadequate. First, the norms are based on very small and probably unrepresentative samples of institutionalized and public school mildly retarded students. It is doubtful that they represent populations of persons in today's schools or institutions. Moreover, there is little guidance given to the user of the test in interpreting the meaning and significance of TSI scores.

TEST DEVELOPMENT

Accepted test construction procedures were not followed in the development and standardization of the TSI. Norms and technical data were derived largely from a number of separate studies conducted by different investigators, and not from a sequenced program of field tests and a standardization study.

Thus, there is little indication that the samples included in the norms were carefully selected for differences in intellectual ability or age. Percentile rank norms are based in many instances on as few as ten people. There was no attempt to sample systematically a quota of persons in various IQ or chronological age strata. Moreover, statistical data on items and test scores are presented using an experimental version of 35 items, while the final test instrument (consisting of 30 items) is limited to the experimental scale. Additional independent studies should be conducted with the final scale version consistent with standards recommended by the American Psychological Association.

RELIABILITY

Two types of reliability are reported in the manual for the Test of Social Inference: interscorer reliability and test-retest reliability coefficients over approximately one-week intervals. Interscorer reliabilities are reported in the high 0.90s and test-retest reliability coefficients are generally reported for a variety of samples in the 0.70s and 0.80s.

VALIDITY

The validity of the scale rests primarily on cross-sectional studies of relationships between the TSI and other measures (e.g., teacher ratings, social maturity scores, adaptive behavior scores, IQ scores, etc.). There is some question as to whether these indices represent the most meaningful measures of validity for this particular instrument. The correlations reported are in the low to moderate range (0.30 to 0.40), and there is no indication as to whether the relationships represent levels of association independent of abilities assessed by intelligence tests. This possible association between TSI scores and measures of performance on intelligence tests is noted in the manual.

Considerably more validation research must be undertaken to establish clearly the TSI as an adequate measure of social perceptiveness and social sensitivity in retarded and nonretarded people. Other forms of validity should be addressed in subsequent editions of the manual, including measures of predictive validity, construct validity, and content validity.

SUMMARY OF UTILITY

The TSI is a potentially important and innovative attempt to measure the social inferential abilities of retarded and nonretarded children. Although it represents a promising area for research, the instrument as presently designed is inadequate for widespread application in educational and other social service settings. It should be used primarily within specialized research and

218

development studies in which attempts are made to alter and improve the social skills of mentally retarded and other handicapped persons.

There are certain technical deficiencies in the test which at this point in time limit its application and usage. Its use should most appropriately be limited to experimental research and evaluation efforts. Perhaps through further refinement many of the deficiencies can be corrected so that it may be used in the development and conduct of special training programs for mentally retarded and other developmentally disabled persons.

TMR (Trainable Mentally Retarded) School Competency Scales

Authors
Samuel Levine, Freeman F. Elzey, Paul Thormahlen, and Leo F. Cain

Distribution
Consulting Psychologists Press, Inc.
577 College Avenue
Palo Alto, California 94306

Alternative Versions
The TMR School Competency Scales contain five separate age and group scales. Form I is used for the 5 to 7 and 8 to 10 age groups; Form II for the 11 to 13, 14 to 16, and 17 and older groups. Both forms assess skills within the same domains.

Date
1976

Revisions in Progress
None

Test Manual
Manual—TMR School Competency Scale, S. Levine, F. F. Elzey, P. Thormahlen, and L.F. Cain, 1976

INTENDED PURPOSES

The Trainable Mentally Retarded (TMR) School Competency Scales were designed to evaluate the current status of trainable mentally retarded students in the area of school-related activities. According to the authors, the scales should prove useful for curriculum and program planning as well as parental guidance. They are intended to serve as a criterion measure for research purposes in determining the relative effectiveness of alternative training procedures.

According to the authors, retarded children of either sex ranging in age from 5 to 17 or more years who have been identified as trainable can be tested with these scales. It is intended that they be administered in a classroom setting.

DOMAINS

Five domains, perceptual-motor, initiative-responsibility, cognition, personal-social, and language, are measured by 91 items on Form I (for ages 5 to 10) and 103 items on Form II (for ages 11 up).

PROCEDURES

Four rated responses describing specific behaviors are given in this scale and the appropriate one is selected after observation of the client in a typical setting. The rater needs no special credentials to administer this scale, although familiarity with the content areas covered would be helpful. The authors do not specify the amount of time required to administer the scales.

A score, converted to a percentile, is obtained for each domain. The sum of these percentiles is converted to a full-scale percentile by using the conversion table provided in the manual.

COSTS

Specimen set	$ 3.50
Manual	2.75
Test, package of 25	11.00
(Indicate whether Form I or II desired)	

REVIEW

CONTENT

Generally, items appear to be placed appropriately within the domains. However, a few items do seem to be misplaced. For example, "keeping time to music" is categorized under the cognition domain. It might better appear under the perceptual-motor domain.

220

While the items within each domain do not appear to be developmentally sequenced (and the authors make no claim that they are), the instrument itself is divided into five subscales by age group. The items assigned to each of these age groups generally appear to be appropriate in terms of developmental expectations.

By and large, the desired behaviors are clearly specified. In a few instances, however, greater specificity might be helpful to the rater (e.g., identifying and matching number symbols).

Given the limited sample of behaviors assessed by the instrument, questions might be raised about the "generalizability" of some items on the scales. For example, in the perceptual-motor domain, why do the authors focus on using a knife in eating, rather than a spoon or fork? Or why, under the initiative-responsibility domain, is there a need for items on both "Keeping Body and Clothing Clean" and "Keeping Nose Clean"?

ADMINISTRATION

As indicated above, the instrument appears to be easy to administer, score, and interpret, although raters may have some difficulty differentiating between the four rating responses. The low costs involved in administering the instrument should result in a favorable cost-benefit ratio in most situations where the scale might be appropriately used. Generally, the manual is succinct and well written. Although the authors do not specify administration time, it should require about 40 minutes for a rater to administer, score, and convert the percentiles.

INTERPRETABILITY

Norms for each of the five age groups are provided by the authors in the test manual to assist the rater in interpreting the results. The percentile tables provided by the authors also appear easy to use and should yield results which are readily interpretable, assuming the instrument is used for the purposes intended.

TEST DEVELOPMENT

The authors provide only limited information concerning the development of the scale, except to indicate that the scale is a response to the need for more precise assessment of the growth of trainable mentally retarded children, and that it is built on the authors' earlier experiences in scale development. They also indicate that the scale's norms are based on teacher ratings in schools located "primarily in urban and suburban communities in California." These districts were chosen for three reasons: (1) they offered extensive curriculum to trainable retarded children; (2) the schools' TMR programs covered a wide range of chronological ages; and (3) the teachers agreed to work with the scale developers throughout the process of standardization. According to the authors, in all, ratings by more than 80 teachers of 302 TMR students are included in the norming sample. The authors provide no information on how the initial items were generated, analyzed, or refined after completion of the field tests.

RELIABILITY

The authors have summarized data on the internal consistency of the scales in the test manual in the form of split-half correlation coefficients for each of the five age groups. These data indicate a high degree of consistency for the subscale and total score for each age group. Correlation coefficients range from a low of .80 for initiative-responsibility among 14 to 16 year-olds to a high of .98 for both 14 to 16 year-olds and the 17+ group.

VALIDITY

The authors also include in the manual means and standard deviations for each subscale by age group and intercorrelations among the scales. The intercorrelations are relatively high and of approximately the same magnitude between subscales, indicating a weak differentiation in content among the subscales. Consequently, differences in score profile should be interpreted with caution. No evidence of validity for the total score is provided.

SUMMARY OF UTILITY

In general, the TMR School Competency Scales appear to be useful instruments for assessing the general developmental level of trainable mentally retarded children between the ages of 5 and 17+. The domains covered in the scales encompass the basic information a classroom teacher requires to develop an instructional plan for a trainable retarded child. The scales would have only limited applicability, however, in other settings (e.g., 24-hour residential facilities, therapeutic recreation programs, etc.) where the trainable child might require services. These limitations can be traced to the few items related to self-help skills which are not specific to the child's performance in a classroom setting. Similarly, the scales offer only limited insights into the child's physical and emotional development and work habits, especially outside the classroom setting.

One of the primary advantages of the TMR School Competency Scales is that they are simple to administer, score, and interpret. For the harried classroom teacher, who already has too many demands on his or her time, the relative simplicity of the instrument is an advantage not to be passed over lightly. The compact design and the way in which the authors have tailored the basic instrument to specific chronological groups of trainable children should make it cost-effective in most school settings.

Finally, even the limited information available in the test manual seems to indicate that the authors did a competent job of developing the instrument, conducting field tests, and gathering data to substantiate the utility of the instrument.

Uniform Performance Assessment System
Birth to Six Years Scale

Author	**Distributor**
Margaret Bendersky, Curriculum Evaluation Coordinator, editor	Vicki Ries
	Child Development and
	Mental Retardation Center, WJ-10
	University of Washington
	Seattle, Washington 98195
Alternative Version	**Date**
There is a version used mostly in the public schools for children age 6 - 12, and a pre-vocational/vocational level alternative is in the process of being developed. These two versions are not reviewed in this study.	1977
Revisions in Progress	**Test Manual**
Yes, including a test manual	None

INTENDED PURPOSES

The Uniform Performance Assessment System (UPAS) is a client evaluation instrument designed to be administered quarterly to monitor pupil progress in an educational setting. Its eventual purpose is to pinpoint the skill level of a child on the continuum of development from birth to vocational placement. The present checklist is intended to measure developmental behaviors of children functioning within the range of birth to six years of development.

DOMAINS

The scale contains 265 items in 25 subdomains intended to indicate developmental level in four domains: preacademic, communication, social/self-help, and gross motor. In addition, a specific inappropriate behavior checklist covers verbal and physical aspects of behavior. Items within a subdomain constitute a behavior checklist of skills, sequenced in the order in which they are agreed to be normally acquired.

PROCEDURES

The checklist is completed by a trained professional through direct observation and measurement of the client's behavior. No administration time is specified in the manual. The number of checked behaviors indicates the pupil's position within a sequence. Computer analysis of UPAS data is available, and includes an individual progress summary for each child tested as well as a group summary.

COSTS

Set of 0-6 year scales	$10.00
Computer results	
first analysis, per child	(approximate) 2.00
subsequent analyses, per child	(approximate) 1.00

(Cost will vary depending upon the number of individual cases analyzed at one time.)

REVIEW

CONTENT

The Uniform Performance Assessment System (UPAS) is a behavioral checklist of items that are stated clearly. Item scoring procedures are described in detail, and generally include a behavioral definition of the concepts being assessed.

ADMINISTRATION

The test materials are weak in explaining the basis for the selection and the arrangement of test items and in giving clear instructions regarding possible interpretation and scoring. Detailed information on the development of the scale, procedures for correct interpretation of performance, and special training qualifications needed to properly administer and interpret the test would be desirable in subsequent editions of the test materials.

Review of this instrument suggests that training or experience in the service delivery field and with instruments of a similar nature are requisite for persons who will administer the UPAS. A good understanding of the early development of children seems desirable. Administration time appears to be one to two hours.

INTERPRETABILITY

As a criterion-referenced device, the interpretation of performance is relatively straightforward and clear. There is little information on the interpretation of test results given in the test materials. There are no normative scores provided, although all behaviors appear to be appropriately sequenced by developmental level. Currently, there is considerable investigation being conducted of the use of computerized methods of scoring and profiling performance. Sample computer outputs suggest that this particular approach could yield meaningful results when available for widespread application.

TEST DEVELOPMENT

No descriptions of the development procedures for the UPAS are contained in the manual or supporting materials available for review. It is not known, for example, what procedures were followed in selecting items for inclusion in the scale, or how (or if) they were field tested. However, it is clear that the scale has undergone some revision as the result of actual program implementation. Unfortunately, there is no description of the rationale for the changes that were made or of the procedures followed to determine which aspects of the UPAS required revision.

RELIABILITY

No reliability estimates are discussed in available test materials. However, in personal correspondence, the author indicated that test-retest reliability coefficients, apparently in percent agreement, are quite high (in the range of 96 percent). However, no information is given on the characteristics of the sample included in this study or the length of the interval between the two administrations.

VALIDITY

The validity of the scale seems to be acceptable if judged in relationship to normal development of behaviors and currently available developmental scales. The test materials and technical report do not discuss the issue of validity in any detail. No mention is made of how the items were selected or developed, and even simple indicators of validity, such as correlations with changes in chronological ages, are not provided. The validity of the scale should be more clearly established before it can be recommended for more widespread use. Items included in the scale, however, are commonly found in early developmental checklists, and, for this reason, appear to possess a good deal of content and construct validity.

The scale's author notes that the content of the UPAS was developed with specific reference to a curriculum and is a summary of the content of that curriculum. While this means that the instrument has a high degree of content validity for users of that particular curriculum, its validity with other curricula is not addressed. Consequently, the content validity of the scale must be determined with reference to the specific educational objectives of a particular user.

SUMMARY OF UTILITY

The Uniform Performance Assessment System appears to be a promising criterion-referenced measure of the development of children from birth to six years of age. It should have widespread applicability in the assessment of developmental behaviors among both handicapped and nonhandicapped children, especially in assessing the status of children for the purpose of designing instructional programs. It has far less applicability as a general program evaluation and service systems planning device.

A promising effort is currently underway to place the scale results into a computer scoring interpretation service. It is too early to judge, however, whether this approach will yield highly useful and economical results. One of the major problems in the use of the scale may be the amount of time taken to secure adequate results. The scale seems quite lengthy to be a routine, quarterly assessment, as is recommended in the test materials. A computerized procedure could eliminate this current problem. However, the cost of such analyses may be prohibitive for many users.

There is still considerable work that could be done to establish the reliability and validity of the scale, and to determine ways of making it more cost-effective for the average user. There is little doubt that scales of this kind are needed in early childhood programs for handicapped students, and the Uniform Performance Assessment System appears to represent a promising approach to this vexing assessment problem in early childhood education. Its widespread adoption and use, however, must await further research and development. Its principal appropriate use at the present time would appear to be in designing individualized programs for young handicapped students on a limited and experimental basis.

Vineland Social Maturity Scale

Author Edgar A. Doll	**Distributor** American Guidance Service, Inc. Publishers' Building Circle Pines, Minnesota 55014
Alternative Version None	**Dates** 1935, 1947, 1965
Revisions in Progress Yes	**Test Manual** Vineland Social Maturity Scale Condensed Manual of Directions, Edgar A. Doll, 1965

INTENDED PURPOSES

The Vineland Social Maturity Scale (VSMS) is intended to measure progress toward independent adult functioning. Practical and research applications of the scale, according to the author, include its use as a standard schedule of normal development which can be used to measure growth and change; as a measure of individual differences, including extreme deviation which may be significant in cases of mental deficiency, juvenile delinquency, child placement, and adoption; as a qualitative index of variation in development of abnormal subjects; or as a measure of improvement which would be useful in evaluating special treatment, therapy, and training. The scale can also be used to discover whether social incompetence accompanies mental retardation. It is intended to be of assistance for child guidance and training and for evaluating the influence of environment, cultural status, and the effects of handicaps such as blindness, deafness, or crippling conditions.

The scale is intended for a population with a chronological and mental age range from birth to adult, with no limitations on the type and severity of disability.

DOMAINS

The scale has 8 domains—self-help, general; self-help, eating; self-help, dressing; locomotion; occupation; communication; self-direction; and socialization—which are measured by 117 items.

PROCEDURES

A qualified examiner with training in use of the Vineland Social Maturity Scale obtains information about an individual client through interviewing someone familiar with the client, such as a parent, guardian, attendant, or supervisor. Each item on the scale states a behavior and includes clarifying phrases to refine what that behavior includes. The item then receives one of the following ratings:

1. successfully performed
2. does not perform because of lack of opportunity or special constraint, but performed previously
3. does not perform and hasn't performed before because of lack of opportunity or special constraint

4. emerging or transitional performance

5. lack of successful performance

A score is obtained for the entire instrument, converted to equivalent social age values. Examination time is not specified.

COSTS

Specimen set	$ 2.10
Measurement of Social Competence (text)	10.50

REVIEW

CONTENT

The content of the Vineland Social Maturity Scale is excellent. It has served as a basis for many later tests of adaptive as well as social behavior and includes a great many behaviors that are generally recognized as significant milestones in normal social development. Although a number of items could be made more current, much of the test content still retains a very contemporary and timely quality.

As a norm-referenced test of social development, the Vineland Social Maturity Scale samples developmentally arranged social behaviors in eight different categories. It does not contain comprehensive item coverage in each of these domains, but presents a useful sample of social behaviors throughout the age range of approximately three months to adult levels.

There is an insufficient number of items at the preschool level to be sensitive to behavioral change in relatively short periods of time. For those interested in measuring change at the preschool level, the Preschool Attainment Record,* which is a downward extension and expansion of the Vineland for the preschool level, may be more appropriate.

Items included in this scale are short behavioral statements. The manual clearly instructs the examiner to determine what the subject can actually and habitually do with respect to each of the items. This approach to assessment clearly stresses the need for information on the specific, expressed behaviors of the individual.

---

*The Preschool Attainment Record is also reviewed in this text.

The manual presents specific definitions for each of the 117 items contained in the scale.

The items are developmentally sequenced in each year level and domain, based upon item difficulty data from a rather large sample of subjects. The concepts underlying the scale or the items within the scale are not particularly outdated; however, there is always continuing need for periodic revision and for restandardization of test items assessing social development skills. Such a revision took place in the 1965 edition. It is quite likely that the age placement of many items is no longer appropriate in that some items might be replaced by more suitable ones, given contemporary standards.

The scale provides special scores for individual behaviors which the person being tested has not had the opportunity to perform. Items can be scored positively if the individual at one time could perform the behavior but currently does not because of lack of opportunity. There is also provision to score items positively when there is no opportunity or occasion to exhibit the behavior, but the respondent clearly believes the individual can perform the behavior in question.

ADMINISTRATION

The Vineland Social Maturity Scale requires rather extensive skill and time (approximately two hours) for administration. It is not a test to be used by the casual, untrained examiner. Under skilled direction the scale can reveal a good deal of information on the social development of people. However, it is not a scale that one would generally use for routine program evaluation purposes.

The technical manual is a most thorough report on the development, administration, and interpretation of test results. There is a very clear statement of the underlying rationale for the test instrument and its usage with a variety of populations. The technical manual includes very extensive case study material, empirical studies, and discussion of the possible uses of the scale under a variety of conditions and with groups of widely variant characteristics. The only major criticism that can be leveled at the manual is that it is perhaps too technical for the average user. However, the Vineland is not intended for use by persons who have not had extensive clinical training in the use and interpretation of psychological tests since administration of this scale requires such extensive formal training. It is particularly useful for the clinician skilled at personal interviews and quite knowledgeable about the normal development of children and adults.

INTERPRETABILITY

Performance on the Vineland Social Maturity Scale is interpreted by means of social age and social quotient scores. Age scores have the relative advantage of being very easy to interpret. And although such scores are subject to a number of limitations, they convey meaning very clearly even to persons without a great deal of background in test construction and interpretation. The limitations inherent in using such scores to interpret performance are described in a number of publications (See Cronbach 1970.) Several texts on test construction comment on the inappropriate use of age scores in describing the development of adult populations and the uneven quality of age score intervals. Use of some alternative scoring system, however, would likely require a much more restricted range of test content and representation by age.

TEST DEVELOPMENT

The procedures followed in the development and refinement of the Vineland Social Maturity Scale were excellent. It has had extensive field testing and considerable research was conducted to improve the clarity and usefulness of the scale. The primary deficiencies in the development of the test were in the use of a rather restricted, unrepresentative norming sample.

This scale was developed through a carefully organized sequential research program. The technical manual (Doll, 1953) provides extensive discussions of the rationale for the initial selection of items as well as of the characteristics of populations used in field testing and results from such studies, item difficulty data for each of the items included in the scale, and the consistency of ratings and performance.

Clinical case studies of instrument application are also included. In general, the Vineland is a very carefully developed scale and follows accepted standards for the development of normative tests. The scale was normed on a sample of 620 subjects in a rural and small town community in New Jersey. The norm sample included 10 subjects per year level between the ages of less than 1 year and 30 years of age. All subjects included in the norming sample were Caucasian. A number of other field tests were conducted on residents of the Vineland Training Center in Vineland, New Jersey. This population could limit the generalizability of the norms, but repeated use of the scale has established the general relevance of its content.

RELIABILITY

Reliability estimates indicate that the Vineland Social Maturity Scale is a rather stable measure of social development. Several studies produced very high test-retest correlation coefficients over intervals as long as three years for samples of mentally retarded and nonretarded people. Moreover, results from the test do not seem to be affected by differences in informants or examiners.

The principal means for establishing the reliability of the scale was through the test-retest method.

The main problem with the studies cited in the manual is that they employed samples with rather wide ranges of ability and age; this generally produces artificially high reliability coefficients. It is quite likely that test-retest reliabilities would have been somewhat lower if the reliability tests had been calculated upon subjects within a narrow range of age and/or ability, as recommended by the current standards manual of the American Psychological Association. Even in light of this criticism, it does appear from the available information that the Vineland will yield relatively stable results in the hands of a sensitive and well-trained clinician.

In one study involving 250 subjects between the ages of less than 1 year and 24 years, a test-retest coefficient of approximately .98 was obtained for intervals of 1.7 to 1.9 years. One hundred ninety-six subjects of this particular sample were then retested after an additional 1.35 years. The test-retest coefficient was again quite high (.97) between second and third testings and remained at a very high level (.94) over the roughly three-year interval. Additional studies were conducted to examine the effects of changing informants on the same subject, using different examiners for the same informants, or using different examiners and different informants. There were no apparent influences detected for the variables of different examiners, different informants, or combinations of examiners and informants. Finally, the reliability of the self-informing method in which the individual acts as his or her own informant seems to be quite high, especially for children above the age of four years.

VALIDITY

The technical manual provides rather extensive information on the validity of the scale. The manual states that the primary source of validity was comparative differences in social development between retarded and nonretarded persons. However, the extensive as well as the citation of developmental psychological literature on motor and social development, indicates that considerable construct and content validity exists for the various items included in the scale. Based on extensive studies, the Vineland Social Maturity Scale appears to be substantially correlated with changes in chronological age, is moderately to highly related to mental maturity as assessed by Stanford-Binet Mental Age Scores, differentiates between mentally retarded and nonretarded persons, and differentiates between the performances of persons exhibiting other handicapping conditions (reflecting lack of social and emotional maturity) and those without evidence of serious handicaps. Evidence regarding the validity of the Vineland Social Maturity Scale seems sound and extensive.

SUMMARY OF UTILITY

A good deal of information on the relative development of an individual's social behavior is provided to the skilled clinician by the Vineland Social Maturity Scale. Used in conjunction with other measures, it can be helpful in making decisions regarding the appropriateness of training programs and the relative need for various types of training experience. It is primarily helpful in selecting training programs and setting the broad goals for services, rather than for designing individual activities and experiences.

The Vineland Social Maturity Scale is generally applicable to the assessment of all groups between the ages of less than one year and adult. It makes special provision for assessing the extent to which the environment provides opportunity for the normal expression of social behaviors, so that it does not possess any serious limitations with respect to assessing the development of particular groups or the assessment of persons in a variety of settings.

As one of the most respected measures of social development, this scale was carefully constructed and has influenced the development of most other measures of adaptive behavior and social maturity since its publication. Early reviews of the scale have been published by Cruickshank and Teagarden in *The Fourth Mental Measurements Yearbook* (Buros 1953). In these reviews, Cruickshank states "the categories of adequacies which the author has set up to facilitate evaluation reflect very well the processes involved in the maturation of social competence" (p. 161). Teagarden further notes that despite a number of limitations, the use of the Vineland Social Maturity Scale has particular value for interviewing and counseling purposes. She states that "when used wisely, the Vineland Social Maturity Scale adds greatly to our clinical insights" (p.163). The reader is directed to this yearbook for more extensive and technical discussion of the uses and limitations of the scale.

There is little doubt that the Vineland Social Maturity Scale can make an important contribution to attempts to understand the development of handicapped and nonhandicapped children. It is most useful as part of an initial screening battery applied under the direction of a very skilled clinician, and can also be very serviceable as a device for interviewing and counseling parents. It is distinctly limited as a measure for widespread use by teachers and others who are relatively untrained in advanced clinical assessment, and it is somewhat limited as a prescriptive assessment device for designing and monitoring individualized educational and training programs.

The American Guidance Service Inc., the publisher of the Vineland Social Maturity Scale, is currently undertaking a revision of the test manual and restandardization of the scale. It is anticipated that this additional work will correct many of the deficiencies in scale standardization and test content. It is likely that this revision will also improve the test manual for the average user, although Doll's technical manual is perhaps the most detailed and scholarly test manual in the field today.

Vocational Behaviors Scale (Experimental)

Author Gordon C. Krantz	**Distributor** Gordon C. Krantz Educational Consultant 5209 Woodlawn Boulevard Minneapolis, Minnesota 55417
Alternative Version None	**Dates** 1971, 1977
Revisions in Progress None	**Test Manual** Vocational Behaviors Scale (Experimental), Gordon C. Krantz, 1977

INTENDED PURPOSES

The Vocational Behaviors Scale (VBS) is an experimental instrument intended to describe several of the behavior dimensions that are important to being employed. It uses direct observation to measure nonabstract behaviors that can be managed. It is not attached to any specific vocational adjustment theory and deals with the general behaviors required for any employment rather than specific factors like mechanical ability or physical strength. According to the author, the scale describes present status rather than potential and can thus be used at successive time periods to measure individual progress and program effectiveness.

DOMAINS

Twenty-six items in 14 subdomains comprise the following four domains: occupational objective behaviors, job-getting behaviors, job-keeping behaviors, and vocationally coupled behaviors.

PROCEDURES

Observations are recorded on a series of rating scales by a teacher or other staff person familiar with the client's actual behavior and with the testing manual. The author does assume that the user is trained and/or experienced in vocational matters.

A rating is obtained for each scale item. No numerical score is recorded. Items may be considered in relationship to other items within the domain for evaluative purposes.

COSTS

Test manual	$1.50
Test copies	free, up to 25, in exchange for an agreement to provide the author with information to assist in refining the instrument. A user report is included with the manual.

REVIEW

CONTENT

The Vocational Behaviors Scale was developed to describe an individual's current status with respect to 26 behavioral dimensions

235

considered by the author as necessary for an individual to be employed. Unlike many vocationally oriented scales, the VBS does not deal with vocational interests, skills, or aptitudes, but rather with behaviors that impact on one's employability.

The scale appears to be comprehensive with respect to the vocational behaviors it intends to measure. Further, the author has deliberately left the scale open-ended in recognition of those factors which were omitted and may affect employability. The user's manual provides instructions on expanding or adapting the scale's behavior dimensions to local circumstances. It is important to reiterate the author's caution that in its present version the scale should be treated as an experimental instrument.

Items, or behavior dimensions, in the VBS seem very functional and appropriately placed within each of the four major classifications of behavior. For example, under the job-getting behaviors domain is included behavior dimensions in the areas of initiative and interview behaviors. Among the items found under vocationally coupled behaviors are social living, and community.

Each behavior dimension is described in benchmarks, usually at three levels or categories—inadequate, marginal/sheltered, or competitive. The competitive level describes the "minimum behavior a person must carry out in each dimension in order to be competitively employed."

The items are not sequenced in any particular order. Some are broadly stated and general in nature while others are narrow and more specific. For example, within the broad category of job-keeping behaviors there are 11 items or behavior dimensions. One of the more specifically stated dimensions in this category is that of attendance. The minimum acceptable attendance behavior for employment at the competitive level is that the individual has less than 12 absences per year. In contrast, the acceptance of supervision, an item also listed within the job-keeping behaviors domain, describes behavior at the competitive level as "supervisor does not report feeling resisted." The author's justification for such a broad dimension is that "the supervisor can usually tell you in a simple way whether he feels resistance to his supervisory role." For the most part, however, the dimensions on the scale are stated in a behavioral way so that they are clearly observable and measurable. To get the most accurate reflection of an individual's employability status using this scale, the user must be familiar with the discussion provided in the test manual which describes the nature of the scale and expands upon the meaning of each behavioral dimension.

ADMINISTRATION

Administration of the VBS requires that the user be trained and/or experienced in vocational matters, and that the rater be familiar with the actual behavior of the individual to be rated. The greater one's familiarity with the client's behavior, the more accurately and easily he or she can use the scale. Further, familiarity with the test manual should provide sufficient orientation for the rater trained or experienced in vocational matters to administer this scale.

No estimate of the required administration time is provided in the test manual. It would appear that familiarity with the client's behavior along the dimensions described in the scale will directly affect the administration time. As the VBS is a kind of behavior checklist and observation guide, the administration of the scale involves the rater circling the appropriate behavior description for each of the 26 behavior dimensions. Once all the observations of the individual have been made, the actual administration should take little more than 15 minutes to one-half hour.

The scale becomes time-consuming only when considered from the aspect of actual observation time, that is, the observation of the scale's behaviors in the individual to be rated. The clearest contradiction between the vocational behaviors as stated in the scale and those of the client to be rated may be found in the individual who is still in a prework or nonvocational setting. If a client is in one of these settings the rater would be forced to "translate student behavior in a nonwork setting into its equivalent behavior in a vocational setting." The author, recognizing that the scale is still in its experimental stage, suggests that time and user experience will show whether or not this translation can be done.

Krantz further points out that many pre-vocational programs have work experience provisions which allow for "work tryout" or time on an actual job; this will more directly provide the individual with an opportunity to perform or demonstrate the behaviors in the scale. Lastly, the author suggests that many of the dimensions lend themselves to observation, practice, and improvement through simulation experiences which can be provided in a prevocational or life preparation program.

INTERPRETABILITY

Scoring of the VBS consists of taking a colored pencil and drawing a circle around the appropriate behavior description in each dimension. There is no numerical assignment to any of the dimensions or behavior descriptions, thus, there is no overall scale total or subcategory scores. When completely scored, the scale should contain 26 colored circles, one in each of the behavior dimensions. The author simply suggests that the rater scan each of the behavior columns to determine something about the individual's level of readiness. Circles found in the left hand or middle columns (the inadequate and sheltered levels, respectively) pinpoint vocational problems. It is the author's position that each of the behavior dimensions chosen are critical to employment and, therefore, that the highest level which the individual attains in an important behavior dimension will limit the level at which he can function vocationally. The scale does not prioritize skill areas or behavior dimensions and thus requires that an individual be highly skilled in vocational diagnosis to determine a goal and plan intended to address an identified vocational behavior concern.

TEST DEVELOPMENT

The author states that the scale dimensions chosen were first found by examining the characteristics of chronically unemployed people to find out why they were not working (Walker 1969). The list of these people's problems was then restated in positive terms of what behaviors a person must carry out in order to be employed (Krantz 1971). The VBS dimensions were chosen from that list of vocational behaviors.

The scale does not follow any particular theories of vocational adjustment; it merely assists in identifying the status of an individual along 26 dimensions of vocational behavior. It is the feeling of the author that examining those behaviors necessary to be employed is important in that it cannot be taken for granted that an individual with special needs "will pick up basic characteristics of a worker during his course of training."

There is no evidence provided in the test manual that a field test of the scale was conducted by the author, nor is there a particular description of the population (in terms of age and level or type of disability) for which the instrument may be used. No discussion is included in the manual of particular item analysis or revisions of this instrument, even in its present experimental version. In the absence of such information, it is not possible to make meaningful comments on the quality of the scale's development relative to construction and further refinements of the instrument.

RELIABILITY

No reliability data were offered in the manual from which to judge the degree of reliability of the scale. The author suggests that repeated administration of the instrument to an individual over time provides an indication of a program's effectiveness as well as an individual's progress. Such an application of the scale would warrant test-retest reliability studies. In addition, given the nature of the scale and its intent to describe an individual's status by observation, tests of interrater reliability would also be appropriate.

The author states his intent to gather both reliability and validity data through data collection from users in the field while the test is in this experimental version.

VALIDITY

No validity studies are reported in the manual. The scale seems to have face or content validity in that it appears to describe directly what it intends to measure. It is built upon behaviors found to distinguish chronically unemployed people from employed people. As the author himself suggests, this type of validity does not demonstrate that the behavior dimensions truly do measure important characteristics of people in relation to employment. In order to obtain concurrent validity data, the author provides directions for field use in order to calculate and interpret a chi square statistic for each item on the scale, or any items a user may wish to add.

The scale is experimental, and as the author suggests, it will require validation through experience and the utilization of studies conducted in the field in local settings.

The author provides a user report form in the test manual for feedback and further refinement of the scale. In addition, he offers technical consultation in order to assist the user in assembling information that will assist in his attempts to validate the instrument.

SUMMARY OF UTILITY

The scale has a number of potential applications. The extent to which the scale is found valid will affect the reliability of the scale's utility for these various purposes and settings. Field use and study will provide this data, which should be analyzed before widespread or statewide use is made of the scale.

The greatest potential application of the scale is in the area of individual program or prescriptive plan (IPP) development. The behavioral nature of the statements in each dimension should translate well into target goals for a program plan. However, as the scale is theory-free, the work adjuster and team developing the IPP will have to develop the strategies needed to achieve the objectives. The scale itself sets no priorities, again requiring the user to examine the individual circumstances to determine an appropriate and realistic goal and program once the scale has assisted in describing an individual's status (and subsequently identifying vocational behavior problem areas). To the extent it is found valid, the scale should also prove useful for screening and making eligibility determinations to determine which individuals are ready for work activities programs, sheltered employment, or competitive employment.

In addition to providing individual needs assessment information for program planning purposes, the scale should be useful with a group of individuals to indicate where program emphasis should be placed based on a larger group picture of client needs. Used as a repeated measure, the tool should be an indicator of client progress and program effectiveness. Thus, the scale could potentially be applied at the outset of a program, intermittently as the individual moves through a program, and for follow-up. The VBS should also be a good vehicle for communication between vocational staff, the client, parents, and the employer to compare perceptions of vocational behaviors and readiness.

The scale may also prove useful in the development of prevocational or life preparation programs in public school settings, work experience programs, work adjustment programs, etc., whether they are based in the community or within an institution. Prework or nonvocational program staff should find it valuable to incorporate information learned about client behaviors through the scale into program activities in order to better insure the employability of individuals within their programs.

Present field use and study should ultimately yield the age, level of disability, and more precise information about the nature of the population for which this scale will prove most useful.

Vulpé Assessment Battery

Author	Distributor
Shirley German Vulpé	National Institute on Mental Retardation
	Kinsmen NIMR Building
	4700 Keele Street
	Downsview, Ontario
	M3J 1P3
Alternative Version	**Dates**
None	1969, 1977
Revisions in Progress	**Test Manual**
None	In Vulpé Assessment Battery

INTENDED PURPOSES

The Vulpé Assessment Battery (VAB) is a developmental assessment procedure intended for atypically developing children from birth through six years. It is designed to do a number of things: provide a test of competencies in various developmental areas; include a sequential teaching approach in the assessment process; provide analysis of the interaction among developmental skill areas and information-processing mechanisms; indicate program goals and techniques to meet the needs of individual children; and provide an accountability scheme, applicable to assessment, developmental programs, and service delivery systems. According to the author, this assessment instrument was specifically designed to be reasonably priced, easily transportable, and easy to use by persons with a variety of educational backgrounds. It is meant to be adaptable to the needs of both the child and the tester, and to be used alone or in combination with other assessment procedures, or to be used as a comprehensive or specific assessment.

DOMAINS

The Vulpé Assessment Battery is divided into eight developmental skill areas (domains) and one environmental domain—basic senses and functions, gross motor behaviors, fine motor behaviors, language behaviors, cognitive processes and specific concepts, the organization of behavior, activities of daily living, and environment. The basic test contains 1,127 items. The author claims that it includes as many items as possible within each age group and skill area in order to provide opportunity for an in-depth picture of the child's developmental functioning pattern.

PROCEDURES

Data about an individual client are collected by direct observation of the child or by obtaining information from a person knowledgeable about the child's behavior. The test consists of a series of tasks requiring the various skills assessed along the above domains.

The author gives no estimate of administration time; she states that the time required will vary according to the child, the environment, and the tester. According to the author, anyone who has had some experience working with handicapped children can use the battery; this includes parents, volunteers, and caregivers from a wide variety of backgrounds, training experiences, and professions. The author states, however, that the reflex test part of the assessment should only be administered by a qualified therapist.

An assessment, rather than a score, is recorded by this instrument. This performance analysis developmental assessment gives a total profile of the individual child and provides the basis for designing an individual program plan.

COSTS

| Complete battery | $15.00 in Canada |
| | 17.00 outside Canada |

The following sections of the VAB are available separately, for use with individual clients:
gross motor, fine motor, auditory language, activities of daily living, organization of behavior and cognitive behavior

Birth to 12 months	$ 3.50 in Canada
	4.00 outside Canada
1 to 3 years	3.50 in Canada
	4.00 outside Canada
3 to 6 years	3.50 in Canada
	4.00 outside Canada

basic senses and functions, assessment of posture and mobility, developmental reflexes, assessment of the environment, functional tests of muscle strength, motor planning and balance

For all ages $ 3.50 in Canada
4.00 outside Canada

REVIEW

CONTENT

Items are appropriate to the domains in which they fall, although several of the domains seem to overlap. Basic test items are sequenced, although the testing of senses and environmental measures do not lend themselves to sequencing.

The basic test includes 6 domains with 43 subdomains and approximately 1,127 items. Several of the domains seem to be measuring the same thing. For example, in the scale measuring social interaction, items such as awareness of rules, courtesy, sharing, etc., are included. The scale measuring organization of behavior, internal control, there are items dealing with control over temperament, verbalization of rules of acceptable behavior, etc. Under the cognitive processes, shape concepts, there are items related to putting puzzles together and under body concepts, completing pictures. Although there may be some clinical differences in these items, it may be that through a factor analysis study some items could be dropped and others merged. According to the author, the problem of overlapping items is a reflection of the fact that many activities involve more than one developmental skill. The cross-referencing of duplicate items in different areas of the assessment was an effort by the author to help cope with this overlap problem by eliminating the need to test an item more than once.

This is one of the few scales that seeks to gain descriptive data as well as test scores. The environment domain seeks to evaluate the characteristics of the learning environment, including the physical aspects and characteristics of the caregivers. A system for evaluating the senses of vision, touch, dominance, motor planning, muscle tone, etc., which are usually only evaluated by a neurologist or a physical or occupational therapist should be useful for other members of an interdisciplinary team serving a multiply handicapped child. Unfortunately, these two domains do not lend themselves to quantification.

243

ADMINISTRATION

There are over 1,100 items on the basic test. A child with a wide scatter and a developmental age of four to five would have to be administered many of these items; this would probably take around three hours. Or, an objective and well-informed individual could tell the examiner about the child. If the examiner were very knowledgeable about the test and could organize the items so that several answers to questions were obtained simultaneously, it might cut the time down somewhat. Because of the overlapping of several domains, it is possible that the test could be shortened if a factor analysis indicated that several of the items were measuring the same skill.

To fully appreciate and utilize the test results, one should have a strong background in normal growth and development, including normal reflexes and the abnormal reflex patterns of the handicapped child. Although the author claims that the test can be used by any person with some experience working with handicapped children, graduate training in a profession—occupational therapy, physical therapy, neurodevelopmental psychology, or speech pathology—is necessary to administer most sections of this instrument.

INTERPRETABILITY

Little information is given about interpreting the child's performance on various tests. The battery was designed to be used along with standardized tests which would provide averages and comparisons of groups of children. It is assumed that the examiner or the supervisor will have training in neurodevelopmental aspects of preschool children and can bring his or her own knowledge to bear on interpreting and using the results. Test items were selected from research and treatment literature; the test user needs to be aware of that literature in order to use the scale meaningfully.

TEST DEVELOPMENT

Although much work went into developing this test (in terms of literature review and clinical experience) there does not appear to have been any systematic field testing of the items or statistical evaluation (such as factor analysis) of the test itself. It has not been tested on a normative population; developmental levels assigned to individual items come from the data of others. This scale greatly needs a series of studies which would evaluate the individual items, its reliability, validity and explore ways in which this test might be shortened.

RELIABILITY

It is likely that reliability studies would find the reliability of the instrument quite good. This is based on the fact that most of the items appear in available clinical exams and in other test instruments that have been found reliable. Except for the use of two judges to score a single child (agreement in 95 percent of 38 test items), little reliability assessment has been done on the scale. One study by the author found a similar level of interrater agreement.

VALIDITY

No validity studies have been done on this instrument, although many of the items have been studied in clinical practice and in other tests. The author accepts the validity of items reported by other test developers from which items were selected. There is a good bibliography given, but users would have to locate and study this material. This instrument obviously has face validity. If a scoring system were devised to produce domain and total scores, it would seem to be more useful and easier to use.

SUMMARY OF UTILITY

This test represents an attempt to reduce many behaviors observed by neurologists and therapists in clinical evaluations to an objective test situation. The test does require a considerable amount of sophistication to be used wisely. For the instrument purpose indicated by the author—neurodevelopmental assessment of handicapped children whose development falls in the birth to six level (particularly birth to three level), the Vulpé is client oriented and not system oriented since it does not give domain or total scores which can be compared.

The test is clearly uneven in quality and somewhat confusing in its organization. A major limitation in its use is that it requires well-trained judgement to use it meaningfully. The number of test items ranges in the different domains from 44 to 206. Some domains have items which go to the six-year level and some only to the two-year level. The test as a whole evaluates the birth to two-year-old child much better than the five- or six-year-old.

This test should be quite useful to physical therapists, occupational therapists, speech pathologists or child development personnel working with the preschool handicapped child. It would be useful in planning and evaluating an individual program for each individual child. Because of the lack of summary scores, it would be unwieldy for group comparisons or for assessing groups of children to evaluate programs and services as a whole. It would be most helpful if a normative sample could be tested with this instrument and a scoring system developed to produce summary scores. This would improve its utility both in evaluating an individual child's progress and evaluating group and program effectiveness.

Work Adjustment Rating Form

Authors James A. Bitter and D. J. Bolanovich	**Distributor** James A. Bitter Univ. of Northern Colorado Greeley, Colorado 80639
Alternative Version None	**Date** 1969
Revisions in Progress None	**Test Manual** None; administration and scoring guide is available

INTENDED PURPOSES

The Work Adjustment Rating Form (WARF) is a rating scale intended for use with retarded individuals of chronological age 16 to 21 and of either sex. According to the authors, the WARF was constructed primarily for use by counselors and workshop foremen working with mentally retarded persons to assess workshop adjustment progress and areas of workshop strength for purposes of training. Further study was conducted to determine its effectiveness as an instrument to predict job readiness.

DOMAINS

There are 40 items organized into eight domains: amount of supervision required, realism of job goals, teamwork, acceptance of

246

rules/authority, work tolerance, perseverance in work, extent trainee seeks assistance, and importance attached to job training.

PROCEDURES

The individual client is rated by a trained professional or other staff person who is familiar with the client's behavior in a workshop setting. Each item in the instrument involves a binary choice ("yes or no"). According to the authors, the administrator of the instrument need possess no special credentials, although observation skills are important. The authors estimate that administration requires three to seven minutes per client, with an additional five minutes for scoring.

A score is obtained for each domain and for the total instrument. The WARF is self-scoring.

COSTS

Single copies are available free from senior author. Author permission is given to reproduce the rating scale.

REVIEW

CONTENT

The behavior components in the various domains of the WARF need improvement. Items were assigned judgmentally to scales, and the scales are not behaviorally defined. The authors acknowledge this as a shortcoming. However, items are sequential, realistic descriptors of skills needed for employment in the community.

ADMINISTRATION

The WARF should take five to seven minutes per client to complete. The ease of administration and scoring makes this a cost efficient test.

INTERPRETABILITY

The rating scale is admittedly judgemental. Although information is not conclusive, according to the authors, it does show that the measurement of job readiness is feasible. No method or instructions for interpretation are discussed. It is not clear what the translation of the "easy-to-administer", "easy-to-score" test means in terms of readiness for employment. No norms or developmental levels are provided as a reference point for interpreting a client's score.

TEST DEVELOPMENT

Items were selected *a priori* by the investigators, on the basis of "judgement." There is no indication of process review. This scale generally attempts to outline the requirements for readiness. However, no score indicators are present to indicate the readiness. Although the WARF is well thought-out, it needs more testing and revisions.

Reference groups are similar to field test groups; however, not many field tests are reported. The focus of the development effort was on interrater reliability rather than item reliability.

RELIABILITY

Interrater reliability is fairly high (.67 to .98). The study design seems sound; authors have noted its shortcomings.

VALIDITY

Predictive validity studies consisted of analysis of the correlations between WARF scores and two criteria of job adjustment—pooled judgements of the same observers in ranking clients as to employability and actual records of employment obtained two years after the program. Correlations between WARF scores and both criteria of job adjustment were reported as significant. A mean correlation of .56 between WARF scores and employment at the later time was observed.

SUMMARY OF UTILITY

The WARF is client-centered, but results could have implications beyond direct client uses. As noted under interpretability, if the relationship of this rating scale to readiness for employment were better understood, it could be used for program development and outcome evaluation as well as client needs assessment and Individualized Habilitation Plans. The WARF is particularly appropriate for use with workshop trainees.

The WARF is designed to predict the job readiness of retarded citizens. The instrument is appropriately designed but needs more testing, and the authors very clearly point out this and other shortcomings. However, through the development of this scale, the authors have added to knowledge in the area by conceptualizing a fine design, listing standards for excellence, and measuring their outcomes (of the scale) against these. There is no substitute for scientific rigor in such matters.

Interrater reliability figures are surprisingly high. Reliance on judgement only in test development is an acknowledged shortcoming and needs to be tackled.

One glaring omission appears to be the lack of an explanation of how the raw scores translate into readiness or relative readiness for employment.

This scale appears to be an acceptable one for client assessment, development of individual plans, program design (job readiness training programs), and outcome evaluations. With more behavioral indicators included, the value of the information can be strengthened several fold.

References

AAMD Adaptive Behavior Scale Public School Version

Aanes, D. and Moen, M. "Adaptive Behavior Changes of Group-Home Residences." *Journal of Mental Retardation,* 1976, *14* (4), 36-40.

Arnold, R.E. "Adaptive Behavior Scales as they Relate to Levels of Measured Intellect within a State School Situation." *Dissertations Abstracts International,* 1974, *34B*(7):3455, Order No. 73-32,091.

Bhattacharya, S. "Adaptive Behavior Scale Refinement." *Journal of Mental Retardation,* 1973, *11,* 27.

Bogen, D. and Aanes, D. "The ABS as a Tool in Comprehensive MR Programming." *Journal of Mental Retardation,* 1975, *13,* 38-41.

Christian, W.P. and Malone, D.R. "Relationship Among Three Measures Used in Screening Mentally Retarded for Placement in Special Education." *Psychological Reports,* 1973, *33,* 415-418.

Coburn, S.P., Schaltenbrand, W.E., Clausman, R.J., Pauly, E.M., de Lesstine, H. and Robinson, R. "Use of Low Pritient Diet Based on Lysine Corn in the Management of Phenylketonuria." *Nutrition Reports International,* 1973, *11*(1), 20-21.

Cohen, H., Conroy, J.W., Frazer, D.W., Snelbecker, G.E. and Spreat, S. "Behavioral Effects of Interinstitutional Relocation of Mentally Retarded Residents." *American Journal of Mental Deficiency,* 1977, *82*(1), 12-18.

Congdon, D.M. "The Adaptive Behavior Scales Modified for the Profoundly Retarded." *Journal of Mental Retardation,* 1973, *11,* 20-21.

Cunningham, T. and Presnall, D. "Relationship Between Dimensions of Adaptive Behavior and Sheltered Workshop Productivity." *American Journal of Mental Deficiency,* 1978, *82*(4), 386-393.

Edmonsen, B. and Wish, J. "Sex Knowledge and Attitudes of Moderately Retarded Males." *American Journal of Mental Deficiency,* 1975, *80*(2), 172-179.

Englemen, D. "Comparative Study of Adaptive Behavior of Ohio Educable Mentally Retarded and Normal Children." *Dissertations Abstracts International,* 1974, *34A*(8):4923, Order No. 74-3157.

Fitzpatrick, A. and Rogers, D. "A Critique of the AAMD Adaptive Behavior Scale (Public School Version)." Northside Independent School District, Public Appraisal Center, 1827 Westridge, San Antonio, Texas, 1977.

Guarnaccia, V.J. "Factor Structure and Correlates of Adaptive Behavior in Non-institutionalized Retarded Adults." *American Journal of Mental Deficiency,* 1976, *80*(5), 543-547.

Lambert, N.M. and Nicoll, R.C. "Dimensions of Adaptive Behavior of Retarded and Nonretarded Public School Children." *American Journal of Mental Deficiency,* 1976, *81*(2), 135-146.

Malone, D.R. and Christian, W.P. "Adaptive Behavior Scale as a Screening Measure for Special Education Placement." *American Journal of Mental Deficiency,* 1974, *79*(4), 367-371.

McDevitt, S., McDevitt, S., and Rosen, M. "Adaptive Behavior Scale, Part II: A Cautioning Note and Suggestions for Revisions." *American Journal of Mental Deficiency,* 1977, *82*(2), 210-212.

Nihira, K. "Dimensions of Adaptive Behavior in Institutionalized Mentally Retarded Children and Adults: Developmental Perspective." *American Journal of Mental Deficiency,* 1976, *81*(3), 215-226.

Nihira, K., Foster, R., Shellhaas, M. and Leland, H. *AAMD Adaptive Behavior Scale.* American Association on Mental Deficiency, 5101 Wisconsin Avenue, N.W., Washington, D.C., 1974.

Cain-Levine Social Competency Scale

Congdon, David M. "The Vineland and Cain-Levine: A Correlational Study and Program Evaluation." *American Journal of Mental Deficiency,* September 1969, *74*(2), 231-34.

Gardner, J.M. and Giampa, F.L. "Utility of Three Behavioral Indices for Studying Severely and Profoundly Retarded Children." *American Journal of Mental Deficiency,* 1971, *76,* 352-56.

The Child Behavior Rating Scale

Dunn, J.A. "Review of the Child Behavior Rating Scale." In Buros, O.K. (Ed.) *The Seventh Mental Measurements Yearbook.* Highland Park, N.J.: The Gryphon Press, 1972, 101-103.

Denver Developmental Screening Test

Frankenburg, W., and Dodds, J. "The Denver Developmental Screening Test." *The Journal of Pediatrics,* August 1967, *71*(2), 181-91.

O'Berry Developmental Tests: Behavioral Maturity Checklist II

Clements, P.R. and DuBois, Y. Reliability of the Behavior Maturity Checklist II. *Research and the Retarded,* 1978.

Preschool Attainment Record

Buros, O.K. (Ed.). *The Seventh Mental Measurements Yearbook.* Highland Park, New Jersey: Gryphon Press, 1965.

Owens, E.P. and Bowling, D.H. "Internal Consistency and Factor Structure of the Preschool Attainment Record." *American Journal of Mental Deficiency,* September 1970, *75*(2), 170-71.

Progress Assessment Chart of Social and Personal Development

Elliott, R. and MacKay, D.N. "Social Competence of Subnormal and Normal Children Living under Different Types of Residential Care." *British Journal of Mental Subnormality* XVII, 1971, *32*, 48-53.

Marshall, A. *The Abilities and Attainments of Children Leaving Junior Training Centers.* London: N.A.M.H., 1967

Social and Prevocational Information Battery

Halpern, A., Raffeld, P., Irvin, L., and Link, R. "Measuring Social and Prevocational Information Awareness in Mildly Retarded Adolescents." *American Journal of Mental Deficiency,* 1975, *80*(1), 31-89.

Irvin, L.K. and Halpern, A.S. "Reliability and Validity of the Social and Prevocational Information Battery for Mildly Retarded Individuals." *American Journal of Mental Deficiency,* 1977, *81*(6), 603-605.

Irvin, L.K., Halpern, A.S., and Reynolds, W.M. "Assessing Social and Prevocational Awareness in Moderately Retarded Individuals." *American Journal of Mental Deficiency,* 1977, *82*(3), 266-272.

Vineland Social Maturity Scale

Buros, O.K. (Ed.). *The Fourth Mental Measurements Yearbook.* Highland Park, New Jersey: Gryphon Press, 1953.

Cronbach, L.J. *Essentials of Psychological Testing.* New York: Harper & Row, 1970.

Vocational Behaviors Scale

Krantz, Gordon C. "Critical Vocational Behaviors." *Journal of Rehabilitation.* July—August 1971, *37*, 4.

Walker, Robert A. "Pounce". *Behavioral Counseling: Cases and Techniques.* J. Krumboltz and C. Thorensen, eds. New York: Holt, Reinhart, and Winston, 1969.

Chapter 4

Primary Environmental Assessment Instruments

INTRODUCTION

In this chapter, eight instruments which attempt to evaluate the environments in which developmentally disabled persons function are reviewed. These instruments, identified in the literature and by practitioners for use in programs for developmentally disabled persons, are included because they assess individual progress from a new and very different perspective than the client assessment instruments reviewed in the previous section.

As discussed earlier, client assessment instruments measure various aspects of an individual's adaptive functioning, that is, the ability to meet the environment's expectations in the performance of social roles and activities. However, a major problem in measuring such ability is the relationship between an individual's functioning and his or her environment. A person with certain functional limitations might be considered disabled in one context, yet nondisabled in another, depending on the expectations imposed on the individual's functional limitations by the environment.

Developmental progress can result from the following two types of changes:

1. changes in the individual's own abilities (e.g., improved socialization skills through maturation and/or training)

2. changes in the environment which facilitate an individual's ability to perform certain tasks (e.g., creating a more integrated, "normalized" environment which may make it easier for an individual to participate in social opportunities and develop socialization skills)

Environmental instruments attempt to assess this second type of change by measuring aspects of the setting which may affect an individual's developmental progress. The underlying assumption of these instruments, as described in a recent review of behavioral assessment instruments by Weigerink and Simeonsson (1977) is that:

> ...if an environment meets certain standards or has certain characteristics, it can be assumed that individuals in that environment are well served, that is, making behavioral progress...assessments of environments accomplish two purposes: (1) they indirectly assess the behavioral development of individuals in them; (2) they focus on evaluation efforts or environmental improvement...this approach appears to be fundamentally more sound and less costly than the other models [focusing on the individuals] (p. A-47).

Most of the existing environmental assessment instruments emphasize the principles of normalization and individual program planning. Environments are assessed in terms of how "normal" the services, programs, settings, or activities provided to developmentally disabled persons are, and how responsive the programs or services are to each individual's needs. These principles are closely tied to other related concepts such as independence, freedom from restrictions, self-reliance, dignity, social and physical integration, and human and civil rights.

According to a 1977 study by Government Studies and Systems, existing environmental instruments focus primarily on measures of process, assessing how well service providers normalize the living environment and protect the rights of persons with developmental disabilities. These measures or standards of process fall into two major categories:

1. the manner in which selected services, especially those related to individual program planning and case management, are provided

2. procedural, organizational, and physical requirements essential to the normalization of the living environment, the protection of individual rights, and the maintenance of adequate record systems

The Use of Environmental Assessment Instruments

Environmental assessment instruments have been used both as an alternative and a supplement to client assessment instruments. It appears that measures of developmental progress based on a dynamic concept of adaptive behavior should take into account both types of information—at the client as well as at the environmental level. Because development is relative to the individual and the specific demands and expectations of his or her environment, it is necessary to look at the interactions which occur between the client and the environment.

Although the kinds of data provided by environmental and client assessment instruments are different, the uses made of the data collected from these instruments is quite similar at both levels. Client assessment instruments measure a person's developmental level and the data can be used as a basis for developing an individual plan for the person which addresses his or her specific needs. Once the plan is implemented, the instrument can be used to monitor the developmental progress of the individual as specified in the plan and carried out in the program.

Similarly, environmental assessment instruments are used to assess a program's functioning. Based on the environmental data, a plan of action can be developed to address identified deficiencies or weaknesses in the program or setting. Following implementation of the recommended plan, the environmental instrument can be used to monitor the progress of the program in making the necessary changes.

In a sense, environmental instruments are used as a general system or information-gathering approach, rather than as a specific research instrument or measurement tool per se. These instruments should be viewed as educational and planning tools, most useful at the administrative level for program reform, policymaking and planning, and staff training. Instead of providing the users with specific measurements and test scores, the instruments offer program information based on a broad continuum of goals or on general sets of guidelines.

The Development of Environmental Assessment Instruments

The impetus for the development and use of environmental assessment instruments has come from several directions. First, many federal policies and legislation directly require or indirectly imply that various aspects of the environment be evaluated. For example, The Education of All Handicapped Children Act of 1975 (P.L. 94-142) mandates that children be educated in the "least restrictive environment" and that states develop plans and mechanisms to ensure the implementation of this process. According to the Developmentally Disabled Assistance and Bill of Rights Act of 1975 (P.L. 94-103) each state is required to implement an evaluation system which includes a "...method for evaluating programs providing services to developmentally disabled persons..." Many of the existing environmental instruments are based, in part, on the requirements set forth in current federal laws and regulations.

Secondly, many of the philosophical trends in the developmental disabilities field emphasize the critical and dynamic role of the environment in the growth and development of individuals. Concepts such as normalization, least restrictive environment, integration, mainstreaming, and right to treatment and service hinge on the ability of the environment to adapt to the needs of individuals.

A final impetus for the development of these instruments has been the increased concern with accountability at all levels of programs. Programs are increasingly being designed with clearer mechanisms for ensuring compliance and provision of required services. Environmental assessment instruments can assist in providing necessary data on program effectiveness and service delivery.

The Role of Program Standards in the Development and Use of Environmental Assessment Instruments

In addition to evaluation requirements set forth in current federal laws and regulations, many environmental instruments are based in part on existing sets of standards developed by various accrediting groups and professional organizations. The set of standards most relevant to environmental assessments in the developmental disabilities field is the Standards for Services for Developmentally Disabled Individuals issued by the Accreditation Council for Services for the Mentally Retarded and Other Developmentally Disabled Persons, a division of the Joint Commission on Accreditation of Hospitals (1977). Although these standards do not qualify as an assessment instrument per se (i.e., the standards do not have many of the technical and psychometric properties of assessment instruments), they have played a major role in the development of many of the other environmental assessment instruments reviewed. Some environmental instruments have attempted to operationalize the standards and/or develop rating scales based on the standards.

The organization of the Standards for Services for Developmentally Disabled Individuals is intended to reflect the conviction that the activities of agencies serving individuals with developmental disabilities must be focused on planning and implementing individual programs in accordance with developmental principles and the principle of normalization, and that these agencies should recognize the rights of individuals and their families and provide for the exercise of their rights. The standards are organized into seven basic sections: individual program planning and implementation; attention to normalization and use of least restrictive alternatives; achieving and protecting rights; case finding; safety and sanitation; research and research utilization; and the agency in the service delivery system.

The most recent draft of these standards represents a merger of two previously separate sets of standards issued by the council, one pertaining to residential facilities, the other to community agencies. The focus of the merged standards is on the total service delivery system, with residential services viewed as part of the total continuum of services.

According to the standards manual, any agency serving developmentally disabled individuals may use the standards presented in this document as a guide for its provision of services and as a means of assessing the adequacy of those services. For maximal benefit to an agency, however, the council recommends that self-survey should be followed by an on-site survey conducted by the council's trained professional surveyors.

Other sets of standards which are indirectly related to environmental assessments of programs serving developmentally disabled persons are the Standards for Rehabilitation Facilities established by the Commission on Accreditation of Rehabilitation Facilities in 1978 and the various sets of service standards issued by specific professional groups (e.g., special educators, occupational therapists, social workers, etc.). Although these standards may not apply in total to developmental disabilities programs, or necessarily be oriented toward individual growth and development, certain sections of them may be appropriate for the developmentally disabled population.

It is recommended that program staffs review various sets of standards in terms of their utility for assessing the quality of programs and services. It may be that some programs will find these standards sufficient for their evaluation needs. For other programs, the standards may be too broad or not sufficiently operationalized. In these cases, some of the assessment instruments reviewed in this report might be useful when used in conjunction with or in place of program standards.

Major Problems in Developing and Using Environmental Instruments

It is extremely difficult to develop measures or indicators of environmental quality for two reasons; first, the concept of normalization and related principles are extremely value-based, connoting various meanings and implications in different contexts, making it difficult to operationalize these concepts in objective and measurable terms, and secondly, research efforts in the field are relatively new and quite unsophisticated. There is not a huge body of theory and literature in this field upon which these new environmental assessment instruments can build.

In the following section, environmental instruments are assessed according to the same criteria used in the review of client assessment instruments—content, administration, interpretation, test development, reliability, validity, and utility. We consider these criteria to be equally applicable to both sets of instruments. However, the reader should note that because the state of the art of environmental instruments is so new, it is not surprising that these instruments generally fall short in the areas of test development, reliability, and validity. This is not to say that these criteria are unimportant in the case of environmental instruments or that these instruments should be excused from evaluation in these areas. To the contrary, major efforts should be taken to improve the possible technical weaknesses of these tools. However, while the research process is ongoing, we strongly recommend that program staff consider some approach to environmental assessments. It is better to gather some data on this very important dimension with instruments that may require further research and development than to neglect the dimension completely or inappropriately use client assessment instruments for this purpose. Environmental assessment instruments represent a promising and unique approach to gathering information about programs for the developmentally disabled and about the developmental progress of individuals within these programs.

Table 4.1 provides summary assessment data across the eight environmental instruments reviewed. The data in this table are based on the reviewers' evaluations of these instruments.

Alternative Living Environments Rating and Tracking System

Author James F. Budde	**Distributor** Kansas University Affiliated Facility/Lawrence University of Kansas 352 Haworth Hall Lawrence, Kansas 66045
Alternative Version None	**Date** 1975
Revisions in Progress In the process of being developed and at present is in the preliminary design stage. A guide for its use for statewide needs assessment and planning is in the final stages of development; it is entitled Residential Services: Statewide Planning.	**Test Manual** In the process of being developed. At present, the available descriptive source is a booklet, *Analyzing and Measuring Deinstitutionalization Across Residential Environments with Alternative Living Environments Rating and Tracking System.*

Table 4.1
Summary Assessments of Primary Environmental Instruments
(Based on Reviewers' Statements)

ENVIRONMENTAL ASSESSMENT INSTRUMENTS	Recommended Purposes — Individual Plan Development	Client Progress Measurement	Screening/Eligibility Determination	Program Planning	Program Evaluation	Population Characteristics — Disability type (Severity)	Age	Setting Characteristics	Domains — Communication	Self-care Skills	Independent Living Skills	Learning and Problem-solving Abilities	Maladaptive Behavior	Physical Development	Emotional Development	Socialization	Work Habits and Work Adjustment	Environmental Characteristics	Summary Ratings — Content	Administration	Interpretability	Utility	Test Development	Reliability	Validity
Alternative Living Environments Rating and Tracking System				X	X	Retardation	Children and Adults	Institutions or Community Residences										X	X			X			
A Normalization and Development Instrument				X	X	Retardation	Children and Adults	Institutions or Community Residences										X	X	X		X		X	
Characteristics of the Treatment Environment				X	X	Retardation	Children and Adults	Institutions or Community Residences										X	X	X				X	
Child Management Scale and Residential Management Survey				X	X	Retardation	Children and Adults	Institutions or Community Residences									X	X	X	X	X	X	X	X	X
Community Adjustment Scale	X	X				Retardation	Adults	Community Programs	X	X						X	X	X	X	X		X	X	X	
Program Analysis of Service Systems				X	X	Retardation and other "Human Problem Areas and Deviancies"	Children and Adults	Human Service Programs (including Institutions or Community Programs)	X	X	X	X	X			X		X	X	X		X	X	X	
Vulpé Assessment Battery	X	X				Developmental Handicaps	0–6	Institutions, Schools or Homes	X	X	X	X	X	X	X	X			X			X			

INTENDED PURPOSES

The Alternative Living Environments Rating and Tracking System (ALERT) is an environmental instrument which is intended to track deinstitutionalization through client movement across a continuum of residential environments and services. Designed as a tool for top level management at the policy and planning level, ALERT is not intended to provide for either individual client evaluation or evaluation of a specific service environment. Rather, ALERT is a generalized way of measuring the restrictiveness of residential environments, the movement of clients through a continuum, and improvement in environments and services.

As described in the ALERT materials, advocacy or parent groups can use the tool to ensure that service systems are deinstitutionalizing. Planners and managers, including state planning councils, can use the tool to study the rate of deinstitutionalization in certain organizations or in certain regions.

DOMAINS

The basic organizing concept of ALERT is a matrix continuum which provides a conceptual framework in which to classify and evaluate residential services at a generalized level. (See Figure 4.1) Nine service delivery models are described to differentiate levels of deinstitutionalization along a continuum. Included in the continuum are descriptors which differentiate service settings according to restrictiveness vs. least restrictiveness, institution-alizing vs. normalizing service provision, and physical and social integration vs. segregation. Scores are not relevant to this broad, nominal set of nine alternate levels. Rather, where a service provider or system falls is reflected in where it is placed along a continuum.

PROCEDURES

The ALERT system evalutes the environmental characteristics of a service provider or system by enabling the user to observe service settings. Each of the nine levels of the continuum is accompanied by a set of narrative observation guidelines. According to the author, users need some training or experience in the service delivery field and general experience with tools of this nature. The length of time required to complete an evaluation depends upon the size of the system being analyzed.

COSTS

A limited number of copies are available free of charge from the distributor.

REVIEW

CONTENT

This environmental tool attempts a laudable goal—to provide a means for managers and planners to track deinstitutionalization based on classifications of residential environments. An important feature of the tool is that it defines deinstitutionalization in terms of normalization criteria and least restrictiveness.

The content is not operationalized beyond rough narrative descriptions of restrictiveness, nor is the instrument accompanied by operational definitions. Further research and development of content would be desirable.

ADMINISTRATION

The booklet gives no instructions, training guidelines, or other administration information. However, methods for using the concepts and the continuum appear to be relatively self-explanatory, given the current stage of development of the tool.

INTERPRETABILITY

While ALERT is conceptually clear and potentially useful in many planning settings, the global nature of the continuum could vitiate the credibility of interpretations and applications. The charts presented in the booklet do offer a useful aid to interpretation.

TEST DEVELOPMENT

There is no information on test development.

RELIABILITY

No reliability information is given.

VALIDITY

No formal studies have been done. ALERT does appear to address valid issues pertaining to normalization and deinstitutionalization.

Figure 4.1
Individuals Residing in Various Environments Within the State

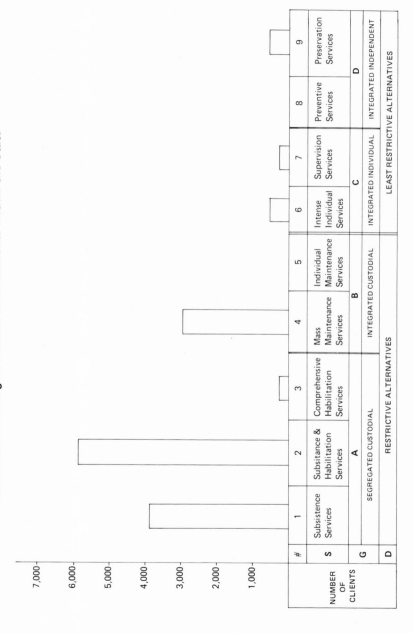

SUMMARY OF UTILITY

ALERT has potential wide application to populations beyond developmentally disabled persons since it uses normalization as a basis for judging residential environments. It is limited to residential settings, however.

If ALERT were to be treated as a measurement instrument (which it should not be in its current state of development), its utility should be considered limited because of its lack of measurement scales and validation and reliability studies.

Overall, ALERT's greatest strength appears to be its utility as a needs assessment, educational, and/or planning tool. It is one of the few instruments developed for top level planners and managers to assess a wide range of residential services over a large geographic area. Its basic aim is to assess the types and quantities of residential services in terms of restrictiveness and normalization. ALERT provides a context for the application of supplemental tools that measure quality of services and a finer degree of deinstitutionalization and normalization. ALERT's approach to the assessment of client distribution across various degrees of restrictiveness and segregation of services allows social planners to take corrective action toward restructuring of the service systems to get them in line with normalization and integration principles. This innovative and useful approach could open new perspectives conducive to planned social change.

A Normalization and Development Instrument:
A Rating Instrument to Evaluate the Quality of Services to Individuals with Developmental Special Needs

Authors Ann G. Flynn and Sandra K. Weiss	**Distributor** ANDI P.O. Box 60964 Sacramento, California 95860
Alternative Version None	**Date** 1977
Revisions in Progress Yes	**Test Manual** Integrated with instrument

INTENDED PURPOSES

A Normalization and Development Instrument (ANDI) was developed in California to provide a means to review the quality of a wide range of residential programs. The authors claim that it is based on the principles of normalization, the developmental model, social integration, the least restrictive alternative, individual program planning, and the rights of clients and their families. According to the authors, ANDI has incorporated many of the basic concepts of two other program evaluation tools—Program Analysis of Service Systems (PASS)* and Accreditation Council for Mental Retardation and Developmental Disabilities Standards for Services (JCAH). In California, ANDI is being used with a measure of client progress, the Client-Centered Evaluation Model* and data on cost and resources in a trivalent design for comprehensive evaluation.

DOMAINS

One hundred eighty-eight items falling into 15 subdomains measure performance in five domains: program, rights, social integration, facility, and administration. The subdomains which fall under these domains are listed below:

Program
    Integrity of service
    Developmental programming
    Individual development plan
    Coordination of client's program
    Personal identity
    Personal relationships

Rights
    Children's and adults' rights and responsibilities
    Legal, civil, and human rights
    Consumer involvement and public information

Social Integration
    Positive interpretations
    Integrated activities

Facility
    Community resources
    Comfortable features

Administration
    Training efforts
    Agency organization and coordination

*This instrument is also reviewed in this book.

PROCEDURES

A quantitative score for the instrument is derived through the application of a weighting system. Generally, the instrument is used for an external review by certified raters who report their findings back to the program. External raters are tested and certified on the basis of specified training, experience, and competencies. These raters can be certified professionals and consumers.

Compliance ratings for each item are made on the basis of direct observation of both setting and clients involved in typical activities. Most programs require a team of two persons for one and one-half days to visit the site, observe the program, conduct interviews, tour the neighborhood, contact family members and staff from other agencies, conduct independent ratings, conciliate results, and prepare a rough draft of the written report.

COSTS

ANDI, per instrument $3.50

REVIEW

CONTENT

Most of the items appear relevant, but additional items could be added in some areas. For instance, there are numerous items that are specific in some areas, although in others items are extremely general (e.g., the areas concerning individual program planning are fairly specific whereas items on administration are not as detailed).

ADMINISTRATION

Training of raters would seem critical. Because of the general nature of many items, rater reliability could be a problem. Administration would be time-consuming but would not take as long to administer as the PASS or the JCAH. Administration time can range from several hours to several days depending on the size of the service evaluated and the number of raters used.

The cost of training raters to use ANDI may be justified in that by educating trainees in normalization theory and creating the opportunity for raters to "internalize" normalization principles, the rating process becomes slightly more reliable, despite the generalization and value orientation of scale items.

INTERPRETABILITY

Two raters determine final scores and combine information in a report. There are no overall scoring or display aids.

TEST DEVELOPMENT

The authors are believed to have analyzed the PASS and the JCAH and extracted what they considered their most important aspects, along with other items. In its initial stage, the instrument underwent several changes as a result of pilot use. It was part of a 1977 large-scale field test of the entire state's evaluation design.

RELIABILITY

There is no information on reliability. However, the generalness of items combined with the subjectivity of raters could affect reliability. The authors indicate that reliability studies will be concluded soon.

VALIDITY

There is also no information on validity, and the generality of items combined with the subjectivity of raters could affect it. The authors indicate that validity studies will be concluded soon.

SUMMARY OF UTILITY

The main advantage of ANDI in relation to the PASS and the JCAH is that it is shorter and requires fewer people and less time to administer. While ANDI provides less information for decision making than either the PASS or the JCAH, it does cover the essential elements of quality. It might best be used in preparation for administration of the PASS or the JCAH, or as a preliminary substitute or "warm-up" session for service providers. The instrument is appropriate for a wide range of direct service environments.

ANDI is not in the more advanced stage of development, as are other related instruments. When the research studies on ANDI reliability and validity are concluded, it will be at a fairly advanced stage of development. Because no formal work has been conducted to determine validity, caution should be exercised in using the data for overall decision making. At the present time ANDI provides a reasonable index of program quality for purposes of comparison, analysis, and service improvement.

Characteristics of the Treatment Environment

Authors	**Distributor**
Original version: Jack Jackson 1960, 1964, 1969 Adaptations: R.E. McLain, A.B. Silverstein, M. Hubbell, and L. Brownlee, 1975, 1977	None. Original instrument is under copyright to Jay Jackson, June, 1960. Copies of the adaptations may be obtained from McLain et al. at Pacific-Neuropsychiatric Institute Research Group, Box 100-R, Pomona, California 91766.
Alternative Version None	**Dates** 1964, 1969, 1975, 1977
Revisions in Progress None	**Test Manual** None

INTENDED PURPOSES

There are several versions of the questionnaire Characteristics of the Treatment Environment (CTE). The original versions of the CTE (1960, 1964, 1969) were developed by Jackson for use in a study of treatment environments of mentally ill persons in hospitals; they will be referred to in this review as the original versions. In 1975, the CTE was adapted by McLain, Silverstein, Hubbell, and Brownlee for use in a study of institutional residential settings for mentally retarded persons, referred to in this review as the hospital version. A second adaptation was developed by McLain et al. (1977a) in which the CTE was revised for use in assessing community residential facilities for retarded persons, and it will be referred to in this review as the community version. The hospital and community versions of the CTE have been used in conjunction with the Residential Management Survey* to assess and compare various residential environments for retarded persons.

---

*The Residential Management Survey is reviewed in this report.

DOMAINS

In the original CTE versions, Jackson factored the instrument's 72 items into five domains: active treatment, socio-emotional activity, patient self-management, behavior modification, and instrumental activity. In the hospital version, a modified scoring procedure yielded two domains—autonomy and activity. (Thirteen of the 72 items of the original CTE do not enter into the scoring of the two domains in the hospital version).

In the community version 13 items are eliminated because their content was deemed inappropriate to the residential life of mentally retarded persons living in the community. The remaining items were reworded to make them more appropriate to community residences (e.g., changing the words "hospital," "patients," and "staff" to "home," "residents," and "caretakers," respectively).

Numbered sample items, those loading most highly on the two domains, which are contained in the hospital version (and reworded somewhat in the community version) are given below:

Autonomy (36 Items)

72. Patients are encouraged to make their own decisions in spending their personal money.

53. Patients are encouraged to start projects with other patients to improve the physical environment of the ward.

62. The staff encourages patients to take over management of their own affairs whenever possible.

49. Patients are not encouraged to take very much responsibility for maintaining their own quarters.

31. Whenever a patient is transferred from one unit of the hospital to another, the reasons for making the change are always explained to him.

Activity (23 items)

24. Patients are kept busy on the ward by frequent social, intellectual, or recreational activities conducted by members of the staff.

61. Patients have many opportunities to express themselves in music, painting, hobby-work, or other creative activities.

34. All members of the staff participate regularly with patients in positive activities.

14. All patients are encouraged to participate in music, painting, handicrafts, or other creative or self-expressive activities.
47. Members of the staff are constantly seeking ways of expanding patients' freedom of movement (about the hospital, grounds, and community).

PROCEDURES

The original CTE was administered to both treatment staff and patients in psychiatric hospitals. In the hospital and community versions, staff respondents are asked to indicate on an 11-point scale how true or false each statement is with regard to activities in their particular residential setting. No special training requirements for administering the instruments are mentioned in the test materials, nor is there a statement about estimated administration time.

COSTS

There are no costs if the CTE is reproduced locally. However, the original versions are under copyright by the author; the hospital and community versions are not.

REVIEW*

CONTENT

The item content of the hospital and community versions seems appropriate for their intended purposes—relating environmental features to client development. These instruments appear to discriminate among staff management practices in a variety of settings. The instruments, which rate two domains in a rather comprehensive manner, seem to have content validity.

The scales attempt to capture the extent to which the environment (primarily based on staff perceptions) promotes autonomy and activity among institution, hospital, and community

---

*This review focuses primarily on the hospital and community versions since they were designed specifically for use in programs for developmentally disabled persons.

facility residents. Items refer to specific staff treatment practices (e.g., "All patients are escorted by a member of the staff whenever they leave the ward"). In the original CTE instrument developed by Jackson and the hospital version the items seemed selected to describe a medical model of care. The rewording in the community version corrects this problem, bringing the instrument more in line with contemporary views on community services for developmentally disabled persons.

ADMINISTRATION

Administration of the hospital and community versions is simple; each should take from 30 to 45 minutes to complete. The questionnaire is completed by staff members following printed instructions. Some information on administration is provided in published articles; no test manual exists.

INTERPRETABILITY

Interpretability of the different versions of the CTE should improve once a data base is adequately established and the scales are used as criterion-referenced instruments, with individual items used in a prescriptive manner to create and implement a facility plan of correction.

Present interpretability is somewhat limited. Staff scores on the instruments are primarily useful for the comparison of various residential or treatment settings. Individual items, appearing as deficiencies, may be used as a basis for corrective action.

TEST DEVELOPMENT

The CTE was originally developed for use in hospitals for the mentally ill. Selection of items was apparently based on significant activities in treatment settings. No formal theoretical basis is evident. However, the author does make reference to operationalizing Goffman's concepts in his description of the instrument's development. The hospital version (with a modification of the scoring procedure for the original CTE) has been administered to a large number (250 or more) of developmental disability staff in a variety of institutional settings. A series of factor and cluster analyses of staff responses yielded two dimensions (autonomy and activity) rather than the author's original five dimensions (Silverstein et al. 1977). In the community version, 13 of the original items were eliminated and other items reworded for use in the community settings described above.

RELIABILITY

Reliability of the hospital and community versions is assessed in terms of the stability of the responses of staff on the same living units for 8 to 12 month periods, assuming that program considerations remain constant over time. For example, a measure of the hospital version's reliability is reported in terms of the correlations of the mean scores of staff responses on specific living units over a one-year period. The results were as follows: autonomy, .88, and activity, .69. These are particularly high in view of the fact that the respondents on the two administrations are not identical. In addition, it is reported that staff responses within living units are significantly more consistent than those among units.

VALIDITY

Since the authors view the use of the instruments as an intermediate step in relating the effects of environmental conditions upon client development, validation (predictive in nature) must await an appropriate and clearcut measure of developmental change, attributable to identified environmental features.

SUMMARY OF UTILITY

The CTE was originally designed for use in hospitals for the mentally ill, being administered to both treatment staff and patients. The adaptations of the instrument, both in scoring and content, have made it applicable to developmental disabilities environmental settings, being administered to staff only, however.

The CTE is helpful but insufficient if used alone for determining the adequacy of a service system. The instrument appears most useful for administrative decisions related to institutional reform and policymaking. Staff trainers may have particular interest in selected items to be used as specifications for creating environments which optimize development.

Child Management Scale

Authors R.D. King, N.V. Raynes, and J. Tizzard	**Distributor** None. A copy of the scale is found in Appendix I of King, R.D., Raynes, N.V. and Tizard, J. *Patterns of Residential Care: Sociological Studies in Institutions for Handicapped Children.* London: Routledge and Kegan Paul, 1971.
Alternative Version The Residential Management Survey is a questionnaire version of the Child Management Scale used in assessing developmentally disabled staff management practices in institutional and community residential settings.	**Dates** 1968, 1971
Revisions in Progress None	**Test Manual** None

Residential Management Survey

Authors R.E. McLain, A.B. Silverstein, M. Hubbell, and L. Brownlee	**Distributor** None. A copy may be obtained from the authors at Pacific-Neuropsychiatric Institute Research Group, Box 100-R, Pomona, California 91766
Alternative Version A shortened version (23 items)	**Date** 1975
Revisions in Progress None	**Test Manual** None

INTENDED PURPOSES

The Child Management Scale (CMS) was devised in England for use as an interview and observation recording schedule in assessing the management practices existing in various residential facilities for retarded persons. The Residential Management Survey (RMS) is a questionnaire version of the CMS. Both the CMS and RMS are designed to evaluate the extent to which staff management practices are client- or institution-oriented, or a mixture of the two.

DOMAINS

The 30 items on the CMS are associated with 1 of 4 intuitively-derived domains: rigidity of routine, "block treatment," depersonalization, and social distance. The 31 items of the RMS are generally rewordings of the CMS (less oriented toward children, more oriented toward adult residents). The RMS items, however, are not particularly associated with the four CMS domains described above.

PROCEDURES

The CMS is completed through observation and/or the interview of appropriate treatment staff. In contrast, the RMS has a questionnaire format completed by staff.* On both instruments each item has three response choices which are said to measure the extent to which management practices are client- or institution-oriented.

According to the authors, test administrators need no special credentials or particular training with the instruments. No information is provided in the materials about administration time required for either instrument.

A simple comparison of the RMS and CMS on salient features is provided on the following page.

---

*This change in administration by RMS authors was not formally assessed in terms of possible impact on data collected.

	CHILD MANAGEMENT SCALE	RESIDENTIAL MANAGEMENT SCALE
ITEMS	30	31
WORDING	original wording is "child"-oriented	revised wording is adult-oriented: "resident"
ADMINISTRATION	interview and observation schedule	questionnaire completed by staff
SEQUENCING		clearer sequencing of response options

COSTS (CMS)

None, except reproduction costs

COSTS (RMS)

None if reproduced locally

REVIEW*

CONTENT

In both the CMS and the RMS, item content seems appropriate for their intended purposes—to yield an index describing how humane the environment is and whether it affects client development. The content of both instruments seems to discriminate among staff management practices in different settings. The content and wording of the CMS tend to make its use most appropriate with young residents.

ADMINISTRATION

The CMS is a short, easily administered survey, based on observations and/or interviews. Procedures for administration of the RMS also appear simple: the questionnaire is completed by staff following printed instructions. The RMS should take 20 to 30 minutes to administer, requiring minimal instruction and supervision. No test manual exists for either the CMS or the RMS.

---

*This review covers both the Child Management Scale (CMS) and the Residential Management Survey (RMS).

TEST DEVELOPMENT

The CMS is a revision of the original Inmate Measurement Scale (King and Raynes 1968) which is based on the theories of "staff-inmate" interaction described by Goffman (1961) in his essay on total institutions. The CMS contains the 15 items of the original Inmate Measurement Scale and 15 new items. The items which formed the initial pool in the CMS referred to everyday staff management practices (as opposed to staff opinions of rarely occuring events). An item analysis was carried out on data provided by initial pilot work to test for discrimination and linearity. Based on an initial pool of 45 items, 30 items were selected in the CMS scale because they were shown to be efficient discriminators and to have linear distributions.

The RMS was the result of a rewording of the 30 items of the CMS and their response choices, and the inclusion of one item which had been discarded during the development of the CMS. On the basis of an item analysis, eight items were eliminated from the scoring.

INTERPRETABILITY

Procedures for interpreting results of both the CMS and the RMS appear simple. The instruments provide a rating on the desirability-undesirability of residential environments. Results seem useful for this intended (limited) purpose.

Although the CMS is evaluated without a score sheet, it appears that scores may be obtained for each of the four domains, as well as for the overall instrument. In contrast, the 31 items on the RMS yield only a total score. A factor analysis study of staff responses failed to support a structure beyond that of a single construct.

RELIABILITY

Reliability coefficients on the CMS were computed between the ratings of observers in numerous settings assessing a variety of staff activities. The coefficients ranged in value from .66 to 1.00 and, in general, they appear acceptable.

Reliability of the RMS was assessed in terms of the stability of the responses of staff on the same living units for 8 to 12 month periods. The resulting "r" for the RMS total scores was .90. Since respondents on the two administrations were not identical, this reliability measure seems very high. In addition, it is reported that staff responses within living units are significantly more consistent than those among units.

VALIDITY

No validation studies are reported for the CMS. However, there are indications that at least some items were rated using both observational and interview techniques.

For the RMS the authors state that a determination of the validity of the tool must await a clearly demonstrated relationship between measures of environment and client development. A preliminary report (Eyman, Silverstein, McLain, and Miller 1977) suggests that a substantial amount of variance in development is accounted for by the RMS's environmental assessment. This instrument has high face, content, and construct validity.

SUMMARY OF UTILITY

Both the CMS and the RMS characterize developmentally disabled residential settings, in particular, client management practices, as imposed by staff and system management. Potentially, these instruments could provide an index of management practices (by staff or management) indicating a developmental/humane environment. Results may be used as guidelines for directing management attention to staff practices.

Ultimately, the CMS and the RMS, like other environmental scales, attempt to capture "quality of life" dimensions. The success with which these two scales operationalize this concept remains to be proven when and if objective measures of client development can be attributed to them. Furthermore, selecting critical operational definitions of an adequate treatment environment is more or less a matter of preference and values.

Their utility for decisions regarding critical issues in the treatment of clients is rather limited. The tools, as a whole, seem more valuable at the administrative level for use in institutional reform and general corrective action. They may also be useful for staff in-service training and job description development.

Community Adjustment Scale

Authors Marsha Mailick Seltzer and Gary Seltzer	**Distributor** Educational Projects, Inc. 22 Hillard Street Cambridge, Massachusetts 02138
Alternative Version None	**Date** Not Specified
Revisions in Progress None	**Test Manual** Instructions for Community Adjustment Scale in *Context for Competence,* by Marsha Mailick Seltzer and Gary Seltzer, Educational Projects, Inc., Cambridge, Massachusetts, 1978

INTENDED PURPOSES

The purpose of the Community Adjustment Scale (CAS) is to assess how well a retarded adult is adjusting to life in the community. The components of community adjustment assessed are whether a person has the skills to act independently; whether a person actually uses his or her skills; whether the physical and social environment promotes the acquisition and performance of skills; and whether a person seems to be motivated to acquire and perform skills. A major goal of the scale is to be able to distinguish between skills and performance.

DOMAINS

The Community Adjustment Scale measures skills along eight domains within the four basic dimensions of skills, performance, environmental opportunity, and motivation. The domains include advanced personal care, housekeeping, communication, social adjustment, community participation, economic management, work, and agency utilization. There are a total of 452 items.

PROCEDURES

Data is collected on the Community Adjustment Scale by obtaining information from a person knowledgeable about the client. The scale contains a variety of items: open-ended (impressionistic) and fact-gathering questions, binary (yes/no) choices, and rating scales. The authors give no information about administration credentials or administration time.

No scores are reported. It is intended that an assessment of the individual's performance on scale items enables the evaluator to assess the person's skills along the four dimensions and to record and plan for remediation where deficits exist.

COSTS

Not available

REVIEW

CONTENT

The content of the scale is quite good in covering eight areas of community adjustment which appear to possess a high degree of construct and content validity. The content of the scale is not appropriate for assessing the community adjustment of persons with severe to profound developmental handicaps. It is intended primarily to assess persons who are capable of placement in the typical group home setting. Generally, items are stated clearly and appear relatively simple to administer and interpret.

The underlying assumption on which this scale is based is that the retarded client's capability to perform a wide range of skills associated with successful community adjustment will be strongly influenced by the motivation of the client and the opportunities to perform provided by his or her environment. The scale, therefore, juxtaposes the dimensions of skill mastery, performance, motivation, and environmental opportunity in reviewing the client's capabilities in each of the eight content areas outlined above.

While the scale offers a unique approach to reviewing the client's adaptation to community living, it also has a number of inherent shortcomings, including the following:

> *Subjectivity.* Many of the items used in the scale do not lend themselves to a completely objective response. For example, under house cleaning (II-E), the respondent is asked: "Does he/she regularly clean own bedroom and other rooms in the house, so that they usually look neat and well cared for?" Obviously, standards of neatness and cleanliness vary from person to person, depending on their cultural background and upbringing. Thus, responses to this and many similar questions

are open to cultural biases which could distort the results. The authors offer no data on interrater reliability and, it seems unlikely that acceptable scores could be obtained if such studies were conducted.

Distortion. The authors point out in the manual that "the interview format may not be the most advantageous method for assessing environmental opportunity," since the respondents (facility staff) "might have an investment in presenting the setting in the best possible light." They suggest that the effects of such response bias might be minimized by directly observing the environment or conducting reliability checks on the staff's responses. Such reliability checks might be of some assistance but they would not obviate the subjective nature of the process. It might be added that some level of response bias can be anticipated in answers to questions concerning skill mastery, performance and motivation, although, perhaps, this phenomenon will not be as pronounced in the latter areas. Unlike reliability checks on the environment, it will not be nearly as simple to validate the respondent's answers in these other dimensions of the scale.

Binary choice. The authors have generally been successful in structuring the items so they lend themselves to "either/or" responses. However, in some instances, what the authors refer to as the "fixed alternative method" of responding does not offer the respondent a means of reflecting nuances in the client's capabilities or performance. For example, under item I-D-1 (clothing care), the question is "does he/she know how to fold clothing and hang clothing upon hangers?" It is possible that a client may have mastered some simple folding tasks (e.g., folding socks) but not more complex tasks (e.g., folding long sleeved shirts). To cite another example (item I-E-2), a client may have mastered sweeping the floor and vacuuming the rug but may be unable to wash the floor effectively.

Sequencing. For the most part, the items are developmentally sequenced within each of the subdomains. However, there are a few instances in which the existing sequences seem questionable. For example, in the subdomain dealing with finding a job it would seem more appropriate if the question about asking friends and acquaintances preceded the more complex tasks of contacting an employment agency and filling out an application. Similarly, the questions under the subdomain of banking should be reordered so that cashing a paycheck appears first, maintaining a savings account, second, and maintaining a checking account, third.

One-year performance criteria. The authors' criterion for mastery of any particular skill is that the client "has independently (without prompts) used the skill at least once in the last year." While this criterion may be appropriate for certain types of skills, it is questionable that such a rate is sufficient to demonstrate the mastery of all skills. For example, given the difficulty in defining what constitutes interest, is a display of "interest in reading for pleasure" sufficient to demonstrate that a client has mastered the skill (item IV-A-2)? Or, looking at the opposite side of the question (i.e., performance), must a resident read a book, magazine, or newspaper for pleasure once a week in order to establish the fact that he can perform the task? Many normal adults would fail to meet that performance criterion.

Availability of training programs. Throughout the instrument, questions are raised about whether the residential facility offers its clients, who lack particular skills, a training program which will assist them in acquiring those skills. Yet, nowhere do the authors define their concept of a training program. Given the response bias mentioned above, some attempt should be made to specify the minimum elements of a structured training program; otherwise, responses to this question are likely to be less than helpful.

One of the unique aspects of this scale is its direct assessment of the individual's opportunity to perform various tasks. There is a separate environmental opportunity subscale which measures, in terms of each content domain, the extent to which individuals have the opportunity to perform the various skills and behaviors.

There is some question as to whether the domains of the test which assess skills, performance, environmental opportunity, and motivation to perform are really independent of one another. The authors were quite sensitive to this issue in the preliminary development of the scale, but there is still some question as to whether the information obtained through additional items in these four areas justifies required time and cost. There may be considerable redundancy in the skills and performance sections of the scale, for example. Future research should establish whether the additional time needed to gather information in these areas is beneficial.

ADMINISTRATION

One of the scale's most serious deficiencies is in the area of administration. While the instructions for administration are relatively simple, the proper use of the scale requires that essentially parallel items be administered in four separate areas: skills, consistency of performance, environmental opportunity or the opportunity to perform, and motivation. In the preliminary development of the test, an effort was made to reduce the redundancy in content across these four areas of assessment, but an inspection of the skills content shows a good deal of overlap, especially between the skills and performance areas of the test. In the instrument's present form, the amount of information gained from assessing environmental opportunity and motivation may not be sufficient to justify the time required to complete the instrument. The present version of the test appears, therefore, to represent considerable costs in terms of the time required for assessment in relationship to the information that can be used for program planning and evaluation of client progress.

Compared with many other assessment tools, this scale would appear to be relatively costly and time-consuming to administer. However, the results may be worth the additional cost and time if the resident staff gains insights into the client's motivation and/or the impact of his or her environment. The needs for such data should be a crucial determinant of the user's decision to employ this scale.

INTERPRETABILITY

This scale would appear to yield relatively imprecise data in behavioral terms, that is, there are no normative scores provided in the test manual, only general behavioral statements that allow the examiner to assess the extent of the person's community adjustment. Nonetheless, it might be useful in gaining insights into the interaction between the client's skills acquisition, performance, and motivation and the surrounding environment.

The authors suggest that the instrument may be used as either a research tool or as a clinical tool. In program settings, the authors claim that the CAS "can be used to generate a clinical profile of a resident." This profile can be used to determine "the resident's present level of functioning and prescriptively (identify) environmental and motivational interventions that would improve independent performance." Since no provision is made for scoring, the scale, norms, percentiles, and graphic displays are not provided. The authors, however, do provide a form which may be used in developing a clinical profile from the CAS.

Few instructions are given in the available manual for interpretation and use of information gained from the administration of the Community Adjustment Scale. Further work should be undertaken to translate the measures of performance more easily into suggestions for training and environmental modification. With some additional investment, the interpretability of performance from the scale could be substantively improved.

TEST DEVELOPMENT

Items from other adaptive behavior scales (the AAMD Adaptive Behavior Scale, the Progress Assessment Chart, the PASS and the PARC project measures) were included in the initial draft of the CAS because "it was felt that the content of the other scales of adaptive behavior was fairly inclusive." The draft instrument was field tested with a sample of 34 retarded adults residing in group homes, institutions, or their family homes. The results of the field test were subject to a correlation analysis, a factor analysis, and a path analysis. Based on these analyses and face validity review by 14 experienced and knowledgeable professionals, the draft instrument was extensively revised.

Although it is clear from the manual that considerable time and effort went into the development of the scale, the original field sample of clients was small (N=34) and selected primarily due to their accessibility rather than because of any statistical sampling basis. Under the circumstances, further validation studies appear to be necessary before the validity and reliability of the instrument are fully established. While other means were used in test development (e.g., the use of an expert panel to rate the value of test items), there is insufficient detail provided in the manual to indicate clearly all the possible procedures that were used in developing test items. For example, very little information is provided on the source of possible items and the extent to which existing scales contributed to the content of the scale. One of the most positive aspects of the scale was the use of path analysis and factor analyses to make modifications in the design of items and in the test structure. Such procedures represent a very promising approach to test development and, with further cross-validation of results, may yield a very useful scale to assess the community adjustment skills of mentally retarded people.

RELIABILITY

Only one form of reliability is reported in the test manual, a measure of internal consistency. Measures of internal consistency using alpha coefficients are reported for the different content areas and domains of the test. The alpha coefficients for these various content areas and domains appear to fall generally into an acceptable range, with somewhat lower reliabilities obtained for the areas of environmental assessment and motivation. The alpha reliabilities for the skills and performance sections appear particularly strong. However, the coefficients were run on a very small sample of subjects (N=32) and no cross-validation was used in computing reliability statistics for the final Community Adjustment Scale subscale scores, that is, alpha reliabilities were run on the preliminary sample and then repeated on the same sample in assessing internal consistency reliabilities for the final subscale scores. The American Psychological Association's manual of standards for test construction clearly regards this approach as unacceptable; an independent sample should have been selected to establish the reliability of scores.

There are other forms of reliability which should be considered in establishing the stability of the CAS. It would seem to be of some advantage to use test-retest reliabilities to establish the stability of the scale and to determine whether different respondents would produce relatively similar information for the same individuals (interrespondent agreement).

VALIDITY

The Community Adjustment Scale appears to possess minimally acceptable validity, although the manual reviewed was clearly inadequate in this area. There is some evidence of construct validity for the concept of community adjustment and the content of the scale, as well as empirical support for the construct of community adjustment obtained through factor analysis and path analysis studies. Unfortunately, the data for these analyses are derived from an extremely small sample of subjects who may not represent the community adjustment status of mildly retarded adults. Therefore, construct validity of the scale should await more detailed cross-validation studies on larger samples of subjects.

There is one additional source of validity used in the development of the Community Adjustment Scale. A panel of 18 persons with expertise in the area of mental retardation was asked to rate the appropriateness of each of the scale items as an assessment of community adjustment. Apparently, decisions regarding the final content of the scale were based in part on these ratings of knowledgeable professionals.

Another possible measure of validity for the scale is the differences in performances found in a study of approximately 150 adults from groups living in institutions and less restrictive living arrangements. It was a general finding of the CAS that persons living in less restrictive settings achieved generally higher scores than those in more restrictive settings. These results could be construed as an indirect measure of predictive validity.

Additional work should be conducted to establish more definitely the validity of the Community Adjustment Scale. More work on larger samples of subjects, assessments of the relationship between the Community Adjustment Scale and other measures of adaptive behavior and community adjustment, and predictive studies of later adjustment and work performance would seem advisable.

SUMMARY OF UTILITY

The Community Adjustment Scale would appear to be useful in helping supervisors and direct care staff in community residences understand the complex interactions which take place between skills development, skills utilization, motivation, and the programming environment. It also should assist such staff in preparing for more sophisticated and targeted intervention strategies.

With the resolution of selected issues in reliability, validity, and interpretability, the CAS can be useful in assessing the community adjustment status of mildly retarded adults. However, it can be of only limited use with more severely retarded and multiply handicapped clients in community settings. Since there is some evidence that such clients are likely to make up an increasing proportion of community placements in the years ahead (as states make further reductions in their institutional populations), consideration should be given to either revising the items so they are more applicable to severely retarded and multiply handicapped clients living in community facilities or developing a subscale applicable to this group.

The CAS should be regarded as a promising experimental measure rather than a finished product. There is considerable work needed to establish clearly the validity and value of the scale as a measure of community adjustment. There is also the need for further work to determine the extent to which the scale yields consistent and reliable measurement and to provide information and suggestions to potential users regarding the interpretation and application of test results for evaluating client progress and designing needed training programs.

Program Analysis of Service Systems

Authors Wolf Wolfensberger, Linda Glenn	**Distributor** National Institute on Mental Retardation York University Campus 4700 Keele Street Downsview, Toronto, Ontario M3J1P3
Alternative Version None	**Dates** 1969, 1975
Revisions in Progress Material for periodic revisions is being collected.	**Test Manual** PASS 3 Field Manual Wolf Wolfensberger and Linda Glenn, 1975 PASS 3 Handbook Wolf Wolfensberger and Linda Glenn, 1975

INTENDED PURPOSES

The Program Analysis of Service Systems (PASS 3) is extensively (but not completely) based on normalization concepts and used to evaluate quality of services, largely as related to normalization principles. It claims to apply universal human service principles in objectively quantifying the quality of a wide range of human service projects, systems, and agencies. As such, it is presented as both a tool for evaluating the adequacy and quality of human service programs and for teaching service personnel through the specification of normalization and other principles. An optional rating instrument, FUNDET, is structured, administered, and scored analogously to PASS for the purpose of funding determinations. PASS and FUNDET scores can be combined. The authors claim that those service systems which might be evaluated with the PASS include child development and special education programs, treatment and training centers, special camps, sheltered workshops, residential homes and hospitals, prisons, and reformatories.

DOMAINS

Fifty PASS 3 items are divided into two major areas: ideology and administration. Major subcategories of the ideological area include physical and social integration, age and culture-appropriate interpretations and structures, developmental growth orientation, quality of setting, ideology-related administration, human service orientation, and regional priorities. The administrative area is subdivided into manpower considerations, and internal administration and financial aspects of operational effectiveness. The 50 PASS elements are rated at defined levels on a scale of 3 (1 item), 4 (8 items), 5 (34 items), or 6 (7 items).

PROCEDURES

According to the authors of the PASS, 21 of the ratings are potentially assessable at a distance, 23 are most apt to require site visits, and the remaining 6 fall between these two categories. Ratings rely on inspection of facilities, program proposals, and other documents, interviews with staff, and observation. A team of no less than three trained raters who may be human service consumers, citizens with volunteer service, or other experienced nonprofessionals, administer the instrument following an extensive five-day PASS training workshop. Administration time varies widely depending on the size of the unit being evaluated and the number of evaluators involved, but would typically require two to four days.

COSTS

PASS set $ 10.50   ($9.50 in Canada)
    (includes field manual and handbook)
Training, introductory 5-day workshop 135.00
    advanced 6-day workshop   165.00

REVIEW

CONTENT

The PASS was one of the first attempts to develop an instrument which evaluates the quality of services. The authors have been careful to maintain current content based on normalization principles.

A short version of PASS was developed by John O'Brien (1977) and based on five PASS factors only. However, this revised version is not recommended by its author for use as a scale, but rather as a staff training tool.

The authors state that, "PASS does not assess every conceivable aspect and feature of service." They go on to say it is necessary to collect additional information. Nonetheless, the major items have been identified at this "stage of the art." For the purposes for which this instrument was developed, the domains appear comprehensive, although some items are vague.

ADMINISTRATION

The manual is comprehensive. Examples are provided and instructions and content are clearly stated. However, because of the scope of the instrument, training for quality control is a must.

INTERPRETABILITY

Scoring and interpretation of the instrument are fairly good. The supplemental report clarifying ratings and alternatives provides an advantage because it yields alternative actions for improving a score. Also worthwhile are the feedback meetings with various staff. This follow-up strengthens the instrument's utility as an assessment and training tool.

TEST DEVELOPMENT

For the most part the PASS was developed on empirical evidence obtained from assessments in numerous services. The system was and is open to feedback. The authors were asked to develop an instrument to evaluate service quality and funding basis. The content of PASS 1 was determined through analysis of the concept of normalization. An empirical approach was used to develop the second and third versions of the PASS, as well as some reliability and validity tests. Care was taken to improve the three versions of the various dimensions. The major field tests resulted from PASS 2 training of raters and trainers. In each version of the PASS, consideration was given to difficulty, sequencing, and consistency. Items have been dropped, added, refined, and rearranged. Plans call for continued work based on both research and feedback from the field.

RELIABILITY

The reliability of the PASS has not been investigated extensively. The handbook provides no reliability data obtained in the authors' own development efforts. However, a study of PASS 2 by R. J. Flynn (1975) was based on 102 service providers and gives strong evidence of the internal consistency of PASS total score (a coefficient alpha of .89). This level of internal consistency is quite adequate. However, a second aspect of reliability in rating scales is interrater agreement. No investigation of this type of reliability has been conducted. Because of the subjectivity inherent in assigning levels to each of the PASS items, this type of reliability could be a problem. The use of multi-person site visit teams and the consequent assignment of ratings by consensus (as recommended by the authors) would minimize this problem. However, this method increases the administration and scoring times and, therefore, the overall cost of assessment. The authors are sensitive to this problem and discuss it at length in their handbook and field manual, and at least one research study addressing this problem is in progress.

VALIDITY

In assessing the validity of the PASS, it is essential to remember that the scale was developed from a particular philosophical viewpoint. Scores obtained measure the degree to which a service program reflects the principles of normalization as explicated by Wolfensberger (1972). Consequently, many scales are highly value-laden. For example, although an optional item, R142 (age group priorities) gives the highest level to programs serving infants and the lowest to those serving adults. This particular aspect of Wolfensberger's concept may not be consistent with the values of some providers. This means that the potential user of the PASS must accept the ideological basis from which the scale was developed.

Empirical assessment of the validity of the PASS has consisted mainly of correlational studies. Some compare PASS scores with subjective assessments of program characteristics, which is a fairly weak validation method. An interesting finding reported in the handbook was that the PASS correlates with data on the number of clients improving in status within an institution. This is construed to be evidence that programs which attend more to normalization are more effective and, further, that such programs can be identified with PASS. This is an important finding, and it is unfortunate that the handbook does not give any details of the study which provided this result.

Two recent unpublished studies of PASS validity were identified by the author. These studies both are based on the same population (245 residents of 96 small community homes in southern California) and used raters whose previous training was not clearly specified. Because of the narrowness and size of the population, conclusions must be made with caution.

One study was a factor analysis of PASS items which yielded six factors strongly supportive of the major PASS rationales (normalization, administration, environmental blending with the neighborhood, ideology-related administration, location/proximity, and comfort/appearance). This factor structure strongly supports several major PASS rationales, but the likelihood that the raters were not adequately prepared was borne out by the fact that they had scoring difficulties and were not even able to compute the total score without considerable mathematical errors. A repetition of the factor analysis using only the levels instead of the scores yielded the same factor structure. From this, the author concluded that the complex weighted scoring system may warrant revision, although an alternate conclusion might be that extensive training is essential.

The same population was used for a study of the correlation of PASS ratings with AAMD Adaptive Behavior Scale scores for the residents over a three-year period. The greatest individual gains observed were found in facilities with high PASS scores on the factors of environmental blending, location, and comfort and appearance. Location and proximity of services was particularly high related to gains by older residents,which suggests that access to resources may be more important for adults who may be able to utilize them on their own. Gains in self-help skills were particularly related to scores in comfort and appearance of the facility, regardless of resident's age or level of retardation. Paradoxically, there was an inverse relationship between ideology-related administration scores and progress in personal self-sufficiency.

Self-sufficiency gains were particularly related to administrative policies, location, and comfort and appearance. The authors of the studies noted that, with limited resources, efforts spent in some of the ideology-related administrative areas may have been conducted at the cost of clinical quality. It is interesting that this once more underlines the dilemma between short-term and long-term benefits, or clinical versus systemic benefits. Strangely enough, the normalization factor, and to some extent the administrative policies factor, did not play a very significant role.

In summary, the validity of the PASS for measuring the extent to which a program adheres in its practices to the ideal model implied by the PASS appears quite high. However, conclusive empirical evidence of its theoretical claims, which can be phrased in correlation terms, is generally lacking. The handbook does not provide enough information to assess even the small amount of data it provides. Consequently, more research is called for and is suggested by the authors.

SUMMARY OF UTILITY

The utility of the PASS is found in supportive training and related software. After training, raters are equipped with both a process for assessment and feedback, and a functional assessment and interpretation tool. The instrument has high utility for making decisions concerning the location, initiation, and improvement of services because various decision makers at various levels are not only provided with ratings but alternatives and the expertise of the raters. It is also highly applicable for the local administrative unit. The instrument has potential to be used at the state and national levels. The FUNDET portion provides a fairly good method for evaluating the existing or potential funding of a project or service. In evaluating the utility of the PASS for a given provider, one must consider the costs and time involved (which are quite high) in training staff and administering the instrument. The expenses may well be worthwhile, given the unique perspective which the PASS offers. However, potential users should weigh the cost and time factors in terms of the information which they hope to obtain from the PASS.

Caution should be exercised in the interpretation of the concept of this instrument's quality. Quality, as operationalized here, is restricted to the concepts of normalization and integration of clients and services. As such, corrective action to improve quality of services based on assessment should not be restricted to the results obtained from the administration of this scale alone.

The potential for improving the quality of human services in the area of humanization is extremely high. This is not only due to the instrument but the backup systems of training, research and development, interpretation, and follow-up. The instrument also provides a functional approach for determining if a project should be funded with the FUNDET section. The utility of determining cost benefits and improvements across agencies and over time is highly desirable. Given the stage of instrument development and the state of the art, the tool should be considered exemplary. It would seem that research and development will continue and the instrument and support systems will continue to be improved. Consequently, the PASS must be viewed as the most sophisticated existing instrument for the quantitative assessment of program quality across a wide range of services and can therefore be extremely valuable to public sector decision makers as they address decisions of funding allocation and prioritization.

Vulpé Assessment Battery

Author	Distributor
Shirley German Vulpé	National Institute on Mental Retardation Kinsmen NIMR Building 4700 Keele Street Downsview, Ontario M3J 1P3
Alternative Version None	**Dates** 1969, 1977
Revisions in Progress None	**Test Manual** In Vulpé Assessment Battery

INTENDED PURPOSES

The Vulpé Assessment Battery (VAB) is a developmental assessment procedure intended for atypically developing children from birth through six years. It is designed to provide a test of competencies in various developmental areas; include a sequential teaching approach in the assessment process; provide analysis of the interaction among developmental skill areas and information processing mechanisms; indicate program goals and techniques to meet the needs of individual children; and provide an accountability scheme applicable to assessment, developmental programs, and service delivery systems. According to the author, this assessment was specifically designed to be reasonably priced, easily transportable, and easy to use by persons with a variety of educational backgrounds. It is meant to be adaptable to the needs of both the child and the tester, to be used alone or in combination with other assessment procedures or as a comprehensive or specific assessment.

DOMAINS

The Vulpé Assessment Battery is divided into eight developmental skill areas (domains) and one environmental domain. They are basic senses and functions, gross motor behaviors, fine motor behaviors, language behaviors, cognitive processes and specific concepts, the organization of behavior, activities of daily living, and environment. The basic test contains 1,127 items. The author claims that the VAB includes as many items as possible within each age group and skill area in order to provide opportunity for an in-depth picture of the child's developmental functioning pattern.

PROCEDURES

Data about an individual client are collected by direct observation of the child or by obtaining information from a person knowledgeable about the child's behavior. The test consists of a series of tasks requiring the various skills assessed along the above domains.

The author gives no estimate of administration time; she states that the time required will vary according to the child, the environment, and the tester. According to the author, anyone who has had some experience working with handicapped children can use the battery, including parents, volunteers, and caregivers from a wide variety of backgrounds, training and professions. The author states, however, that the reflex test part of the assessment should only be administered by a qualified therapist.

293

An assessment, rather than a score, is recorded by this instrument. This performance analysis/developmental assessment gives a total profile of the individual child and provides the basis for designing an individual program plan.

COSTS

Complete battery	$15.00 in Canada
	17.00 outside Canada

The following sections of VAB are available separately for use with individual clients:

gross motor, fine motor, auditory language, activities of daily living, organization of behavior, and cognitive behavior

birth to 12 months	$ 3.50 in Canada
	4.00 outside Canada
1 to 3 years	3.50 in Canada
	4.00 outside Canada
3 to 6 years	3.50 in Canada
	4.00 outside Canada

basic senses and functions, assessment of posture and mobility, developmental reflexes, assessment of the environment, functional tests of muscle strength, motor planning, and balance.

For all ages	$ 3.50 in Canada
	4.00 outside Canada

REVIEW

CONTENT

Items are appropriate to the domains in which they fall, although several of the domains seem to overlap. Basic test items are sequenced, although the testing of senses and environmental measures do not lend themselves to sequencing.

The basic test includes six domains with 43 subdomains and approximately 1,127 items. Several of the domains seem to be measuring the same thing; for example, the social interaction scale contains items assessing awareness of rules, courtesy, sharing, etc. Under organization of behavior-internal control, there are items dealing with control over temperment, verbalization of rules of acceptable behavior, etc. Cognitive processes, shape concepts assesses items related to putting puzzles together, and under body concepts, completing pictures. Although clinically there may be some differences in these items, it may be that through a factor analysis some items could be dropped and others merged. According to the author, the problem of overlapping items is a reflection of the fact that many activities involve more than one developmental skill. The cross-referencing of duplicate items in different areas of the assessment was intended by the author to help cope with this problem by eliminating the need of testing an item more than once.

This is one of the few scales that seeks to gain descriptive data as well as test scores. The environment domain seeks to evaluate the characteristics of the learning environment including both the physical aspects and characteristics of the caregivers. A system for evaluating the senses of vision, touch, dominance, motor planning, muscle tone, etc., which are usually only evaluated by a neurologist or physcial or occupational therapist, should be useful for other members of an interdisciplinary team serving a multiply handicapped child. Unfortunately, these two domains do not lend themselves to quantification.

ADMINISTRATION

There are more than 1,100 items on the basic test. A child with a wide scatter and a developmental age of four to five years would have to be administered many of these items. This would probably take around three hours (or else an objective and well-informed individual could tell the examiner about the child). If the examiner was very knowledgeable about the test and could organize the items so that several answers to questions were obtained simultaneously, it might cut the time down somewhat. Because of the overlapping of several domains, it is possible that the test could be shortened if a factor analysis indicated that several of the items were measuring the same thing.

To fully appreciate and utilize the test results, one should have a strong background in normal growth and development, including normal reflexes and abnormal reflex patterns of the handicapped child. Although the author claims that the test can be used by any person with some experience working with handicapped children, it is the reviewer's opinion that graduate training in a profession—occupational therapy, physical therapy, neurodevelopmental psychology or speech pathology—is necessary to administer most sections of this instrument.

INTERPRETABILITY

Little information is given about interpreting the child's performance on various tests. The battery was designed to be used along
with standardized tests which would provide averages and
comparisons of groups of children. It is assumed that the examiner
or the supervisor will have training in neurodevelopmental aspects
of preschool children and can bring their own knowledge to bear on
interpreting and using the results. Test items were selected from
research and treatment literature. Therefore, the test user needs to
be aware of that literature in order to use the scale meaningfully.

TEST DEVELOPMENT

Although much work went into developing this test (in terms of
literature review, clinical experience, etc.), it does not appear that
any systematic field testing of the items or statistical evaluation
(such as factor analysis) of the test itself was conducted. It has not
been tested on a normative population; developmental levels
assigned to individual items come from the data of others. This scale
greatly needs a series of studies which would evaluate the individual
items, reliability, and validity, and explore ways in which this test
might be shortened.

RELIABILITY

It is likely that reliability studies would find the reliability of the
instrument quite good. This is based on the fact that most of the
items appear in available clinical exams and in other test
instruments that have been found reliable. Except for the use of two
judges to score a single child (agreement in 95% of 38 test items),
little reliability assessment has been done on the scale. One study by
the author found a similar level of interrater agreement.

VALIDITY

No validity studies have been done on this instrument although
many of the items have been studied in clinical practice and in other
tests. The author accepts the validity of items reported by other test
developers (from which the items were selected). There is a good
bibliography given, but users would have to locate and study this
material themselves. This instrument obviously has face validity. If
a scoring system was devised to produce domain and total scores, it
would seem to be more useful and be easier to use.

SUMMARY OF UTILITY

This test represents an attempt to reduce many behaviors observed by neurologists and therapists in clinical evaluations to an objective test situation. The test does require a considerable amount of staff sophistication to be used wisely. For the purposes indicated by the author, neurodevelopmental assessment of handicapped children whose development falls in the birth to six level (particularly birth to three level), the Vulpé is client-oriented and not system-oriented since it does not give domain or total scores which can be compared.

The test is clearly uneven in quality and somewhat confusing in its organization. A major limitation in its use is that it requires well-trained judgement to use it meaningfully. The number of test items ranges in the different domains from 44 to 206. Some domains have items which go to the six-year level while others go only to the two-year level. The test as a whole evaluates the birth to two-year-old child much better than the five- or six-year-old.

This test should be quite useful to physical therapists, occupational therapists, speech pathologists or child development personnel working with the preschool handicapped child. It would be useful in planning and evaluating an individual program for each individual child. Because of the lack of summary scores, it would be unwieldy for group comparisons or for assessing groups of children to evaluate programs and services as a whole. It would be most helpful if a normative sample could be tested with this instrument and a scoring system developed to produce summary scores. This would improve its utility both in evaluating an individual child's progress and evaluating group and program effectiveness.

References

Commission on Accreditation of Rehabilitation Facilities. *Standards Manual for Rehabilitation Facilities*. Chicago, Illinois, 1978.

Government Studies and Systems. *Model Standards to Assess the Quality of Services and Programs for Persons with Developmental Disabilities*. Philadelphia, Pennsylvania, November 1, 1977.

Joint Commission on the Accreditation of Hospitals. *Standards for Services for Developmentally Disabled Individuals*. Accreditation Council for Services for Mentally Retarded and Other Developmentally Disabled Persons, Draft 3, September 20, 1977.

Weigerink, R. and Simeonsson, R. "Behavioral Assessment and the Developmentally Disabled: A Review." In *The Feasibility of Product and Outcome Measurement in Quality Assurance for Services and the Developmentally Disabled*. Government Studies and Systems, Philadelphia, Pennsylvania, May 11, 1977.

Characteristics of the Treatment Environment

Goffman, E. *Asylums: Essays on the Social Situation of Mental Patients and Other Inmates*. New York: Doubleday, 1961.

Silverstein, A.B., McLain, R.E., Hubbell, M., and Brownlee, L. "Characteristics of the Treatment Environment: A Factor Analytic Study." *Educational and Psychological Measurement*, 1977, *37*, 367-371.

Child Management Scale and Residential Management Scale

Eyman, R.K., Silverstein, A.B., R.E., and Miller, C. In P. Mittler (Ed.), *Research to Practice in Mental Retardation* (Vol. 1). Baltimore: University Park Press, 1977.

Goffman, E. *Asylums: Essays on the Social Situation of Mental Patients and Other Inmates*. New York: Doubleday, 1961.

King, R.D. and Raynes, N.V. "An Operational Measure of Inmate Management in Residential Institutions." *Social Science and Medicine*, 1968, *2*(1), 41-53.

Program Analysis of Service Systems

Flynn, R.J. *Assessing Human Service Quality with PASS 2: An Empirical Analysis of 102 Service Program Evaluations*. Toronto: National Institute on Mental Retardation, 1975.

O'Brien, J. "Normalization-oriented Short Form of PASS (experimental)." Unpublished manuscript, 1977.

Wolfensberger, W. *The Principle of Normalization in Human Services*. Toronto: National Institute on Mental Retardation, 1972.

Chapter 5

The State of the Art of Assessing Developmental Progress

ANALYSIS OF REVIEW FINDINGS AND RECOMMENDATIONS

This final chapter looks across the instruments reviewed in order to assess the overall state of the art of measuring developmental progress. Based on the reviews and ratings given the individual instruments, a summary of findings, implications, and issues is presented.

The review findings are organized according to the major dimensions on which instruments were evaluated in the individual reviews. Following the findings for each of these dimensions a list of recommendations regarding future instrumentation efforts is presented, along with a summary profile which describes the most frequent characteristics of instruments, as well as those aspects most notably lacking. In the final section of this chapter the implications of these review findings for the design and operation of statewide evaluation systems are discussed.

Content

In general, the content of most instruments was judged by their reviewers to be acceptable, very good, or exemplary. No single instrument reviewed covered all of the domains with which we were concerned; some focused on only one domain and others attempted to obtain an overall picture of the individual's functioning by touching on a variety of related domains. The domains most frequently covered (in one-half of the instruments or more) were communication, socialization, and self-care. The areas of functioning least frequently measured (in one-third of the instruments or less) were environmental characteristics, maladaptive behavior, and emotional development.

It is not surprising that the areas of communication, independent living, and self-care are so popular in these instruments. These domains represent areas of functioning considered vital for the community adjustment of disabled persons. The lack of attention paid to other domains, however, is disconcerting. The scarcity of instruments measuring environmental characteristics shows that the role of the environment in fostering the development of clients has not been adequately examined. Most of the instruments which do measure environmental characteristics are relatively new, and as su ı, are technically not as advanced as many of the client assessment tools. It is likely that more instruments of this type are or will be developing as the state of the art in this field advances.

The lack of instruments measuring emotional development and maladaptive behaviors is also noteworthy. The behavioral and emotional problems of developmentally disabled persons are often their most difficult handicaps. Recent studies have shown that these kinds of problems pose the biggest obstacles to effective integration of clients into jobs, schools, and communities. Perhaps because behavioral and emotional problems are so difficult to manage, little has been done in developing instruments appropriate to these problems. It is likely that adequate instrumentation in this area might help to focus on effective treatment strategies for behavior and emotional problems.

The quality of the coverage of these domains varied widely across instruments. The domains which were most frequently rated by their reviewers as adequately covered or better (i.e., judged adequate, very good, or exemplary in 80 percent or more of the cases) were self-care, independent living, socialization, and communication. The domains judged to be least adequately covered (i.e., judged poor or unacceptable in 25 to 40 percent of the cases) were work habits and work adjustment, learning and problem solving, maladaptive behaviors, emotional development, and physical development.

In over three-fourths of the instruments, items were judged to be appropriately placed within the domains covered. In terms of the quality of the behavioral specification of items, about three-fourths of the instruments were judged to be adequate, very good, or exemplary.

The authors claimed that items were sequenced in a developmental order within domains in more than half of the instruments. However, in many of these cases, the instrument reviewers felt that the sequencing was inappropriate or inadequate. Frequently, reviewers claimed that the levels of items within a given sequence were uneven, that is, some distinctions between levels were extremely fine whereas others in the same sequence were too gross. These problems in sequencing have a definite effect on the scoring and interpretation of test results, especially when the scale is to be used to develop programs for individual clients or to measure their progress.

Approximately one-fourth of the instruments contained items which evidenced bias or stereotypes or which might be considered offensive to particular groups. These items took several forms. The most frequent form of bias was items inappropriate or not applicable for physically handicapped persons. For example, many items related to independent living require mobility of the individual (e.g., use of public transportation, participation in community social and recreational programs, going shopping, etc.). Most instruments did not take into account the presence of a physical handicap in scoring and interpreting such items. Of those instruments which did consider this factor, they generally did so by instructing testers to skip items not applicable to physically handicapped persons. However, the client's score is affected and the applicability of any normative data is reduced when items are skipped.

A second form of bias in some tests was an assumption of deviance, particularly in instruments measuring maladaptive behaviors. Some items were phrased in a manner or direction which excluded the possibility of normal client behaviors or skills; the only response alternatives were varying levels of negative or deviant behavior. Tests including such items are considered objectionable because they promote the negative stereotyping of developmentally disabled persons.

In five of the instruments the concepts underlying the scale or items within the scale were considered outdated and not relevant to contemporary mores. Most of these cases involved ratings of maladaptive behaviors no longer necessarily considered deviant—particularly in the areas of sexual behaviors and attitudes and appropriate masculine and feminine behaviors and roles.

Administration

Almost all of the instruments were rated as acceptable or better in terms of administrative ease and cost/benefits. Most of the instruments consisted of rating scale items or checklist items. The sources of data in the overwhelming majority of cases were observations of individual clients and interviews with informants about the clients. Five instruments involved observations of the settings of clients, nine were based on interviews with clients, and one was intended to be self-administered by clients.

In most cases, trained professionals or other staff persons are intended to administer the instrument, being responsible for the collection of data and completion of forms. In only nine cases did the manual or supporting materials suggest parents as potential administrators of the tests. Of those instruments which specified the general professional credentials required of the persons administering the instrument, about one-half required training or experience in the service delivery field and about one-half did not require any special credentials. Either extensive formal training in test administration of the instrument or general experience with instruments of a similar nature was recommended with approximately one-half of the instruments reviewed. For the other half, instructions in the test manual were considered sufficient, with practice or no particular practice required.

Of those instruments with test manuals available, most were rated as acceptable or better in terms of comprehensiveness and clarity. Although the estimated administration time required to complete the instrument was not provided in most manuals and materials, reviewers estimated that administration would require 40 minutes or less in about one-half of the instruments. In about three-fourths of the cases, administration time required 90 minutes or less. Of the remaining instruments requiring more than 90 minutes to administer, estimates for administration of these ranged up to 5½ hours.

Interpretation

In terms of the interpretability of the data provided by instruments, most were rated acceptable, very good, or exemplary. A total score was reported for about half of the instruments. Also, for about half of the instruments, scores were reported for each domain. Other types of scoring procedures used with some instruments included scores for each subdomain, scores for each item, and graphed profiles. Graphic display procedures were considered extremely helpful in those few cases where they were available.

Appropriate norms for the instrument were sometimes lacking. For example, some instruments intended for use with all levels of retardation had been normed only on mildly and moderately retarded persons. Or sometimes an instrument intended for use in community as well as institutional settings was based only on reference groups of institutionalized clients. The lack of appropriate norms prevented adequate interpretation of test data in some cases.

Utility

The overall utility of more than 80 percent of the instruments was rated to be acceptable or better. Assessment instruments were evaluated in terms of their utility for certain specific purposes. Instruments were most useful at the individual client level and least useful at the program or systems level. About two thirds of the instruments were rated as acceptable or better for individual plan development and monitoring client progress. About one-half of the instruments were considered acceptable or better for screening needs assessment and overall program planning. The utility of instruments for overall program evaluation was most limited—only seven were rated as acceptable or better for that purpose.

Some of the characteristics of instruments which were cited as extremely useful for the development of individual plans and monitoring of client progress included:

fine discriminations and sequences of the behaviors measured;

sensitivity to development of the individual over time;

easy translation or incorporation of data into developmental goals and objectives for individual clients; and

high reliability and validity.

303

Instruments appropriate for screening and needs assessment did not need to be so finely attuned to individual development and progress. Screening instruments were generally broader in scope than those used for individual plan development and client progress measurement. They often were less time-consuming and less costly to administer since the data which they gathered were less detailed. Instruments appropriate for program planning and program evaluation generally had the following characteristics:

quantitative data was easily aggregated into group totals or means;

data could be compared or converted across programs; and

limited time and costs required to collect and interpret the data.

Most of the instruments specifically geared to individual plan development or client progress monitoring were not considered appropriate for overall program planning and evaluation purposes because the individualized data were too detailed, difficult to aggregate, unwieldy to compare across programs, costly, and time-consuming to collect. Similarly, most program planning and evaluation tools yielded data which were not sufficiently detailed or reliable to be useful at the client level. However, there were some instruments which managed to offer some utility at both the client and program level by avoiding the extremes of too much or too little data. In general, however, no instrument was equally appropriate for all purposes.

Two additional purposes which some instruments served well were as research and staff training aids. Some instruments were considered potentially useful in research settings, that is, in efforts to advance the state-of-the-art of research related to client or program evaluation. These instruments were generally recent developments, not yet field tested or advanced enough in development to be applied in treatment programs, but promising enough to be explored further in research settings. And many of the instruments, particularly the environmental ones, were often cited as being useful in staff training, especially in the areas of management and policy making.

The appropriateness of existing instruments for specific populations and settings was also examined. The overwhelming majority of client assessment instruments are intended for use specifically with mentally retarded persons, and most of these are oriented toward mildly and moderately retarded persons. The types and levels of items appropriate for more severely retarded persons are often quite different from those appropriate for the less handicapped. For example, scales appropriate for severely handicapped persons must include a large number of items in the basic areas of self-care and communication. The gradations of behaviors and skills within these items must be quite fine in order to be sensitive to changes in the development of severely handicapped persons over time. In contrast, mildly and moderately retarded persons require scales with items focusing on higher level skills and behaviors such as independent living and work habits and adjustment.

Although some client assessment instruments are intended to be used with persons of all disabilities (e.g., nonspecified developmental disabilities, special needs, impairments, etc.), there were few instruments identified to be used with specific disabilities other than mental retardation.

For example, only four instruments were identified as appropriate for persons with emotional disturbances, two for multiple handicaps, and one for cerebral palsy. Individuals with these specific disabilities may have unique needs in terms of test item content (e.g., items sensitive and appropriate to the communication skills of a person with cerebral palsy or the emotional development of an autistic child) or in terms of test administration procedures (e.g., physical requirements of test setting). In terms of coverage of developmentally disabled persons, it is evident that mentally retarded persons are most adequately covered by existing instruments. Other groups included within the developmental disabilities rubric are least adequately covered, for example, persons with epilepsy, autism, or cerebral palsy. Not only are these subgroups inadequately covered, they are often, as mentioned earlier, discriminated against by existing tests which are biased against physically disabled persons.

In terms of age, the majority of instruments are intended for children and young adults. Once persons reach adulthood, there are fewer instruments available for assessment purposes. Instruments appropriate for adults may focus on different items and levels of skills than child-oriented instruments. Whereas instruments for children generally contain items appropriate to school, home, and play situations, instruments for adults focus more on community living and independent functioning, work behaviors and skills.

There seems to be a wide variety of instruments appropriate for use in institutional and community settings. About half of the instruments reviewed were developed and are considered appropriate for institutional settings; fourteen of these are intended as well for use in community settings. However, items appropriate for institutional settings may be irrelevant or inappropriate to community settings and vice versa. For example, the kinds of social and communication skills and behaviors considered acceptable by a resident in an institution may be regarded as unacceptable on the "outside." And on the contrary, the independent living and community skills required of a person living in a community residence may not be appropriate or even permitted in an institutional setting.

Test Development

In assessing the quality of a scale's psychometric development, reviewers considered all aspects of the initial development and subsequent field testing of an instrument. The extent to which authors provided evidence that a rational basis (either empirical or theoretical) was used initially to generate items was important, as was evidence of field testing and subsequent revision of the instrument with a developmentally disabled population. Of the instruments reviewed, about half were judged to be adequate or better with respect to their development.

Most instruments were subjected to a variety of field tests in their developmental phase. However, evidence of the specific role played by the field testing in development (e.g., item analysis or simple rewriting of items or instructions to improve their clarity) was often lacking. The authors simply claim a scale has been "field tested".

The generalizability of the setting in which the field testing was performed is another common problem. Many scales were developed for use by a single service provider, often a residential institution, and the instrument was developed by the institution's staff and field tested on its client population. Since these populations are not often described in much detail, it is difficult to determine the extent to which their responses are representative of a larger developmentally disabled population. Further, given that many scales had their developers present during the testing (conducted in an institution with which the developers were very familiar), there could be some degree of observer bias in the testing as well as a tendency of the authors to write for specific characteristics of the environment.

Related to the above issues is the original intent of the test developers. Many scales reviewed were initially developed for local, not broad, application. Others were developed for research purposes (and not well tested) but have been picked up in the literature. It is therefore important to examine the original purpose for which a scale was conceived.

Reliability

The reliability of a measurement instrument is important in determining how much the scale measures the true characteristics of the client(s) being assessed and how much variation observed in behavior is simply measurement error. Overall, 34 instruments (65 percent) reviewed were considered to have a level of reliability that was adequate, very good, or exemplary. Many of the ones with poor ratings received them because no evidence of their reliability was presented in available materials. This is not to say that these scales are without reliability, but that reviewers had no evidence to indicate their reliability. Further examination and testing of a scale of this type may lead one to conclude that it does in fact have adequate reliability.

Most of the reliability data presented for scales concerned the reliability of raters or observers rather than the statistical properties of the scales themselves. A variety of interrater reliability study designs were implemented, many indicating nearly perfect agreement among raters using particular scales. Unfortunately, while this type of reliability data is important, especially given the number of scales which require someone other than the client being assessed to provide judgemental data, it does not explicitly address the question of the internal consistency of a scale.

In fact, many instruments reported data for "domains" which consist of only one or two independent items. Such subscales are very prone to unreliability. This is a potentially serious problem because the type of scale in which this is most likely to occur is the detailed behavioral assessment tool, intended by its authors for use in making judgements about individual clients. Unfortunately, this is the application of a scale which is most sensitive to unreliability. If a scale will be applied one time by one rater to a client (as at the time an IHP is developed), then data about interrater agreement is irrelevant to determining the extent to which that scale contains measurement error. Interrater agreement data are most useful when data are to be aggregated and the information obtained from more than one rater (or the same rater over time) is to be compared and/or combined for analysis.

Validity

The scales reviewed in this project fared most poorly when their validity was assessed. Only 40 percent of the scales presented evidence of their validity that was considered adequate or better. Nearly as many were rated unacceptable on validity, most often because no validation of the scale was conducted or reported, empirical or otherwise. In fact, many scales that were judged to be acceptable were found to be so on the basis of conceptual arguments rather than empirical studies, that is, content validity was considered acceptable if a convincing rationale for item content and selection was presented or if a group of experts rated the items as acceptable. While somewhat weak, this level of validation is better than none at all.

When empirical data were presented, the form of the validation study was most often correlational: correlations of the scale with other instruments (similar measures or IQ tests) were reported or the intercorrelations of subscales of the instrument were examined. While these approaches to construct validation are perfectly appropriate, the authors often did not state their assumptions about the behavior of the construct with regard to the other measure, so whether a particular correlation coefficient is evidence of validity or invalidity is sometimes in doubt. For example, if a particular subscale correlates strongly with IQ (as many did), is that validity? If the scale measures social competency, it may indicate validity; if it measures motor skills, it may not. However, are self-care skills correlated with IQ? Many authors simply reported a correlation matrix and, with little additional discussion, claimed it to be evidence of the validity of the scale.

With the exception of a few vocational and work-oriented scales, very few validation studies addressed the predictive validity of a scale. Those that did often involved well-constructed followup studies of clients who were administered a scale and whose subsequent performance in a work setting was assessed. Given the intent of many scales to be used for client program development, it would seem important to assess the degree to which predictions of appropriate treatment approaches made by a scale were in fact borne out.

IMPLICATIONS FOR EVALUATION SYSTEMS

A current issue in the operation of programs serving develop-mentally disabled clients is the need to establish statewide systems for the evaluation of these programs. The Developmentally Disabled Assistance and Bill of Rights Act of 1975 [P.L. 94-103 (Section 110)] requires each state to implement an evaluation system which assesses the effectiveness of programs in terms of client progress. In order to measure the developmental progress of these clients, instruments such as those reviewed in previous sections must be used. In this section we will discuss some implications for statewide evaluation systems (and for national evaluation systems designed to use these state-provided data) which have emerged from our investigation of available measures of developmental progress. This discussion will focus primarily on the implications for evaluation as mandated in P.L. 94-103, although many of the issues examined are also important for evaluation systems required in other legislation, regulations, and standards, such as the Education of All Handicapped Children Act of 1975 (P.L. 94-142) and the Rehabilitation Act of 1973 (P.L. 93-112).

Evaluation system structures and measurement requirements.

A simplified conceptual model of a statewide evaluation system calls for service providers within the state to regularly collect and report data on the developmental status of their clients. Assessments of the effectiveness of the providers, both individually and collectively, could be made on the basis of these data which would be centrally received. Effectiveness would be reflected in client progress, in absolute terms, relative to some reference group or standard, or relative to the individualized plan established for the client by the provider. Programs of different types (e.g., community homes vs. residential institutions) could be compared for their relative effectiveness. The differential success of different types of clients (e.g., different severity levels) could be monitored. To conduct these and other possible analyses, the evaluation data system would collect information about current client developmental status; describe the client, the provider and the services delivered/received; and maintain a longitudinal file of client data so that progress relative to prior assessments could be measured. If gain was to be measured relative to Individual Habilitation Plans (IHPs), as specified in legislation, a quantification of the plan and its specific goals would be developed and made part of the system.

The system described briefly above is certainly technically feasible. Based on the instruments which were reviewed in this study, we can assume that adequate data collection procedures exist for many aspects of test development in which an evaluator would be interested. Data processing and analysis techniques are well developed. However, there are some constraints on this evaluation process which limit its feasibility.

First of all, in order for data from different providers to be combined for analysis, each provider must collect exactly the same data from its clients. If one provider, for example, uses the Adaptive Behavior Scale and another the Progress Assessment Chart, it is impossible to conduct any statistical analysis of the scores since they are not comparable or even in the same metric. Although some interesting work is being conducted to explore the areas of overlap between these two particular instruments and other instruments, it is not yet possible to translate a score from one into a score on another. Consequently, the evaluator must require that all providers utilize the same assessment instrument. This will be a hardship for providers who may be familiar with different but equally sound instruments since they must retain their staff and lose the benefit of several years of historical data on their clients.

How would a state go about selecting such an all-purpose instrument? Our reviews of existing measures indicate that there is no single instrument that distinguishes itself on totally technical grounds. Rather, there are a number of scales which are technically acceptable but which differentiate themselves in terms of other dimensions such as content or purpose. Consequently, the selection of an instrument must be based on substantive grounds; the technical data on available instruments is not a sufficient basis for making this selection. In fact, as was discussed in Chapter 2, the appropriateness of the content or purpose of an instrument to the programmatic goals and objectives of a provider is a primary factor in selection since any number of technically acceptable instruments are likely to be found.

What should be the basis for the selection of the content of state evaluation? Obviously, the set of providers within the state will be diverse in terms of their own program goals and procedures for operationalizing them. At minimum, what is necessary is an instrument which is independent of specific programs or curricula and which measures important developmental constructs (e.g., adaptive behavior or vocational adjustment).

For example, some instruments measure client performance against the goals of a particular curriculum. Although these instruments are appropriate for evaluating providers that use the curriculum, they are not suited to evaluating other providers. It is then incumbent on the state—actually, on the ultimate users of the evaluation data—to determine which constructs are important enough to measure and how they are defined. The legislation which requires these evaluation systems provides no content specifications, only stating that the system should be "comprehensive". This could lead to collection of excessive amounts of data, much of which will never be used. The content design should therefore be parsimonious.

If providers are to collect and report evaluation data, they and their staff must expend considerable effort in the assessment of clients. However, client assessments are also required as a part of establishing and monitoring a client's IHP. An efficient method of operation would, therefore, be to utilize the available IHP data to assess client outcomes, not necessitating an additional data collection effort. While this idea is attractive, it has some serious drawbacks. As we noted above, standardization of data collection in terms of both procedures and content is essential if any meaningful analysis is to be performed. Development of an IHP is a clinical process that must be tailored to the specific characteristics of the individual client. Requiring the collection of a standard set of data using a standard set of instruments as part of the IHP development process undermines the concept of individualization which is central to the IHP notion. In practice, were this approach implemented, provider staff who complied with the procedures would undoubtedly administer any number of additional instruments to a client for diagnostic purposes. These instruments, which are essential to the client's receiving a useful IHP, represent additional burden on providers. Worse yet is the possibility that a harried staff member would not run additional tests on a client, only using the required measures, or would apply the required measures when others are more appropriate to the client. An evaluation system cannot result in the reduction of the quality of services received by clients because of requirements of the evaluation.

Another issue relates to client populations. Existing instruments by and large have some implicit or explicit target population (e.g., specific disabilities, levels of severity, age ranges, settings). While the populations covered in instruments vary in their breadth, none is truly comprehensive because of the diversity of the developmentally disabled population and the providers serving them. And because no single instrument is uniquely appropriate for assessment within all segments of this population, a problem exists if one accepts the fact that data collection procedures must be standardized. A compromise would be to utilize different instruments for different client types (functioning level, disability) in different settings. This could become quite a complex process and still precludes direct comparisons among the groups so defined.

Given the political and practical realities of the service delivery system, it appears that the only structure for an evaluation system which is likely to be accepted by those who will provide the data and still yield useful information is one which is external to the providers. It will be impossible to reach consensus among providers as to the most appropriate instrument for their client population; in fact, it is not clear that such a consensus should be reached. So, despite the added burden, the evaluation designers must specify their own set of measures which provide the minimum amount of data necessary for analysis and decision making. Allow providers to use whatever instruments they prefer internally while having them provide additional data for the evaluation system.

The process of evaluation system design

Despite the problems stated above, it is necessary to establish statewide evaluation systems. Not only are such systems required by law but they also provide information useful to planners and administrators at all levels which can enhance the efficiency and effectiveness of service delivery to developmentally disabled people. In this section we would like to specify some of the decisions that must be made by evaluation designers in setting the specifications for a system. Note the similarity of these points to the process described in Chapter 2 for the selection of instruments: the same principles hold true. Here, however, we do not attempt to be comprehensive and only address issues that might not be obvious. We will not repeat recommendations that evaluators examine the reliability of their instruments, etc. As was the case in Chapter 2, many of the decisions in evaluation system design are judgements and will require exploration of the substantive and political context of the evaluation. There are not technical or methodological guidelines; one must choose among a number of technically acceptable alternatives the design most likely to yield acceptable results.

The first step in evaluation design is to specify the purposes of the evaluation. This is done by clarifying the possible decisions that will be informed by the evaluation data. Will funding of providers be an issue? Will decisions about program or service components be made? These decisions imply both data requirements and analytic design issues. An evaluation conducted simply for the purpose of "obtaining data" will not be satisfactory to anyone.

The framing of a research design and analytic strategy questions are next. Although we have talked so far about an evaluation data system that is like a management information system in that data are collected from all providers, the use of sampling is also an option. It may not be appropriate to sample providers, but evaluation data on all clients within a provider may not be necessary. This is an analysis issue: at what level will generalizations be made? If decisions will be made about individual providers, then extensive client data for each provider is needed. However, if the analysis will address only provider *types*, then fewer clients per provider could be assessed without undermining the quality of the research effort.

Data requirements must also be specified. These include client outcome measures and possible environmental outcome variables. If you want to examine the effects of different service mixes or environments, data on these variables must be collected systematically. Client characteristics (age, sex, etc.) can be used as covariates in an analysis. If the evaluation data collection requirements are not designed to serve additional purposes, the content only needs to reflect those variables that the evaluation data users think are important. However, there will be multiple users and there is a need (mandated by P.L. 94-104) to be comprehensive.

Given these design specifications, it will be necessary to explore the operational implications of the system. Far too many reporting systems have been designed by overzealous researchers or administrators who did not realize the burden compliance would place on the suppliers of the data. Also, far too much data are often generated than can be used meaningfully by the evaluators. The practical considerations of the evaluation system must be worked out and examined critically. Are the costs of the system justified by the benefits? If not, you should consider redesigning the system to bring its demands more in line with what can be realistically expected.

Also necessary to such a design is specification of the subjects and settings of the system. Which providers must comply? Which of their clients (if not all) must be assessed for the evaluation system? Should the characteristics of the specific settings or environments be assessed? Given this information, how many providers and clients will be involved? This number could be unwieldy and may produce more data than can be processed or than is needed to inform the decisions the evaluation was designed to address. Definition of who must comply will be necessary to make the system run in the field.

Likewise, the questions of who will collect the data and what procedures will be used must be answered. We have stressed issues of administration elsewhere in this volume. It is exactly in situations involving data collection from a variety of locations by a variety of people that standardization of procedures is essential. Without clear and explicit instructions for data collection, together with some quality control and validity checking of data returns, the evaluation system could be rendered useless. Incomplete or poorly completed forms undermine all analysis.

Given data requirements and procedures, what is compliance likely to cost? Will this cost—direct or indirect in the form of extra responsibilities for existing staff—be perceived by providers as unreasonable? Since compliance represents an added cost, will the state increase its funding of providers to compensate for the added cost, will providers operating on fixed budgets be forced to cut back in other areas such as client services or, will the cost be so high that providers will not comply with the requirements at all? These costs need to be considered explicitly in designing the system.

Finally, consider the political reality of it all. Will the system be acceptable to the providers who must supply the data? If not, cursory, grudging compliance can bring with it poor quality data. Noncompliance can be an even more severe problem. Is the perceived benefit of participation in the evaluation system worth it to providers? Will they receive useful information for their own purposes or are they just supplying to a state agency information that could ultimately be used against them? Is there a threat of loss of funding because of noncompliance and is this threat enough to cause providers to comply? If the funding level received by providers is already low, it may be worth the risk to refuse cooperation. There is already a well-established mood among some program staff (if not the public at large) which is resistant and hostile to government data collection.

A second aspect of political reality is the content validity of the instrumentation selected. Will there be general agreement among evaluation users and providers on two basic content issues— whether the instruments selected measure content which providers feel is useful for their programs and whether the instruments selected really measure the construct(s) they claim to. Because almost every provider is currently using some instrument to measure developmental progress, it is very unlikely that a single instrument will be totally acceptable to everyone. However, what kind of compromises are possible? Instruments which take a very strong philosophical stand in their measurement will be more difficult to use with wide acceptance than will those which try to be objective.

SUMMARY

Based on our analysis of existing measures of developmental progress and our examination of the process of instrument selection at both the provider and the state levels, we have come to the following conclusions:

A uniform data collection strategy must be followed within a state. The same instrument must be used to measure developmental progress in all providers' reporting data. Otherwise, data from different sources will not be comparable and the analytic aims of the evaluation system will be defeated.

The data collection procedure must be defined at the system level and be implemented by providers in addition to any other developmental assessments they might perform. In order to assure uniformity of content and procedures the evaluation agency must specify such uniformity. To avoid interference with ongoing assessment programs (such as those needed for IHP development) the evaluation reporting requirements should be separate and distinct. The need for comparability and parsimony of statewide evaluation data is in conflict with the need for detail and flexibility at the individual client level possessed by more clinical applications. Both purposes cannot be served efficiently by the same instrument.

The evaluation designers must clearly and specifically define their data needs based on decision making requirements, not simply data availability. In order to provide useful evaluative information, the data collected must explicitly address the decision needs of the users of the system.

The evaluation system data requirements should be parsimonious. Collect no more data than is actually needed or than can be used effectively. This applies both to the scope of the data collection (i.e., do not ask unnecessary questions) and to the number of units of data collected (i.e., consider sampling of clients or even providers whenever possible). Collecting data on a particular variable which might be useful later is wasted effort and increases the burden on respondents.

Ultimately, the selection of outcome measures is subjective and must reflect the substantive and political context of the state. Decisions about which variables should be measured are often value judgements regarding the importance of variables. There are few objective technical grounds on which to base the selection of an instrument. Inadequate ones can be rejected on a technical basis but selection of the best strategy among several acceptable approaches is a subjective process. Consequently, all interested parties must be actively involved.

Index